SAFARI PRESS

The Accurate Rifle... and Rifleman

The Accurate Rifle... and Rifleman

Craig T. Boddington

With a contribution by
Phil Massaro

Safari Press

Boddington, Craig T.

Second edition

Safari Press

2017, Long Beach, California

ISBN 978-1-57157-469-5

Library of Congress Catalog Card Number: 2016934657

10 9 8 7 6 5 4 3 2

Printed in China

Readers wishing to see Safari Press's many fine books on big-game hunting, wingshooting, and sporting firearms should visit our website at www.safaripress.com.

To the memory of

my old friend and mentor

Sergeant Charles "Chub" Eastman, U.S.M.C.

October 11, 1940–August 3, 2014

Marine sniper, varmint shooter,
buffalo hunter,
consummate rifleman

Chub, this book would have been
a whole lot better
if we could have worked
on it together!

Table of Contents

AUTHOR'S NOTE

Accurate rifles are interesting. So are accurate rifle shooters. Generally speaking, however, the shooting sports are not spectator events. There are exceptions: Cowboy action shooting is very visual, and so are some of the modern "running and gunning" practical pistol and three-gun events. But unless you're a participant, many formal shooting disciplines are a lot like watching paint dry. Come to think of it, as many non-hunting spouses will attest, there are also probably better ways to observe and enjoy nature than as an "observer" on a hunt. Donna figured that out pretty quickly the first time she tagged along on a hunt: Participating is a whole lot more interesting, and she's been a hunter ever since.

I'm a shooter, and have been since before I was ten years old. I certainly do not participate in all, or even very many, of the myriad shooting games available today, and don't claim even passing knowledge of some. Although it may seem that way from much of my more recent writing, it is not true that it's only the rifle that I find interesting. I grew up as a shotgunner, and I learned to shoot pistols before rifles. Back in the 1970s, more of my earliest scribbling (much of which is best forgotten) was devoted to scattergunning and handgunning than rifle shooting! However, I am fascinated by rifles and rifle shooting, and for many years now I've spent a lot more time with the rifle than with other firearms.

I do follow the old admonition that "only accurate rifles are interesting" . . . provided that phrase is always put in context. An elephant rifle doesn't have to be as accurate as a varmint rifle. A rifle for timber whitetail hunting doesn't have to be as accurate as a rifle for reaching out across Alberta wheat fields or southern soybean fields. A .22 suitable for head-shooting rabbits and squirrels for the pot doesn't have to be as accurate as a .22 for smallbore competition. Thus, at least to me, what makes a rifle interesting is that it is *accurate enough for its intended purpose*, and accurate enough to give its user confidence to take and make his or her shots.

While rifle shooting may not be the ideal spectator sport, I can honestly say that I really enjoy watching a good shooter do his or her work. And the reverse: I find it extremely painful to watch a shooter struggle. Bad shooting habits are easy to acquire and often hard to fix. Good shooting habits are also fairly easy to acquire, but many of us in the shooting world are more or less self-taught . . . or taught by mentors and family members who have had no formal training. There are many ways to skin a cat and shoot a rifle. Results are all that matter, so technique isn't necessarily a matter of good/bad or proper/improper, but shooting is hardly a new sport, and proven techniques and positions do work.

I have never claimed to be more nor less than what I am: A career gunwriter, and thus a student of the shooting sports . . . but not necessarily a master. We all miss now and then. Unlike some of my colleagues, I have never been shy about recounting my misses and errors. I'm very happy with what I do and who I am, and I have never wished to create a larger-than-life persona. There are many better rifle shooters than I, especially folks who truly specialize in one or another discipline. On the other hand, there are some who are not as skilled, and, fortunately, we are blessed with a steady stream of newer shooters coming into our ranks. I don't have all the answers or all the knowledge, but I've been fortunate to have learned from some really great shooting coaches at several stages in my career. In this book there will undoubtedly be some technical information as well as techniques that will be useful to beginners. However, since we all have different experience, there will probably be nuggets here and there of use to veterans.

Speaking of veterans, longtime (and long-suffering) readers of my work will be aware that this is not the first book I've written on rifle accuracy, nor the first book on rifle shooting. Some repetition is unavoidable because basics are basics. However, earlier books on these subjects are now out of print. That's a good thing, because one of the wonderful things about shooting is no one ever quits learning. I know a lot more now than I did ten or twenty years ago. Also, while basic shooting techniques have changed little, technology continues to advance. Rifles and ammunition are more accurate and more consistently accurate than ever before, and optics are immeasurably better than when I was a young shooter.

So there is plenty of new material, and in this effort my treatment is considerably different. It is not exactly a two-part book. However, as you study the table of contents and decide whether you want to read front to back,

back to front, or start with selected chapters of particular interest, you will note that there is a progression. I start with a clinical discussion of technical factors that influence raw accuracy: barrels, actions, triggers, ammunition, sights, and more. Then I shift to *shooting*, including both physical and psychological factors that either help or deter a shooter from realizing the potential of his or her rifle.

It's no secret that I'm a hunter. Use of a rifle in the field is one of my greatest passions. I make no apologies for that, or for using examples from the field in many of the anecdotes in this book. It follows naturally that many of my readers are also hunters. Hunters will almost certainly pick up some tips and techniques they may find useful. However, shooting is shooting. It really doesn't matter whether your goal is to punch tight groups in paper targets, ring steel at long range, or cleanly take down a fine buck. I enjoy doing all of these things and, with infinite modifications, I use the same techniques across the board.

Unless we're talking formal competition with strict rules, shooting is a free-form activity. The basics of trigger use, breath control, and sight alignment are fairly rigid, but beyond that there's a lot of flexibility in techniques and positions. Ultimately *you* must learn what works for *you*, and as much as I wish it were otherwise, that can't come out of a book. So please enjoy the book, but get out to the range!

Craig Boddington
Elk City, Kansas
October 2015

Accurate. Deadly. Dependable.
Cartridge:
Powder:
Bullet:
Primer:

Lands and Grooves

CHAPTER 1

The action is the heart of a rifle, but the barrel is its soul. The barrel is always the single most important factor in accuracy. You can try an endless array of loads and all sorts of little tricks to improve accuracy, but this is an irrefutable fact: Nothing can make a bad barrel shoot well.

The challenge is you often can't tell much about a barrel by looking. Ideally, of course, when you look through a barrel you want to see rifling that is sharp and bright, with no apparent blemishes. Unfortunately, some barrels shoot better than others (and some worse), and looks can be deceiving. A barrel that appears to have worn rifling, an eroded throat, and even serious pitting may still shoot

A really good borescope like this Hawkeye is really the only way to examine a barrel properly, but the only way to be certain what the examination is telling you is to actually shoot the rifle. Some barrels that look great don't shoot, and others that look horrible shoot well.

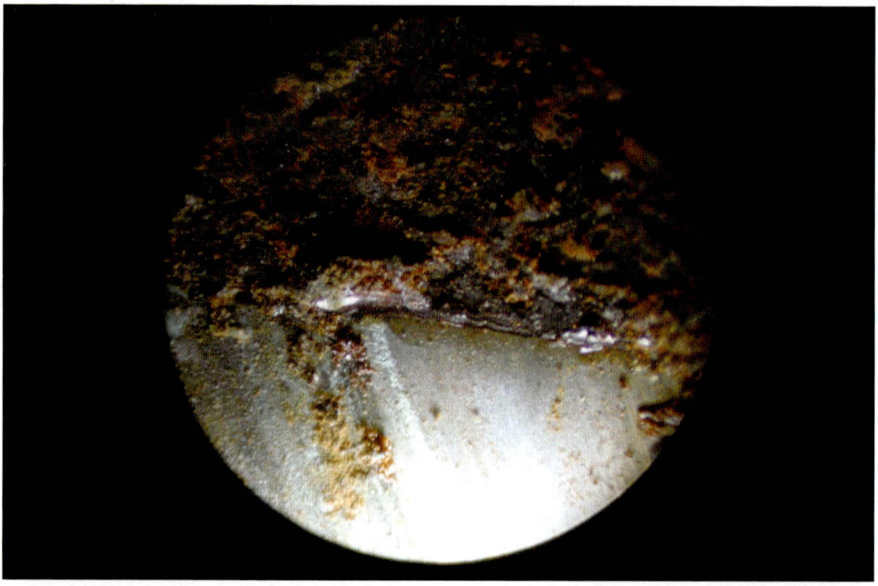

These are two macro photos of badly pitted and rusted bores taken with a Hawkeye borescope. You wouldn't buy *a rifle with a barrel in such condition, but you never know; some barrels still shoot very well even after such neglect.*

very well . . . and a barrel that looks perfect could be, well, the pits. If one is *buying* a rifle it would be foolish to take a chance on a barrel that looks worn, but the reality is the only way to tell how well a barrel shoots is to shoot it. Shoot it a lot, with different loads. Much later we'll talk about troubleshooting accuracy, but for now let's stick with the inside of the rifle's barrel.

Rifling is a series of spiraling grooves cut into a barrel. The intact segments remaining between the *grooves* are called *lands*. The purpose of this system is to impart a spin to the bullet, and the spin tends to stabilize the bullet in flight and increase accuracy. This is hardly new. The first known rifled barrels appeared before 1500, and rifling has changed relatively little since the sixteenth century.

Rifling was, however, problematic in the era of muzzleloaders. In order for the rifling to make the bullet spin, the projectile must be the same diameter as the groove-to-groove measurement, meaning it is larger than the land-to-land diameter. Upon firing, the bullet obturates or "squishes" into the rifling. Thus, even with soft lead projectiles, loading a rifle by pushing a bullet down the

Although an upgraded "75-year" commemorative Model 70 patterned after a pet rifle of Jack O'Connor's, it's still just a Featherweight Model 70 with a very light barrel. Out-of-the-box accuracy was spectacular, clearly proving that light barrels can shoot, though groups will usually open quickly after more than three shots.

barrel from the muzzle was slow and required a lot of force. Bullets patched with paper or thin cloth helped, but a better solution was the hollow-based "Minié ball," a conical bullet. Invented in France but made famous in our Civil War, the Minié measured slightly less than the land-to-land diameter and was thus easy to load. Upon firing, the hollow base expanded into the rifling, so accuracy was very good.

Bullet design, however, could not overcome the tendency of black powder to rapidly foul the barrel. It quickly filled the grooves with gunk and, in effect, reduced bore diameter after repeated firing. Breechloaders solved the loading problem, but until nitrocellulose-based "smokeless" propellants came along, a black-powder rifle would lose accuracy quickly as the bore fouled. With reduced bore diameter, recoil also increased dramatically.

The spin imparted by the rifling is not random; it depends primarily on the length of the bullet, but velocity also comes into play (faster bullets require a faster twist). Accuracy is reduced very quickly if the spin is too fast (over-stabilized) or too slow (under-stabilized). Rifling twist is generally designated by the number of inches of barrel required for a full revolution, so "one turn in ten inches" is usually written as "1:10." A rifling twist of 1:8 is "faster" than a twist of 1:10, meaning that the bullet is spinning faster when it exits the barrel. Shorter bullets don't need to spin as fast to stabilize, so the shorter the bullet, the slower the required twist. A muzzleloader intended to fire round balls might have a twist of 1:48, which, practically speaking, means that the ball has exited the muzzle before a complete revolution can be made. Rifles intended for extremely long bullets, such as heavy-for-caliber (70 grains and more) bullets for .22 centerfires, must have a very fast twist of perhaps 1:8.

This is about as fast a twist as you will see. The slowest twist in use today on a centerfire rifle cartridge is probably 1:20, which is standard for the .44 Remington Magnum, .444 Marlin, .45-70, and .450 Marlin. These cartridges have in common relatively low velocity and short-for-caliber bullets, so they require a slow twist. In general this is not something we need to worry about since rifling twists were more or less standardized generations ago.

Most modern rifle cartridges use barrels with rates of twist between 1:9 and 1:12, and these will stabilize the general run of popular bullet weights in

The .243 Winchester and 6mm Remington were both introduced in 1955. Envisioned as a combo varmint/big-game round, the .243 was introduced with a 1:10 rifling twist and gained instant acceptance. The 6mm, originally called the .244, was envisioned as a varmint rifle and had a 1:12 twist that couldn't stabilize bullets over 90 grains. In this case Winchester guessed right!

Fluting reduces barrel weight and actually strengthens the barrel by creating raised "ribs." Top, horizontal fluting in various patterns is most common, but helical or spiraling fluting is occasionally seen. The effect is the same; the difference is mostly cosmetic.

A group of barrel blanks, in this case at the Musgrave factory in South Africa. Most smaller firms "source" their barrels from other makers already rifled, and then they chamber, turn, and fit them as required.

the various cartridges and calibers. A barrel with a 1:10 twist is standard for most .30-caliber cartridges, and this rate of twist will stabilize bullets between at least 150 and 200 grains.

Just supposing, however, you wanted to shoot the extra-heavy, 250-grain .30-caliber bullets sometimes used in long-range competition. *Hmm.* Maybe you should think about a custom barrel with a 1:8 twist. Or the reverse: Perhaps you want to use the short, light-for-caliber, 110-grain .30-caliber bullet. Chances are you will need a slower twist to get the best accuracy.

Again, optimum rifling twists have been known and standardized for many years . . . but there have been some interesting twists, pardon the pun. Remington and Winchester both introduced 6mm cartridges in 1955, the .244 Remington and .243 Winchester. Remington saw its cartridge as a long-range varmint round, so the company introduced it with a 1:12 twist suited for short, light bullets. Winchester envisioned a dual-purpose cartridge for varmints and deer-size game and gave its .243 barrels a faster 1:10 twist. With a slower 1:12 twist, the .244 Remington was unable to stabilize bullets heavier than 90 grains, while

Winchester's faster twist worked fine with lighter varmint bullets and equally well with 100-grain deer bullets. The .243 took off like a rocket, while the .244 languished. Some years later Remington renamed it the 6mm Remington and changed the twist to 1:9, but the damage was done. The 6mm Remington is a great cartridge, but it has never approached the .243 in popularity.

Gene Stoner's original AR-15 rifle had a 1:14 twist. Standard today with the .223 Remington is 1:12. Either is fine for bullets in the 50-grain class, but a faster twist is needed to stabilize the heavy-for-caliber .223-inch bullets in use today. A major, though invisible, difference between the M16A2 and the M16A1 it replaced is a barrel with a faster twist, which is needed to stabilize our current 69-grain 5.56mm service round.

Over the years many arrangements of lands and grooves have been tried, but today the most common in rifle barrels is probably six grooves, the grooves cut with walls perpendicular to the line of the bore. There are exceptions. In the early years of World War II we made a lot of two-groove barrels as a time-saving wartime expedient—but this came with reduced accuracy. Marlin is famous for its "micro-groove" barrels that have numerous closely spaced lands and grooves. Modern artillery and tank gun barrels are often rifled in much the same way.

"Gain twist" rifling surfaces now and again, meaning that the spirals start near the chamber with a slower twist, the twist "gaining" in revolutions toward the end of the barrel. This can reduce pressure and throat wear and, if perfectly executed, can be conducive to increased accuracy. But because it's very difficult to execute correctly, better accuracy with gain twist rifling is not the norm.

Three primary methods are employed in manufacturing rifle barrels:

- *Cut rifling* means just that: Grooves are cut into a barrel blank with a machining tool of greater hardness than the barrel steel. Rifling can be cut one groove at a time, sort of the old-fashioned way, or all at once with a broaching bit.
- *Button rifling* is done by pushing or pulling a tool or "button" down the barrel blank with great pressure, essentially pressing the grooves into the barrel steel.
- *Hammer forging* is done by placing an oversized barrel blank around a mandrel holding the reverse image of the lands and grooves, then forging the barrel into the mandrel with heat and pressure.

Loading a muzzleloader is obviously slower . . . but as the barrel fouls and internal diameter increases, it gets slower. At a local sports fair these muzzleloaders are being loaded on an "assembly-line" basis.

Many rifle nuts argue that cut rifling is the best and most precise. Personally I think hammer-forged barrels are generally the most consistent. The primary drawback to this method is the machine required to make these barrels. This machine is both huge and costly, so this method is generally an option only for major manufacturers. To me, however, the most important thing isn't *how* the barrel is rifled, but that it is well executed.

Some years ago I did a tour of the Savage plant, a "make your own rifle" sort of a thing. I'm a clumsy guy, and I consider a screwdriver a complex tool. So, while I did some of the assembly, I can assure you I didn't rifle my own barrel. I did, however, watch a veteran Savage employee button-rifle barrels, inspect them, and occasionally give one a straightening tweak. At some point in the process I picked a chambered .22-250 barrel at random from a bin and it was mated to the action and nestled into a stock. We put a scope on it and took it upstairs to the 100-yard testing range that ran the length of the factory.

I'm left-handed, but the bench was in such a small space that the only way to properly access the narrow tunnel was to shoot right-handed. Well,

I can do that, especially off a bench, but it was obvious that having to shoot wrong-handed made Ron Coburn, then CEO of Savage, nervous. It took just a couple of shots to achieve an approximate zero, and then I settled down and fired a three-shot group. I don't recall the load—it was just a factory load with a decent bullet—but I do recall that the first three-shot group out of that rifle, fresh off the line, measured 0.18-inch.

That particular rifle was a heavy-barrel varminter, stainless steel in a heavy laminate stock. Within the Savage lineup, it would have been a comparatively costly rifle, but still retailing under $1,000 today. Savage prides itself on building a fairly basic rifle that has an exceptional reputation for out-of-the-box accuracy.

So let's put this in perspective. If you wanted to build a rifle that was almost certain to produce exceptional accuracy, you would pay extra for a "match-grade" barrel from a "name" barrelmaker. There are many good names: Krieger, Lilja, Obermeyer, Pac-Nor, Shilen, Lothar Walther, and more. But here's the point: You will pay around $500 for a top-quality cut-rifled or hammer-forged barrel from a great barrel maker. If it's properly mated to a

This is a heavy-barrel Ruger Number 1 in .204 Ruger. Heavy barrels don't necessarily shoot better, but they usually fire longer shot strings before overheating . . . and are often less finicky about both bedding and the range of loads they will shoot well.

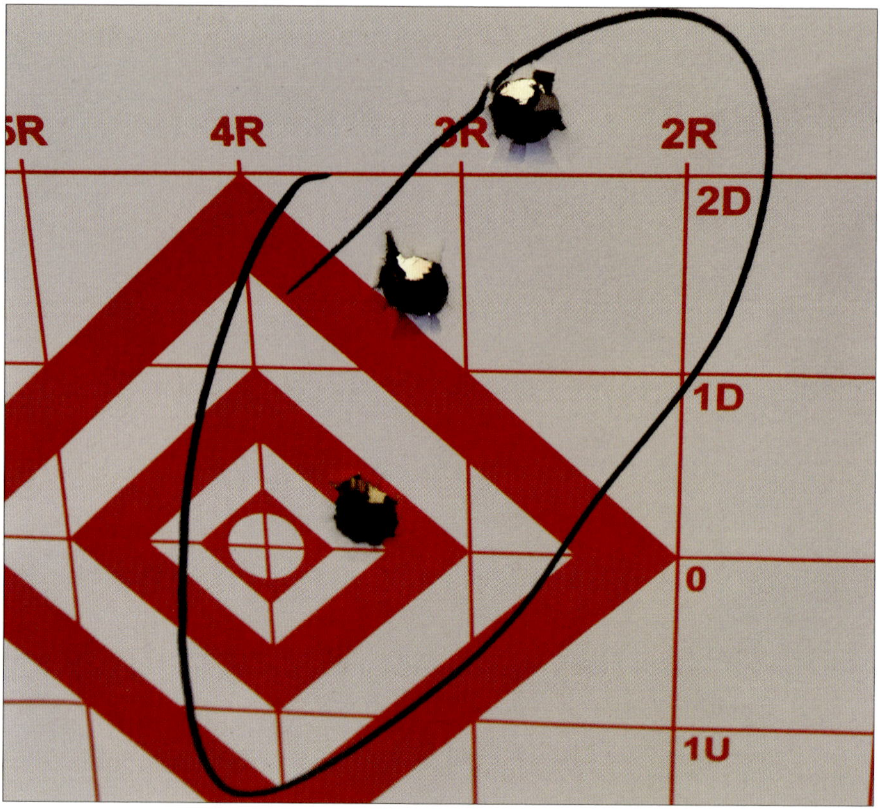

Vertical stringing like this could reflect a bedding issue, or it may simply be a matter of a barrel heating up very quickly. Many extremely light barrels can only fire a couple of shots before barrel heat makes bullet impact walk—usually vertically.

good action, bedded well, and fed good ammo, you can expect such a barrel to deliver good accuracy, and it will. However, even the very best barrels cannot always exceed the sub-one-fifth-inch group that the button-rifled Savage barrel produced that day for me. Considering that barrel was just one component of a complete rifle, it is unlikely that Savage invested much more than thirty bucks in that barrel.

This is the frustrating part about not just rifle barrels, but this entire subject: The ultimate level of accuracy of any given rifle is impossible to predict. In fact, today's production rifles, even without the benefit of costly "extra-good" barrels, are often capable of delivering genuinely exceptional accuracy.

Rifle barrels today are generally either carbon steel or stainless. Stainless steel is a bit harder and more resistant to wear (inside and out), but in terms of accuracy there are no real advantages or disadvantages. The military shifted to chrome-lined barrels to improve both reliability and barrel life. Today other coatings are used, with nitride probably the most common. Chrome lining reduces a barrel's internal dimensions, so it is optimally applied to a slightly oversize barrel. A salt-bath nitride (SBN) coating does not change the internal dimensions but makes "rough spots" or imperfections in the barrel permanent, so at its best should probably be applied to a barrel that has already been broken in. In barrels there are no absolutes, but most knowledgeable riflemen seem to agree that the most accurate barrels, whether for traditional or modern sporting rifles, are not coated.

Barrel contour, the external dimension of the barrel, does not actually relate to raw accuracy. Very slender barrels can shoot extremely well . . . and extremely heavy varmint-weight or benchrest barrels aren't necessarily tack drivers. Accuracy depends primarily on the quality of the rifling and the consistency of the internal dimensions—and a whole lot of other things we'll talk about as this book progresses.

As a bullet passes down a barrel, it creates vibration, almost like ringing a bell. Heat is also created, both through the burning of the propellant and friction from the bullet's passage. The heavier the barrel, the more subdued the vibration and the longer it takes to heat up. So a heavier barrel will allow a longer shot string before the barrel overheats and the impact starts to "walk." A heavier barrel, with less vibration, is therefore likely to be less finicky about the loads it shoots well than a pencil-thin barrel.

Ultimately, however, the barrel contour you want really depends on the purpose of the rifle and how much weight you're willing to carry around. When I was younger, the gold standard for accuracy was an average of five-shot groups. Today maybe we've gotten lazy, but three-shot groups are more commonly cited. With a really slender barrel on a lightweight mountain rifle, you may be wasting your time and ammo even attempting to fire five-shot groups. Many very light barrels are incapable of firing five shots without the barrel heating up and bullets starting to walk.

For raw accuracy you can always fire a shot, wait ten minutes for the barrel to cool completely, then fire again, and so forth. But, again, it depends on

A hammer-forging machine at the Ruger factory in New Hampshire. My opinion is that hammer forging is the most consistent technique for making rifle barrels, but the equipment is huge and costly, so this technique is generally limited to larger manufacturers.

the rifle's purpose. If you want sustained fire in a prairie dog town, you're clearly better off with a heavy barrel that will handle five, ten, or a dozen shots in succession before barrel heat causes accuracy to deteriorate. With a big-game rifle, you care mostly about the first shot from a cold barrel. You will occasionally need a second shot and, less frequently, a third, but do you really care about five-shot groups? I think not.

There are ways to reduce the effects of heat without increasing barrel weight. *Fluting* is a machining process that removes barrel steel. It can be longitudinal in a variety of patterns, or helical (spiraling). Done properly, the raised portions essentially act as "ribs" that strengthen the barrel while exposing more surface area for more rapid cooling.

Cryogenic stress relief is a process by which a barrel is essentially deep-frozen in liquid nitrogen, altering and "smoothing" the molecular structure. "Cryo" was a big thing a few years back, and I've played with several barrels so treated. Once again, nothing will make a bad barrel shoot well, but cryogenic relief may make a good barrel shoot better, and it generally extends barrel life and reduces the effects of heat. Obviously both fluting and cryo also add significantly to the cost of a barrel.

Finally, let's talk about carbon-fiber barrels. The term is actually a misnomer. These are actually conventional steel barrels, turned down very thin and then *reinforced* with a wrapping of carbon fiber. Christensen Arms was a pioneer in this technology, and more recently I've spent quite a bit of time with Proof Research carbon-fiber barrels. Although the contour is generally thick, similar to a heavy varmint barrel, the "wrapping" is very light, so the result is a very light barrel that is extremely resistant to heat.

This is probably not of huge importance in a big-game rifle, except that you don't spend nearly as much time on the range waiting for your barrel to cool. Obviously it has great advantages for a varmint rifle or an AR, and the accuracy can be astounding. About a year ago I had a Proof Research AR on the range. Using different loads, I shot five, five-shot groups as fast as I could fire accurately. Groups varied because no rifle provides equal accuracy with all loads, but the best group was the last one, shots twenty-one through twenty-

This is a Proof Research 7mm-08 with a carbon-fiber-reinforced barrel. Carbon fiber reinforcement retards heating, but actual accuracy depends on the quality of the steel barrel within the reinforcement.

This target represents five, five-shot groups fired rapidly *with a Proof Research AR with a carbon-fiber reinforced barrel. The center group is the fifth group. Using different loads, the groups are not equal, but the center group is the last one, clearly proving that the carbon fiber greatly reduces overheating.*

five. This would not be possible with any all-steel barrel. Except for cost, there is no disadvantage to a carbon-fiber reinforced barrel, but even the very best of them are no more accurate than traditional barrels. Rather, they offer an option for achieving stability without adding weight.

ACTIONS AND ACCURACY

CHAPTER 2

There are essentially four types of repeating actions in common use today, although all have significant variations: bolt, lever, self-loading (semi- or fully automatic), and slide action. In addition, there is the single-shot action, of which there are two major types: the fixed-breech action like the falling block (Ruger No. 1, Dakota Model 10, Browning High Wall and Low Wall) and the break-open action such as those made by Harrington and Richardson and Thompson/Center (Contender/Encore).

A Mozambique buffalo taken in 2014. The rifles are a brand-new English Rigby (left) and a 1929 English Rigby, both in classic Mauser actions in .416. The classic controlled-round-feed Mauser action is still preferred by many for dangerous game, although actual superiority in reliability is hard to quantify.

Break-open actions also come in double-rifle versions with two barrels and two sets of firing mechanisms. Although cost is a major drawback, the double rifle has its uses: Nothing else is as fast or as reliable for the second shot, so the double rifle in powerful chamberings remains a standby for hunting the largest and most dangerous game. Many Europeans prefer doubles in lighter cartridges for driven hunts, especially for wild boars. Although rarely so employed in North America, a double chambered to appropriate cartridges would be ideal for a lot of our close-cover hunting, from black bears and boars to big-timber whitetails. However, because this is a book focused on accuracy, we will leave the double rifle right here because it is impossible to make a rifle with two barrels as accurate as a rifle with just one.

Just as with barrels, the choice of the most accurate action is not an exact science. High-quality, match-grade barrels will, on average, deliver better accuracy than inexpensive factory barrels or "replacement barrels" that cost less. However, any barrel of any design and make can defy this tendency. Similarly, bolt actions, on average, are probably the most accurate of all action types, but a good barrel

Traditional Winchester lever actions are rear locking and have two-piece stocks, both of which theoretically reduce accuracy. This Winchester M1886 built by Doug Turnbull in his propriety .475 Turnbull cartridge appears to defy these long-accepted concepts!

This is Remington's 50th Anniversary edition of the M700, introduced in 1962 with the 7mm Remington Magnum cartridge. A push-feed action, Remington's advertising touted that the cartridge was surrounded by three rings of steel. The 700 has remained a standby for both accuracy and reliability.

Remington was among the first of the major manufacturers to go to a push-feed bolt. There is at least a theoretical increase in strength, and although not a controlled-round-feed, there is a long track record of absolute reliability.

is more important to accuracy than the action it is mated to . . . and proper and concentric mating, good bedding, and consistent ammunition are also probably more important than action type when it comes to delivering accuracy.

This is a long way of saying that *any* rifle action can deliver awesome accuracy. Even so, there are trends. Forward-locking actions tend to be more accurate than rear-locking actions. Most bolt actions are forward-locking, meaning that lockup occurs with the front portion of the bolt just behind the chamber and cartridge head. ARs are forward-locking with a rotating bolt, and so are some lever actions like Browning's BLR. Rear-locking actions include traditional Winchester lever actions (such as the Model 94) and the Savage 99 action. The issue here is rigidity. Rear-locking actions tend to flex more during firing, which is not conducive to accuracy. This also applies to all break-open single-shot actions, which attempt to unhinge or open during firing. And yet any individual rifle with a rear-locking action can make a lie of this trend.

I've seen Savage 99s that were spectacularly accurate (and others that were not), but perhaps the most classic example was the long-discontinued Remington Model 788, a basic, inexpensive, and unlovely rear-locking bolt action. My experience with this rifle was that it was, consistently, exceptionally accurate right out of the box. This is almost certainly because the action was a massive hunk of steel that, despite its rear-locking lugs, was extremely rigid. Also, in the day of the Model 788, Remington was producing consistently excellent barrels, and their top-of-the-line Model 700 had perhaps the best reputation for out-of-the-box accuracy. Accuracy can almost never be attributed to just one factor.

Actions designed for use with one-piece stocks tend to be more accurate than actions designed for two-piece stocks. This is, again, a matter of stability and rigidity, and also the greater difficulty of obtaining a sound and stable bedding arrangement with a small fore-end ahead of the action. This removes most semiautomatic, lever, slide, and single-shot actions from consideration as ideal choices for the most accurate actions. (Individual rifles can always belie this trend.) An easy action to pick on is the once-popular Savage 99 because it's no longer made and probably never will be again because of its complexity and cost to manufacture. It was not only rear-locking, but tied to a two-piece stock. I've seen few that could be described as exceptionally accurate . . . but those few exist.

The Winchester M88, regrettably no longer made, is a departure from most lever-action designs in that it uses a forward-locking bolt and a one-piece stock design. A Model 88 in .308 Winchester was used to take this exceptional Columbian black-tailed deer.

The various falling-block single-shot actions, although they achieve extremely rigid lockup, also fall into this trap because of their two-piece stocks. But rigidity of the barrel also makes a big difference because heavier barrels tend to be less finicky to bed.

The Ruger No. 1 is one of my favorites, to my eye one of the most elegant and beautiful of all factory actions. Over the years I've owned a number of them, and have had many more in as test rifles. I wish I'd kept every one of them—this is a rifle I really like. However, the Ruger No. 1 has a reputation

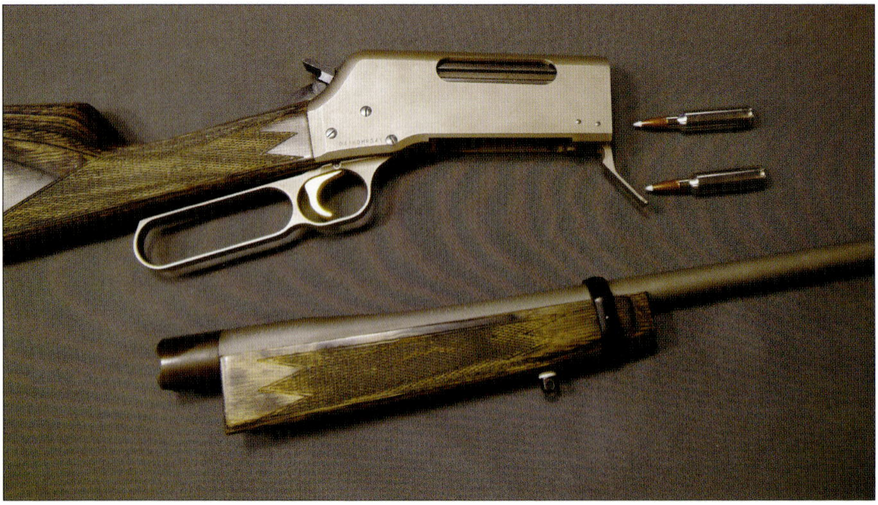

Browning's BLR, shown in takedown form in .270 WSM, is a forward-locking lever action, and the only lever action currently offered in modern high-intensity cartridges.

for finicky accuracy. It has a two-piece stock, with the fore-end attached to the barrel by a forward screw. My experience has been that No. 1s with heavier barrels, whether a lighter-caliber varmint model or a large-caliber Tropical model, are not especially finicky and tend toward excellent accuracy. "Medium sporters" are also often very accurate. For years a go-to varmint rifle was a heavy-barrel Ruger No. 1 in .22-250, consistently accurate with a wide variety of loads. I should have kept that one, but a stainless/laminate No. 1 in .204 Ruger with heavy barrel has taken its place and is just as accurate. Perhaps the most accurate No. 1 I've ever had, however, is a .300 H&H Medium Sporter with a 26-inch barrel.

Over the years, the No. 1s I've had the most trouble getting to shoot well are the "Light Sporters," light, handy rifles with very slender barrels. Sometimes the accuracy is there, but the rifle is finicky and it's just a matter of finding the right load. This is the situation with a 7x57 Light Sporter I've been messing with: It likes what it likes, but it is pretty awful with loads it doesn't like. Perhaps that was also the case with a Light Sporter I had in .270 Winchester, but I never found a load it really liked and I eventually passed that one along. When the No. 1 was relatively new, my colleague Jon Sundra did almost all of his hunting with them. He actually modified the fore-end attachment and got rid of the forward screw, which he said tended to significantly stabilize accuracy. I have never tried that, but I have no doubt it would help.

Oddly, however, two-piece stocks are not consistently a problem, let alone the kiss of death to accuracy. The Blaser straight-pull system, both the older R93 and the newer R8, has a two-piece stock, but accuracy is consistent and generally superb. In theory, the two-bolt system by which the interchangeable barrels attach to the fore-end could, and perhaps should, cause at least occasional accuracy issues, but in my experience it does not. So perhaps we really don't know what we think we know. Or perhaps other factors overcome this potential issue: The Blaser action is extremely rigid, the bolt is forward-locking, and the hammer-forged barrels are excellent.

I've been fortunate to have Blaser as a sponsor for a couple of outdoor TV shows I work with, so I've messed with the Blaser R8 on multiple actions with several barrels chambered to different cartridges. Not only has accuracy been consistently superb, but also the modular system actually works. You can switch

Although falling block actions like the Ruger Number 1 have extremely rigid lockup, the two-piece stock can create finicky accuracy . . . but not always! This Ruger Number 1 in .300 H&H is one of the most consistently accurate Number 1s I have owned.

Break-open actions have a natural tendency to try to unhinge during firing, which is not conducive to accuracy. The barrel is actually much more important, and many break-open actions like the Thompson/Center break-opens are extremely accurate.

barrels back and forth, change bolt heads (for different case head sizes), detach and reattach the scope, and everything comes right back into place. The system essentially defies everything I thought I'd learned about the accuracy potential of modular rifles.

Another system that defies the rules of accuracy is the popular semiautomatic AR-15 action. It is, of course, an action that requires a two-piece stock. More than forty years ago, when I started training with the heavy, stable, and wonderfully accurate M14, then had to switch to the M16A1, the military version of the AR-15, I wasn't impressed. Nor should I have been. The rifle was lighter, kicked a lot less, and was easier to shoot, but raw accuracy, though adequate, wasn't impressive. But the military ammo wasn't all that good, nor were the barrels. Today we know that when mated with a good barrel and fed

A Mauser-type controlled-round-feed bolt (left) with a much more modern three-lug bolt from a Ruger American. The three-lug design allows more concentric lockup, which is at least theoretically more conducive to accuracy . . . but it doesn't have controlled-round-feeding.

good ammo the AR can be, and often is, a spectacularly accurate platform. Check out an AR from a top-end custom maker like Les Baer, MGA, and so many more. The accuracy can be amazing. Come to think of it, it's pretty darned good from virtually all the ninety-odd manufacturers now offering commercial models on the AR and similar actions.

One of the things the AR has going for it is a rotating, forward-locking bolt that completely encircles and supports the rear of the cartridge case. That brings us back to our discussion of bolt actions, as this is another design feature worthy of discussing as regards accuracy. Across the board, the conventional bolt action with rotating forward locking lugs is probably on average the most accurate of our sporting rifles. Contributing factors include the stability of the one-piece stock, which can be bedded in numerous ways, and the ability to house virtually any cartridge (some of which are inherently more accurate than others).

However, purely as regards accuracy, bolt actions are not created equal. In the early years of the twentieth century the Mauser system with its dual-opposing forward-locking lugs became dominant. The American Springfield, the Pattern 14 (and U.S. 1917) Enfield, and the Winchester Model 70, among others, were nothing more than Mauser clones. One of the features of the Mauser design was controlled-round-feed, whereby the cartridge fed up out of the magazine, slid against the bolt face, and was trapped or held against the bolt face by the extractor and carried or "controlled" into the chamber. In order for this to be possible, the bottom part of the bolt face must be open. This means that, during firing, the bottom of the case head is not fully encircled or supported by the bolt face.

In the post-World War II era many manufacturers abandoned the Mauser controlled-round-feed, fully encircling the bolt face. This creates a "push-feed" action in that the cartridge is pushed into the chamber ahead of the bolt, not carried or controlled. There is a theoretical loss in reliability, but there is also an increase in action strength. Remington was among the first to go to this type of action, and they made advertising hay in asserting that the cartridge was surrounded by three rings of steel: The fully enclosed bolt face, the barrel, and the forward action ring of the receiver.

I mentioned that the loss of reliability in a push-feed is largely theoretical. Push-feeds work! As a left-handed shooter, until very recently the only left-

The AR action, initially designed by Gene Stoner some sixty years ago, has become incredibly popular, with some ninety manufacturers now making rifles on the AR and AR-type action.

Although the AR bolt has a multiple locking-lug arrangement, it is a forward-locking, rotating-bolt design, thus it should be considered a modern advancement of Peter Paul Mauser's design.

hand actions I had available were push-feeds, and while I've seen virtually all actions jam, the difference between push-feed and controlled-round-feed has never been the culprit. In fairness, the increase in safety from a fully enclosed bolt face is also largely theoretical. All modern bolt actions have redundant features to contain and channelize the blowback in case of a catastrophic failure. However, there is one point to be made regarding accuracy: All things being equal, a bolt face that completely encircles and *supports* the case head during firing is more conducive to accuracy than the partial support offered by the Mauser system.

So, if accuracy is the primary driving factor, one might be better off choosing a push-feed action that fully supports the case head. This is no secret; it has been known for a long time. Interestingly, however, a fairly large portion of the hunting public prefers the confidence instilled by a controlled-round-feed action. This is also not new. In 1964 Winchester made the most colossal blunder in the history of sporting firearms when it discontinued the beloved pre-1964 Model 70 in favor of the easier-to-manufacture push-feed post-1964 Model 70. The post-'64 Model 70 worked just fine and shot very well, but very few shooters loved it. Today's Model 70s are again controlled-round-feed. Ruger's Model 77 was a push-feed action for years. The M77 Mark II brought in controlled-round-feed.

Does the choice really matter in terms of accuracy? Again, if all other things were equal, it might. A benchrest competitor would be extremely unlikely to choose a controlled-round-feed action. In practical terms other factors are far more important, so for most sporting applications the difference would be extremely difficult to discern. But there is something about the stability of a beefy, rigid action that I am certain contributes heavily to accuracy.

Let's take a look at Ruger's new American bolt action. The rifle was designed from scratch to be easy to manufacture, and thus to be much more affordable than the Model 77 (which is a Mauser clone). I was present when the rifle was introduced, a dozen writers shooting a dozen pre-production Americans in .30-06. Accuracy was just plain spectacular, and has remained so, especially considering this rifle goes off the dealers' shelves at less than $400. For many years Ruger had a reputation for varying barrel quality, but this was long since fixed. Ruger invested in the equipment, and their barrels are hammer-forged and just fine. The synthetic stock on the American is extremely light, about 1.25 pounds, and yet the finished rifle weighs about seven pounds. The barrel is sort of medium contour and that contributes to weight. The action, however, is a massive chunk of steel. The bolt is large diameter (heavy), and it's a push-feed short-uplift action locking with three opposing locking lugs as opposed to the Mauser system's dual opposing lugs.

This is, of course, hardly the only three-lug system out there. Sako, long known for accuracy, went to a three-lug action years ago. The Weatherby Mark V is sort of a three-lug action in that, although it has nine lugs, they are arrayed in three rows of three. When accuracy guru Kenny Jarrett designed his own action he went to a three-lug design. I am no engineer, but if supporting the case head is important, then supporting it concentrically is probably also important. This design, combined with the beefy, rigid action, is part of the reason the Ruger American, inexpensive though it is, has achieved such a reputation for accuracy.

I haven't said anything about the slide action, so let's finish with another rifle that breaks all the rules. The slide action remains a popular shotgun action, and in the 1890s it was second only to the lever action in popularity

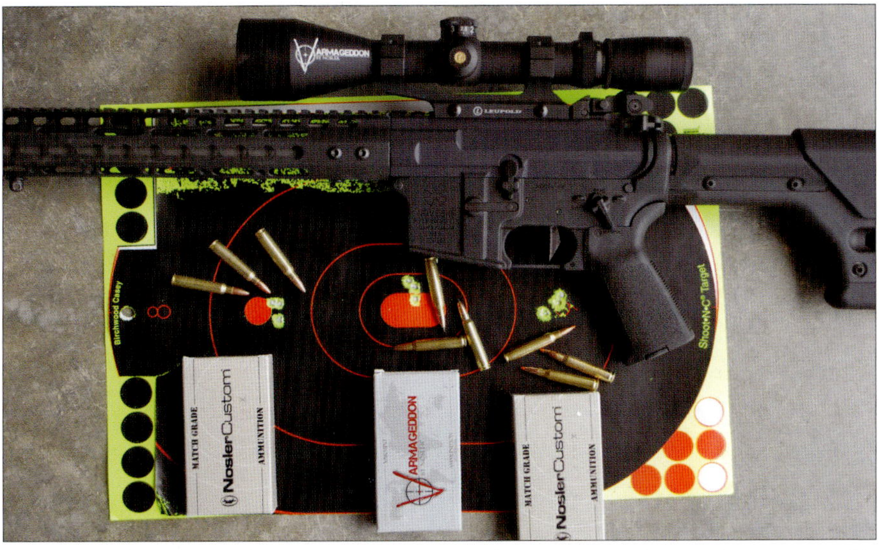

This is a Nosler Varmageddon in .223 Remington, demonstrating the amazing accuracy this action is capable of when mated to a good barrel.

with American riflemen. Today a slide-action rifle is kind of a rare bird, very fast in the woods and certainly adequate for that work, but traditionally its accuracy has been hampered by a two-piece stock and the near impossibility of traditional bedding with a moving fore-end.

Enter the Krieghoff Semprio. Although irrefutably a slide action, it's sort of a reverse slide action in that the action is cycled by pushing the fore-end forward and then back, rather than the traditional reverse. The forward motion unlocks and ejects; the rearward motion carries a round into the chamber. Uniquely, the massive bolt does not move.

My belief is the rifle was designed for European driven shooting. This activity often requires fast offhand shooting, ideal for semiautomatics, but in many European countries semiautomatic actions are not legal. The Semprio is fast and positive, although from a steady rest (or prone) you have to get at least partially out of position to work the action. This is true of all slide actions. But

The Blaser system defies all the rules. Despite its two-piece stock, detachable barrel, and detachable scope, it is a spectacularly accurate platform, and remains repeatable no matter how many times you switch barrels and detach and reattach scopes.

The Krieghoff Semprio is another rifle that breaks all the rules. Although the action is forward and back rather than back and forward like American slide actions, it has a two-piece-stock slide action. This group was produced after assembling the rifle and attaching the scope.

here's where the Semprio breaks the rules: Accuracy is astonishing! I took a Semprio in .300 Winchester Magnum on a hog hunt in Texas, packing it in its handy attaché-style takedown case. I'd shot it on my range and accuracy was surprisingly good, but of course I wanted to check it. So we went to the range. I opened the case, put the barrel onto the action, clamped the detachable scope into place, and shot a quarter-inch group with Winchester factory ammo, exactly where I'd left it at home. If, as Townsend Whelen said, "only accurate rifles are interesting," then this is a very interesting rifle. And it proves once again that while action type affects accuracy, it is only one of many factors.

Stocks, Bedding, and Vibration

CHAPTER 3

Accuracy is very much about stability: stability of the shooter (which we will get to) and stability of the action and barrel. Although we can all appreciate the beauty of fine gunstock wood, the rifle's stock is, after all, just a handle with the primary purpose of helping provide both levels of stability.

Regardless of how the stock is shaped and what it's made of, it is essential that the action be securely nestled—*bedded*—into the stock so that no movement is possible. If it is able to slip even the slightest bit during firing, maximum

Although the barrel is free-floated, the action of this synthetic-stocked LAW Model 704, sort of a semicustom rifle, has obviously been bedded with extreme care.

A group of exceptionally fine walnut stocks, these were partly finished and drying at the Rigby shop in London. Good walnut is my personal preference for "looks"—but it is neither as strong nor as stable as the other options, and good walnut is getting scarce and extremely costly.

accuracy is impossible, and if the stock is wood, any movement during recoil will eventually destroy it. (Barrel bedding is a slightly different subject with several different options, and we'll address that in a bit.)

Synthetic stocks are molded (more or less) to fit the contours of the intended action, while wooden stocks are inletted to fit. Today this is done primarily by machine, although a few custom makers still do this painstaking work by hand. In all cases the fit must be nearly perfect, and the more recoil there is, the closer to perfect it must be. Fiberglass bedding compound is often used to improve the fit and to reinforce critical areas such as behind the magazine well and recesses for recoil lugs and action screws. Action-to-stock fit cannot be sloppy!

The shape of the stock depends on personal preference, but also on the rifle's purpose. The rifles used by benchrest competitors are often built with handles so massive they barely resemble sporting rifles, but weight gives stability, and stability is essential to accuracy. Varmint rifles are often housed in beefy stocks with wide, flat-bottom fore-ends for stability when shooting off sandbags, and

The action bedding of these two production rifles isn't especially pretty, but looks aren't nearly as important as ensuring a tight, uniform, and consistent fit between the action and stock.

The good old "American classic" style of buttstock is my personal favorite, wiht its very straight comb that brings recoil straight back. It is critical that the comb be the proper height so a perfect sight picture can be achieved without raising the cheek or scrunching it into the stock.

tactical rifles usually also have a heavier stock of generous proportions. With hunting rifles, well, there's a limit to how heavy and bulky a rifle you really want to carry, and how far you can carry it.

Also, it depends a whole lot on how you intend to shoot. A rifle intended for benchrest competition will only be shot off the bench. The only limitation to its weight is the class in which its owner wishes to compete. A rifle intended for sustained shooting in a prairie dog town will probably only be used from a solid rest. It's a varmint rifle, yes, but a varmint rifle intended for hiking in the hills while calling coyotes is quite a different thing. A deer rifle intended for use in a stand overlooking a big agricultural field may be different from a deer rifle intended for use in a tree stand in the woods.

I'm not a benchrest competitor, but I do have heavy varmint rifles. I appreciate their stability, but I don't much like to carry them. My personal preference is for a lighter, trimmer stock with a straight comb in the American classic style, and I can make that work under most circumstances.

Provided the action is solidly bedded and the barrel is soundly and evenly bedded, the stock's remaining purpose is to help you shoot better. To do so, it must fit you. The length has to be right, but, of equal importance, height of comb must allow proper use of sights or scope. You should be able to weld your cheek firmly to the stock and get a good sight picture without having to lift your cheek or crane your neck because the comb is too low, or scrunch your face down into the stock because your comb is too high.

While I have little involvement with the tactical arena, I notice that many tactical stocks are adjustable for height of comb (and often length of pull). This is a very good feature. The larger scopes many of us are using today must be mounted high in order to clear the barrel, and a lot of perfectly good riflestocks weren't made with that in mind. A viable alternative is a strap-on comb that can be shimmed until it's perfect. A good recoil pad is also a near-essential feature. This is not because you need it to attenuate recoil—although you might—but so that the pad will grip your shoulder and preclude slipping during firing.

My daughter Caroline is fairly short. The laminated stock is the proper length for her, but we discovered that she needed a bit more height of comb to achieve a natural spot-weld when she cheeked the rifle. A strap-on cheekpiece solved the problem.

The classic varmint rifle has a heavy, beefy stock as well as a heavy barrel. This is a Remington 40-XB in .243 Winchester, consistently a quarter-inch rifle.

There are three primary options in stock material: wood, synthetic, and laminated wood. The choice doesn't impact accuracy *per se*, but a traditional wooden stock is the most likely to warp, and if it warps so that it is causing uneven pressure on the action or barrel, this is going to cause trouble. Synthetic stocks are more stable than wood and usually stronger, especially in the fragile grip area. Synthetic stocks, however, are not necessarily lighter than wood; this depends on the construction of the stock and the density of the wood. Laminated wood is probably the strongest of all, but also the heaviest. Unless you know you'll be shooting or hunting in wet country where warpage is likely—or doing really tough horseback hunts—there is no clear-cut advantage to any of the three materials as far as accuracy is concerned. Whatever the stock material, it remains essential that the stock fits you so that you don't have to fight it to get into a steady shooting position and obtain a clear sight picture.

In chapter 1 we talked a bit about barrel vibration. Although it can't be seen, the barrel actually oscillates during the passage of the bullet. Traditionally, bedding a barrel is a way to dampen that vibration or at least make it consistent.

The emerging new class of "tactical rifle" is pretty much an extension of the old "varmint rifle." Adjustable stocks are becoming more common, and with the larger scopes in common use today, this is a very sound feature.

Today, however, a great many barrels are free-floated, meaning that there is no contact between barrel and stock. This is the cheapest and easiest way to bed a barrel, as it is actually not bedding at all, but total *absence of bedding.* The barrel is allowed to vibrate as it will, and many barrels shoot extremely well this way.

Most heavy barrels are free-floated. They don't vibrate as much as light barrels, and they are unlikely to respond to other bedding techniques. Actually, any straight barrel of good quality may shoot very well free-floated, but the thinner the barrel is the more it vibrates, so a lot of sporter-weight barrels need a bit of help. A barrel that is fully bedded is the opposite of one that is free-floated: There is complete and consistent contact between barrel and stock throughout the barrel channel. This is the most difficult bedding to execute. A great craftsman can fully bed a wood stock by fitting the wood, but it is usually done by removing more wood than needed, then filling in with bedding compound to ensure a perfect fit.

There are numerous other techniques that lie somewhere between fully bedded and free-floated. It is very common to bed the first few inches of the barrel, then free-float the rest. Pillar-bedding or block-bedding (sometimes with fiberglass or plastic, sometimes with aluminum blocks) lays a foundation for the barrel to rest upon. In years gone by, Winchester often bedded Model 70s with just a bit of upward pressure on the fore-end tip, created by a pad of bedding compound just behind the fore-end tip.

The campfire arguments about which bedding technique is best are a lot of fun because most serious riflemen have a preferred technique. The arguments are also endless because there is actually no right (or wrong) answer. Bedding is about barrel vibration, but no two barrels are exactly alike and no barrel ever made is absolutely perfect, so no two barrels vibrate exactly the same. This means that some barrels will respond best to one bedding technique, and some to another. And with heavy barrels—and lighter barrels that are very straight and nearly perfect—the bedding technique may not matter much as long as there is no uneven pressure.

Here is a Kenny Jarrett Ridge Walker in .300 Winchester Magnum. With synthetic stock and both barrel and action by Jarrett, this rifle should shoot . . . and it obviously does!

Free-floating is essentially the absence of bedding; the barrel is allowed to vibrate as it will. A good barrel will usually shoot well when free-floated, but if it doesn't, there are numerous options that may improve accuracy (or may not).

In a later chapter we'll talk about troubleshooting accuracy. Right now, however, it needs to be said that when a rifle doesn't shoot the way its owner thinks it should, too many riflemen assume bedding is the culprit, so they immediately start hacking and sanding to change it. I don't agree with this. Rifle barrels are indeed individuals that respond differently to different bedding techniques. On the other hand, today's riflemakers know their actions and their barrels, and have a pretty good idea of what works for their products. It's always OK to question bedding, and never a bad idea to check for high spots; sideways pressure on a barrel is almost sure to cause erratic accuracy. However, it's not often a good idea to change the bedding system, at least not until a lot of other possibilities have been checked out.

There is one exception to this. Free-floating is extremely common these days; many barrels shoot very well free-floated, and many shoot well when partially bedded, then free-floated the rest of the way. There is a very quick and harmless experiment you can run that enhances accuracy with a shocking number of barrels. Shoot some groups with the barrel free-floated. Then loosen the action screws enough to slip a business card between barrel and stock, just behind the fore-end tip, and retighten the screws. Sometimes two or three thicknesses are needed, depending on the space between stock and barrel, but the idea is to create just a bit of even upward pressure, maybe two-and-a-half to three pounds. This seems to have the effect of dampening barrel vibration, or at least making it more consistent. Obviously this doesn't work all the time, but over the years I've been amazed at how many times this simple trick shrinks groups significantly. If it works, it can be made permanent with brass stock, or just by using trimmed business cards. If you use paper or thin cardboard, soak it in oil so it won't draw moisture and create rust.

To me, a full-length Mannlicher-style stock is one of the most beautiful of all stocks, but I've seen very few that would shoot well. This is probably a simple matter of too much wood contact, and the fact that the stock is "pinned" near the muzzle by a cap. The same shimming technique, right at the midpoint of

This is a new Mossberg Patriot .375 Ruger with a laminated stock. Today synthetic stocks are more common than conventional wood. Laminates, strongest of all, are becoming much more common.

Although very strong and impervious to warping, a disadvantage to laminate is weight. This laminated stock from E. R. Shaw weighs three pounds; the factory synthetic stock on the Ruger American is just 1.25 pounds, a big difference (page 41).

the barrel, often works wonders. Barrel vibration cannot be stopped, but it can sometimes be managed to improve accuracy.

This is exactly what the Browning/Winchester "Ballistic Optimizing Shooting System" (BOSS) attempts to do. The BOSS is simply an adjustable barrel weight, different in appearance but no different in effect than barrel weights used in certain classes of serious competition firearms. (Some BOSS systems incorporate a muzzle brake and some do not.) When we're trying various types of ammunition, part of what we're doing is finding a load that

suits the harmonics—the vibration—of the barrel. The goal is to create a situation so that, as the barrel oscillates, each bullet exits the muzzle at the same point in the vibration. With the BOSS you're doing the opposite: By moving the barrel weight forward and backward you are adjusting the barrel's vibration to the load. Sometimes it takes a lot of groups and sometimes it falls quickly into place, but when the groups start getting smaller you're nearing the point the designing engineers called "the sweet spot." The system works, and fiddling with it is a good lesson in the effects of barrel harmonics.

While we're on that subject, keep in mind that the exact position of the muzzle when the bullet exits is what determines accuracy and group size, and remember that, however microscopically, the muzzle is vibrating as the bullet exits. Anything that messes with the muzzle, such as a muzzle brake, can affect accuracy. Muzzle brakes work, of course. On heavy-recoiling rifles that may be shot from the prone position, they may be essential. I don't care for them, simply because I have long had more hearing loss than I can afford, but they work. Without question, however, they do change how the barrel vibrates.

I borrowed this vintage Mannlicher .30-06 with full-length stock on a brocket deer hunt in Mexico. The Mannlicher-style stock is gorgeous and handles wonderfully—but in my experience properly bedding a full-length stock is difficult, with accuracy often suffering.

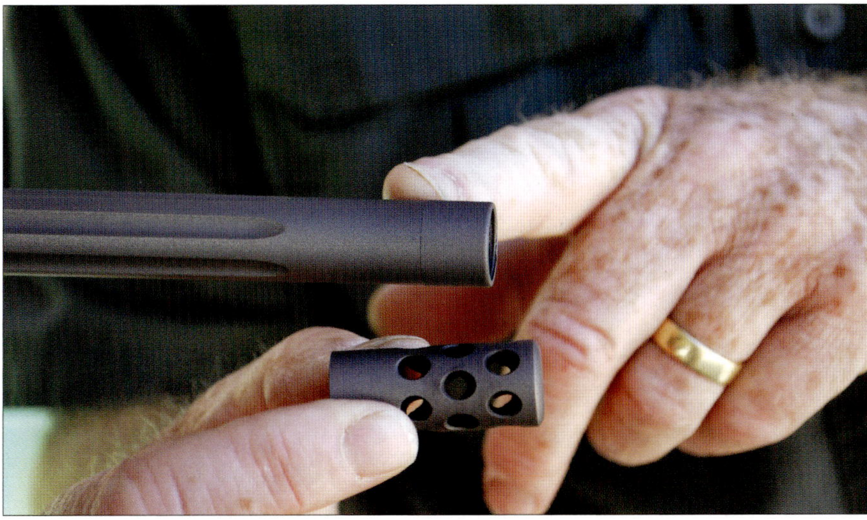

Anything on the end of the barrel can impact accuracy. A detachable muzzle brake that can be replaced with a thread protector is a wonderfully versatile option . . . but always check zero with and without the brake because point of impact can shift.

This doesn't matter if the brake is permanent. Popular today, however, are removable muzzle brakes. These brakes can be taken off the rifle and replaced by a thread-protecting muzzle cap. This is really the best of both worlds: You can practice on the range (using both earplugs and earmuffs) with the muzzle brake in place, and then remove it to go hunting. Just remember that when you remove the brake, you remove weight from the muzzle. Not all rifles will change zero when the brake is removed, but many will. This is something you absolutely must check. Never forget: When you remove a muzzle brake, you'd better check your zero.

TRIGGERS AND TRIGGER CONTROL

CHAPTER 4

The rifle's trigger system is totally unrelated to the potential accuracy of the rifle. There are, however, two factors related to the trigger system that have a great deal to do with the shooter's ability to maximize the rifle's accuracy. The obvious one is trigger pull, and the not-so-obvious one is lock time: the few milliseconds between the trigger "breaking" and the firing pin igniting the primer and starting the bullet on its way.

The ideal trigger pull depends a bit on the rifle's purpose. A dangerous-game rifle like this Rigby in .416 should definitely have a heavier trigger pull than, say, a heavy varmint rifle intended to be shot from a steady rest.

The best rifle shooting happens when the trigger breaks cleanly and crisply with relatively light pressure. A clean "break" is often likened to a glass rod suddenly shattering after steady and constant pressure is applied. Other terms often applied to trigger pull include "overtravel" and "backlash." Both of these are negative and, ideally, are minimal. Although some travel after firing is inevitable, overtravel means the trigger continues to move rearward excessively after the rifle fires; it isn't good because it creates additional finger movement during and after the shot. Backlash means the trigger springs back against the finger after the shot is fired. It is negative for the same reason, specifically in that it makes smooth, consistent follow-through very difficult. We'll talk about that later.

Trigger pull weight is the feature mentioned most frequently. Pull weight is very important, but doesn't exist in a vacuum. For instance, a trigger that is somewhat heavier but breaks cleanly may actually be easier to use than a lighter trigger that has significant overtravel and noticeable backlash. Also, it depends a whole lot on what you're used to.

In a perfect world, ideal pull weight depends on the rifle's intended purpose. A benchrest rifle, never intended for field use, may have a trigger pull measured in ounces, difficult to master but causing fast ignition with minimal human involvement. A varmint rifle intended to be fired from a steady rest can also have a very light trigger. On a hunting rifle, most of us with a lot of experience reckon a trigger pull between and 2.5 and perhaps 3.5 pounds to be about right. However, a large-caliber rifle intended for dangerous game should probably have a bit heavier trigger pull. You don't want any surprises as you gear up for recoil, and of course such a rifle is intended for close-range use under pressure, so a more conscious effort should be required to fire the rifle, perhaps more like a shotgun trigger.

Unfortunately our world isn't perfect, and triggers—especially *factory* triggers as supplied by manufacturers—are not created equal. To some extent, effective trigger control depends a lot on what you become accustomed to. Remember the old adage, "Beware the one-gun man?" Most of us shoot better with a good trigger, but with practice and familiarity it is very possible to shoot well with a truly horrible trigger. Perhaps toughest of all is to switch around. As a gunwriter I'm very conscious of this. Most of my own rifles have good

The two-stage "military-style" trigger remains standard on many ARs. It's a sound system if you're used to it, but there are now numerous aftermarket options with single-stage triggers.

triggers, but there are lots of circumstances where I'm obligated to use unfamiliar rifles for magazine articles and such.

It's pretty easy to get spoiled by a really good trigger, and then it's very difficult to switch back to a heavy, creepy trigger. As a caution, however, the reverse is also true. If you're used to, say, a really nasty seven-pound factory trigger, it can take some serious range time before you are not only comfortable with but also *safe* with a trigger pull one-third the weight.

Some triggers are designed to be adjustable. Others are more or less adjustable, but you void the warranty by fooling with them. Either way, messing with triggers is not something to be taken lightly; it is work for skilled gunsmiths—certainly not for beginners (or unhandy veterans like me!). Even then, not all triggers can be safely adjusted. The bolt action is the most likely for trigger adjustment or, if that isn't safely practical, for replacement. There are plenty of excellent aftermarket triggers available for most bolt-action rifles, with good names including Can-Jar, Jewell, and Timney. Other action types, by nature or design, are usually a lot trickier and often their triggers simply cannot be either adjusted or replaced.

The original AR-15 trigger was a typical military two-stage trigger (meaning significant slack or let-off before you hit pressure and begin the "real" trigger squeeze); it was heavy and creepy. Today, with more than ninety manufacturers making rifles on the AR action, there are lots of aftermarket triggers available, and of course the higher-end ARs have better factory triggers than the more basic models. Ruger has just offered a drop-in AR trigger, available in both two-stage and single-stage, that offers a trigger squeeze that is somewhat lighter, and a whole lot cleaner and smoother than standard. Simultaneously, they offered a drop-in trigger assembly for the 10/22 semiautomatic, which is now the world's most popular rimfire rifle.

Timney is one of many aftermarket triggers. It is a favorite not only as a replacement trigger, but it is also offered as "standard" by many custom and semicustom makers.

Trigger development continues. This is a new replacement trigger from Alaska Arms, offering a Model 70-style trigger for '98 Mauser actions.

To some extent, I've seen factory triggers come full circle. In the 1960s, at least on bolt actions, factory triggers were pretty darn good (and could usually be fixed if they weren't). As time went on, manufacturers became increasingly wary of the product liability specter hanging over their heads. In the 1980s and 1990s, factory triggers got heavier and creepier, and many were specifically designed to foil attempts at improvement. In many cases a trigger pull of five pounds was good news; I've seen quite a few that were seven pounds and more.

Some of those triggers are still out there (certainly on used rifles), but it appears the people have spoken, and rifle manufacturers have worked pretty hard at making improvements. Some rifles, including the current Remington Model 700, Ruger Model 77 Mark II, and Winchester Model 70, have new, improved trigger groups. Then there's the relatively new style of trigger that has a little vertical bar (usually skeletonized) protruding forward from the center of the trigger. The first of these was the Savage AccuTrigger, but a similar design is now seen on Mossberg rifles and the Ruger American. The little bar is actually a trigger safety, preventing the trigger from firing the rifle until the bar is pressed back into its recess in the trigger itself. Although it has been refined, this is actually not a new design; it dates back to a patent issued to a J. H. Brown in 1883! Brown's patent was for a complete rifle that was never manufactured, but the protruding trigger safety is a very clear part of his patent.

My first centerfire rifle was a surplus Springfield with a two-stage military trigger, and of course the rifles I qualified with in the Marines also had two-stage triggers. I'm comfortable with the feel, and the new trigger-safety designs are similar in that you are conscious of placing pressure on the little bar before your finger comes into contact with the actual trigger. The majority of sporting rifles, however, have a simple trigger that is more or less curved, sometimes smooth and sometimes with vertical striations. I don't think it matters much, except that, whatever trigger you have, it's important to spend time with it, both dry firing and actually shooting, so that you are comfortable with it and understand how much pressure is required for it to break.

"Set" triggers are much more common in Europe than in the United States. This is a vintage Mannlicher in 6.5x54mm Mannlicher-Schoenauer, featuring a double-set trigger. The rear "trigger" serves only to "set" the front trigger for a lighter pull.

The CZ 550 is one of very few rifles readily available in the U.S. with a single-set trigger. Used conventionally, the pull is normal. When the trigger is pushed forward, it is "set" for a much lighter pull. If you intend to use this feature, it's best to practice with it . . . a lot!

Whether on the range or in the field it isn't unusual to find a strange rifle in your hands. This can range from a simple "Hey, you wanna shoot this?" to having a rifle thrust into your hands because your own rifle has a mechanical or scope issue. The first thing you should do is make sure the rifle is completely empty, then dry-fire the rifle a few times to get the "feel" of the trigger. Dry-firing is not a good idea with rimfires, but it does no harm to modern centerfires. Again, a trigger that is a whole lot lighter *or* a whole lot heavier than what you are used to can cause an unpleasant surprise.

Although it is rarely seen on current American firearms, a common European trigger design is the "set" trigger. In a "double set" trigger the trigger guard appears to contain two triggers, but usually the rearmost "trigger" simply activates or "sets" the real (usually forward) trigger for a very light pull. In "single set" triggers there is just one trigger, but the trigger must be pushed forward to cock or "set" it, and then it releases with a very light pull. The single set triggers I have seen actually offer two trigger pulls. Without pushing it forward, the trigger pull is normal; when pushed forward to set, the trigger pull is greatly reduced. The CZ 550, for example, comes from the factory with a single-set trigger as standard. If you're going to use it in the field you'd better spend some time with it on the range! Once you're used to it, however, such a system does give the best of both worlds: A heavier trigger pull for fast-breaking situations, and a very light trigger pull for situations where you're in a steady, rested position and can really concentrate on your trigger squeeze. I have used this system, setting the trigger, in a couple of field situations, but you shouldn't try it unless you've spent plenty of time practicing with it and are familiar with the distinct feel of both trigger pulls.

OK, let's talk about trigger control. To shoot accurately, the trigger needs to break with pressure that is steady and constant. You do pull or slap a shotgun trigger, but we all know that "pulling" a rifle trigger is a bad thing (though perhaps not quite as bad as "jerking" the trigger). The preferred description is "squeezing" the trigger, but since we don't really squeeze anything with just one

A heavy, creepy trigger was a traditional disadvantage to the early ARs. Today's AR triggers have gotten much better, and to a great degree they enable the amazing accuracy this platform is capable of.

Although based on an 1880s patent, the "trigger safety" design is now growing in popularity. Savage was the first modern manufacturer to use this type of trigger. Mossberg followed, and now this trigger is found on the Ruger American (bottom). It is similar in feel to a military two-stage trigger . . . I like it!

finger, I'm not sure that's the most perfect word. A rifle trigger is activated by slow, deliberate pressure that builds steadily until the trigger breaks.

Trigger control starts with the whole hand. The pistol grip or "small of the stock" shouldn't be too large for your hand; ideally you can wrap your fingers comfortably around the stock, and then place the forward portion of your trigger finger on the trigger. Exactly where the finger makes contact isn't all that critical, and depends somewhat on the size of your hand. You don't want to use your fingertip or the joint itself, but contact should be comfortable somewhere between the pad of the fingertip and just outside the first joint. Pressure is exerted with the trigger finger only, "pressing" more than "squeezing," and the force should be horizontal. So, henceforth, let's call it a trigger "press" rather than a "pull" or a "squeeze."

While the press itself is critical, "follow-through" is equally important. Here's an important concept to remember: The shot doesn't stop until the bullet hits the target. Anyone who has done any shotgunning knows that it's important to keep the shotgun swinging during and after slapping the trigger; if you stop the gun, you will shoot behind the target. This is of equal importance in riflery. There's still a lot going on after the trigger breaks: The sear releases the hammer or striker, which still must travel forward. The primer has to be ignited, which in turn ignites the propellant charge. Smokeless powder doesn't actually explode; it burns very rapidly, the gases expanding at something over 5,000 feet per second, pushing the bullet down the barrel. All of this happens in milliseconds, but there's still plenty of time for you to mess up the shot through aberrant movement of your trigger finger.

"Barrel time" is the short period while the bullet is traveling down the barrel. The amount of time this takes depends on the velocity of the cartridge.

"Lock time," the period between the trigger breaking and the primer igniting, varies quite a bit. Serious benchrest shooters are very aware of the evils of lock time. They not only prefer ultra-light triggers; they gravitate toward actions that are very fast. In sporting rifles we don't worry about lock time too much, but to illustrate the point let's take two opposite examples. Have you ever fired, or seen fired, a flintlock firearm? The flint strikes the frizzen, creating a spark. The priming charge is ignited and burns through the flash hole, ig-

Lack of follow-through with the trigger press is a common problem, especially with long-range accuracy. At the SAAM shooting school, students quickly learn to study the trigger pull when a perplexing problem occurs, and often it's a matter of "coming off the trigger" too soon!

niting the main powder charge. There is an agonizing delay between pressing the trigger and the bullet starting down the barrel, long enough that one must not only concentrate on continuing the trigger squeeze, but also consciously maintaining the sight picture.

Pennsylvania, uniquely to my knowledge, maintains a flintlock deer season. My friends who follow that season tell me that, aside from dealing with vexing but almost inescapable failures of a flintlock rifle to fire in damp weather, the hardest part is maintaining the sight picture while the rifle goes off.

From this we'll move to the opposite end of the spectrum. Some years back an Austrian company (Voere) developed a "cartridge" that was actually a bullet seated in solidified propellant, no cartridge case. It was ignited by an electric impulse, instantaneous with the trigger breaking. Developed with military applications in mind, it came along before the First Gulf War, in a time when no one was buying. They tried the civilian market and apparently no one was buying there, either. I suspect the problem was that the ammunition was pricey, and also there was no practical way to vary the load. The concept died, but I had a chance to do some shooting and a bit of hunting with a sporting rifle that chambered this oddity. Wow, the action was fast! I've done enough shooting that I recognize some actions are faster than others, but I've never shot anything that was as noticeably and obviously as fast as that. It actually took a lot of the work out of shooting. More recently Remington has also offered electronic ignition with conventional brass-cased cartridges, although I gather demand has not been high. Still, to understand lock time you really need to shoot a flintlock . . . and then shoot a firearm with speed-of-light electronic ignition.

For now, just keep in mind that both lock time and barrel time are factors in accuracy, and the only solution is to follow through: Keep pressing the trigger steadily and consistently (and maintaining your shooting position and sight picture) until after the bullet exits the barrel. Since there is no way to know precisely when this occurs, the rule of thumb is: The shot doesn't end until the bullet hits the target.

Proper trigger use is a constant throughout all rifle shooting. Where the finger makes contact isn't so important, but it is critical to be consistent and to follow through. Practice doesn't require sustaining recoil; shooting with a good .22 is ideal training for learning and maintaining a good trigger press.

In recent years I've spent quite a bit of time at Tim Fallon's ranch in the Texas Hill Country, where his Sportsman's All-Weather, All-Terrain Marksmanship (SAAM) rifle-shooting courses are conducted. Here's an interesting thing: When a student is having a perplexing accuracy issue, especially at longer ranges, the instructors get up close and stare at the student's trigger finger while shots are fired. More often than not, the culprit is lack of follow-through: coming off the trigger too soon rather than maintaining steady and consistent pressure during and after the firing of the shot. Obviously it's just as important to maintain your position and sight picture, but if you really concentrate on your trigger press, you'll find that everything else tends to follow along and remains stable. Remember: The shot doesn't end until the bullet strikes the target.

Cartridge Design

Chapter 5

It is irrefutable that cartridge design is a factor in accuracy. We can state as a fact that the .308 Winchester is a more accurate cartridge than the .30-06, and that the .300 Winchester Short Magnum is a more accurate cartridge than the .300 Winchester Magnum. Mike Walker, longtime mainstay at Remington and one of our greatest benchrest champions, designed the .222 Remington for accuracy, and you can put in the bank that it is a more

Although I'm a huge fan of the .30-06 (right), I concede that the .308 Winchester (left) is a more accurate cartridge. This is because the case is shorter and wider in relation to the powder column; thus, it burns more efficiently. This may not have been known when the .308 was introduced in 1952, but today we know the "short, fat" case design works!

accurate cartridge than the more popular .223 Remington or the faster .22-250 Remington. But don't get carried away with this thought, because in practice, good barrels, rigid actions, true assembly, and consistent ammunition are more important factors than cartridge design. There are lots of .30-06 rifles that shoot better than lots of .308 rifles, and so forth. Even so, in any clinical discussion of accuracy it would be improper to overlook cartridge design as a factor, even though the actual gains are often theoretical rather than practical.

The first self-contained rifle cartridges were weak rimfires designed to fit into fledgling repeating actions like the Henry and Spencer. Single-shot actions could be made larger, so in the 1870s, with the advent of centerfire ignition, cartridge design diverged. A host of large-cased black-powder cartridges were chambered to an equally diverse host of single-shot actions. In those days it became less a matter of fitting the cartridge to the action than cramming enough black powder into the case to get the job done: .45-70, meaning .45-caliber, 70 grains of black powder; .50-90, meaning .50-caliber, 90 grains of black powder, and so forth.

Smokeless powder changed that, enabling unprecedented velocity and much higher energy per grain of propellant burned. Calibers and cartridge cases got smaller, and although pressures were much higher it was a great deal easier to design practical repeating actions. In the early days of smokeless powder, propellants weren't anywhere near as good as they are today, even though the basic formula for nitrocellulose propellants hasn't changed much since 1890. Also, it's fair to say that barrels were not as good as they are today. Until fairly recently, cartridge design was primarily about increasing velocity or power, or designing a cartridge that would fit into a certain action.

It is perhaps an accident that the .308 Winchester is more accurate than the .30-06. Over time, as propellants got better, standard velocities for the .30-06 increased significantly. In both World Wars, it was the most powerful cartridge employed by any major power, and, great battle rifle that it was, the M1 Garand was probably the heaviest rifle in common use. While .30-06 performance was legendary, the only way to reduce gun weight and increase magazine capacity was to use a smaller cartridge. The M14, fielded in 1957, has its origin as a shortened Garand with a detachable box magazine. Its cartridge was ready a few years earlier. The .308 Winchester was introduced

The mild .44 Henry (left) with rimfire priming was one of the first successful self-contained metallic cartridges. Winchester's centerfire .44-40 (right), introduced in 1873, was a major step forward. In those days cartridge design was mostly about creating cartridges to fit rifle actions.

in 1952 and officially adopted as the 7.62x51mm NATO in 1954. It is nothing more than a .30-06 with its case shortened from 2.494 inches to 2.015 inches. Powder capacity was lost, but the .308 Winchester lags barely 100 feet per second behind the .30-06, and is considerably faster than the original .30-06 developed in 1903 (as the .30-03 version).

Part of the reason is that propellants, although chemically similar, were much advanced over what was available a half-century earlier. The design of the cartridge was another factor, but whether this was fully known in 1952 is unclear. Experiments with tank cannons showed that the wider a cartridge is in relation to its length, the greater percentage of the propellant is instantly accessed by the primer flame. This tends to allow a smoother and more consistent burning curve, which has multiple benefits: Complete burning (and thus full velocity) can be obtained in a shorter barrel; more energy can be obtained per grain of powder burned; and the smoother burning curve is conducive to more consistent accuracy.

The .308 Winchester has the same .473-inch base diameter as the .30-06, but the case is nearly a half-inch shorter. It is thus comparatively "short and fat," coming surprisingly close to .30-06 velocities while burning considerably less powder—and most experts agree that, if everything else could be made exactly equal, the .308 is more accurate than the .30-06.

So, continuing this thought, the ideal cartridge case would probably be triangular in shape, about as wide at the base as it is long. The problem is this is an impossible configuration for any rifle action as we know it, so that won't happen any time soon. But now that we understand this dynamic, we do have some short, fat cartridges that tend to be accurate.

Years ago, spurred by American wildcatters, Remington standardized the Benchrest Remington (BR) case, a much-shortened .308 that was necked to .22, 6mm, 7mm, .30, and God knows what else. The BR cartridges were popular for a time, especially in specialty pistols like Remington's XP-100, but seem

An important part of cartridge design is creating an index for headspacing, essentially the fit of the cartridge to the chamber. Various headspace means, left to right: rim (.30-30); shoulder (6.5x54); belt (.375 H&H); case mouth, common in pistol cartridges but unusual with rifles (.30 Carbine); and semirimmed (.401 Winchester Self-Loading and 6mm Lee Navy).

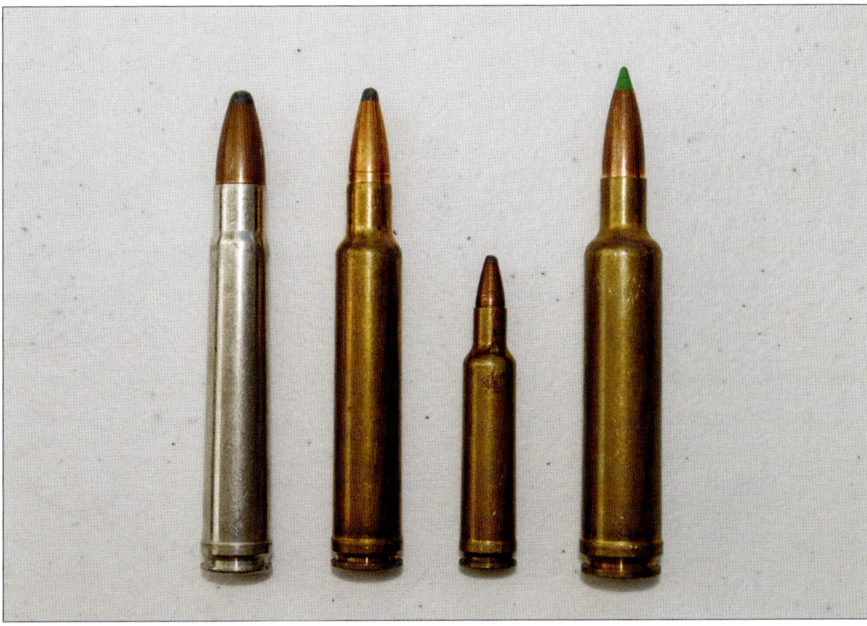

Left to right: .375 H&H, .300 Weatherby Magnum, .224 Weatherby Magnum, .30-.378 Weatherby Magnum. Most belted cartridges, including the majority of the Weatherby line, are based on the .375 H&H case. The Weatherby line also includes some of the exceptions, like the .224 and the cartridges based on the big .378 case.

to have almost vanished. A similar family is the PPC, developed by R. Lou Palmisano and Ferris Pindell and based on a shortened 7.62x39 case. Only Sako ever chambered commercial firearms to a PPC cartridge, but the 6mm PPC remains popular in benchrest competition. Interestingly, both the BR and PPC family have "small rifle" primer pockets, thought to also be conducive to accuracy, but both families of cartridges are very short, and thus "short and fat" relative to length.

Of course you know where I'm going with this. In the late 1990s, in what appears to be parallel development, both Winchester and Remington were working on new families of magnums based more or less (more with Remington, a bit less with Winchester) on the old .404 Jeffery case, a large-diameter (.550-inch base) unbelted case. This was not an entirely new concept. Most of the proprietary Dakota Magnums are based on the Jeffery case, and although there are internal differences, several of John Lazzeroni's proprietary

Lazzeroni Magnums are based on one of the fattest of all commercial cases, the .416 Rigby, as is the .338 Lapua.

In addition to the wide case, which makes a cartridge relatively "short and fat" unless length is extreme, all of these cartridges are unbelted. This is another consideration for accuracy. Clear back in 1912, when the .375 H&H took the world by storm, some idiot decided that a belted case suggested higher velocity and thus "magnum" performance. For the next eighty years almost every cartridge to be called a "magnum" wore a belt, and most of them were based on the .375 H&H case, necked this way and that and either left full-length or shortened. But the belt actually had nothing to do with case strength or cartridge performance.

It is crucial to both safety and accuracy that the case of a self-contained rifle cartridge fits its chamber. We call this fit "headspacing." There are essentially four ways for a rifle cartridge to headspace. A rimmed cartridge headspaces on the rim, and a belted cartridge headspaces on the belt. A rimless cartridge with a straight or slightly tapered case headspaces on the case mouth; this is common in pistol cartridges but uncommon with rifle cartridges. A rimless cartridge with a bottleneck shape headspaces *on the case shoulder*. This has always been considered a more precise method of fitting than on belt or rim, and, clearly, a more precise fit of cartridge to chamber is conducive to better accuracy.

Now back to the Great Magnum Race of the late 1990s and early 2000s. John Lazzeroni is a great friend of mine, and I respect him immensely. He makes loud and seemingly exaggerated claims for the performance of his cartridges, but I've run nearly all of them over my chronograph, and John Lazzeroni's cartridges do exactly what he says they will do. In the 1990s he spent a lot of money on advertising and a lot of ink was spilled. He developed extensive families of both short (.308 Winchester-length) and full-length (.375 H&H-length) cartridges, using the extra-large rim and base diameter of the old .416 Rigby cartridge for the majority of his designs. By the mid-1990s Lazzeroni was making the major manufacturers nervous, just as Roy Weatherby did in the 1950s. The simple thing would have been for the majors to co-opt him and adopt his cartridges, but he used a full-diameter rim on a big case, and there were very few commercial actions that would house his cartridges without extensive (and expensive) redesign.

John Lazzeroni is setting up for a shot with his 7.21 Fireball. As Roy Weatherby did in the 1950s, Lazzeroni in the 1990s made the major manufacturers nervous with his ultra-fast, proprietary cartridges. Because of size, few adopted Lazzeroni's cartridges, but he almost certainly gave rise to the large number of magnums introduced in the late '90s and early 2000s.

So the majors went their own way, using the slightly smaller .404 Jeffery (.550-inch) case diameter with a rebated rim of smaller diameter than the case head. It is said that Remington already had short, unbelted magnums on the drawing board, and this is probably true. Whatever, Remington struck first in 1999 with the .300 Remington Ultra Magnum: 2.850-inch case, same as the old .375 H&H, base diameter of .550-inch, and rim rebated to .534-inch (almost the same as the .375 H&H and all of its progeny). I missed that introduction, but in 2000 I joined my old friend Chub Eastman, then of Nosler, in Tanzania for a workout of the whole family of full-length Remington Ultra Magnums (RUMs): 7mm, .300, .338, and .375 RUM.

The 7mm RUM is overbore capacity, a term that simply means the size of the hole down the bore isn't big enough to properly burn all the powder. As far as accuracy goes this is not the kiss of death, but a cartridge that is overbore capacity will be finicky in the powders that can be used, and rapid throat erosion is likely. Still, it's a very fast 7mm! The .300, .338, and .375 RUMs are among the fastest cartridges we have in those bullet diameters, and the unbelted design is sound. They are excellent. Neither the .338 nor .375 have been popular, almost certainly due to extreme recoil, but it appears to me that the .300 RUM is finally catching on, as it deserves to.

So in 2000 we had four full-length RUMs, although their future was unclear. That was the year that Winchester started with the opposite approach, introducing the .300 Winchester Short Magnum (WSM): 2.1-inch case, .555-inch base diameter, rim rebated to .535-inch. Using the "short and fat" concept, the .300 WSM produces velocities very similar to the longer, belted .300 Winchester Magnum. Combining the short, fat case with shoulder (instead of belt) headspacing, it is technically a more accurate cartridge. It did reasonably well, and the floodgates opened. A year later Winchester added the .270 and 7mm WSMs, and in 2002 Remington countered with the 7mm and .300 Remington Short Action Ultra Mags (RSAUM), based on the Ultra Mag case shortened to 2.015 (same length as the .308 Winchester).

Although Lazzeroni's pressures are a bit higher than standard, he uses nonstandard extra-heavy brass. In my experience his claimed velocities were consistently accurate. This 7.82 (.308) Warbird with 130-grain Barnes X-Bullet came very close to 4,000 feet per second!

I used a .300 Remington Ultra Mag to take this greater kudu. Introduced in 1998, the .300 RUM was the first of what would be four full-length Remington Ultra Mags: 7mm, .300, .338, and .375. Without question the .300 RUM has been the most successful of the four.

Things were already confusing enough. Winchester beat them to the short-action cartridges, so why did Remington bother? Well, Remington had a problem. The WSM case was just a wee bit too long for their compact Model Seven action, and undoubtedly they already had their cartridges on the drawing board. So by 2002 we had five new short, fat factory magnums, and in a short time Winchester added the .325 WSM. Neither 7mm has done especially well—maybe we already had enough 7mm cartridges? The .325 WSM is a great cartridge, but above .30-caliber the American market drops like a rock, so it's hard to judge its lasting impact. The .300 WSM has probably been the most popular of the bunch, but the .270 WSM is doing fine, and the .300 RSAUM has a following, in part because it fits into actions that won't house the WSMs.

In 2003 Winchester surprised me (if not everyone else!) by introducing the Winchester Super Short Magnums (WSSM), the WSM shortened to 1.67 inches—a real little fireplug of a case necked to .22, .243, and .25 caliber.

These carry the short, fat concept almost to its ultimate extreme. They were fast and accurate, but there were issues. The grim reality of all the short magnums (including WSM and RSAUM) is that, after more than a century of actions based on either the .30-06-size .474-inch rim cartridges or belted .532-inch rim cartridges, the new short, fat cartridges caused feeding problems with many actions. The WSSMs were worse. Despite initial hype, they have already been dropped. Perhaps there are two lessons: First, and most important: The shooting community can only absorb so many new cartridges in a given period. Second: Performance in terms of increased velocity and accuracy is wonderful, but the cartridges still need to feed.

This was the issue addressed by Hornady's and Ruger's collaboration in yet four more cartridges. They started with the .375 Ruger, an incredibly sound design that uses the .375 H&H's .532-inch rim and belt diameter, but extends it forward in an unbelted case with a length of 2.580 inches. They started out to create a case that could be housed in a .30-06-length action, but would equal the performance of the .375 H&H. In this they exceeded their expectations; because of the efficiency of the shorter, fatter case, the .375 Ruger exceeds the .375 H&H by about 100 feet per second. Despite the fact that we still have too many new cartridges, this one has legs. It was probably the most successful introduction of a large-caliber cartridge in history, and it seems to be gaining ground. In a radical departure for the brand, Mossberg has just introduced a version of its Patriot bolt action in .375 Ruger, so this cartridge is here to stay.

The Hornady/Ruger team followed up the .375 with the .416 Ruger, obviously necked up to .416. It's an equally good cartridge, but when you get above .30-caliber the market drops, and when you get above .40-caliber it's very small. The .416 Ruger is a great little cartridge, but it won't win any popularity races.

The .375 Ruger case is a great case not only because it's short and fat, but also because it isn't extremely fat. It will feed properly in actions of appropriate length, and it can be manufactured without significant retooling. This was the concept when they shortened it to create the .300 and .338 Ruger Compact Magnums (RCMs) that followed. Thanks to Hornady's proprietary blended propellants that created their Superformance ammo line, both RCMs are incredibly fast for their size (they are the same length as the .308 Winchester).

Left to right: .270, 7mm, .300, and .325 Winchester Short Magnum; .25 Winchester Super Short Magnum; 7mm and .300 Remington Short Action Ultra Mag; .and 300 and .338 Ruger Compact Magnum. This lineup includes the majority of the new short magnums released in just a few years. Obviously these were more than the market could bear, and not all have been successful.

The .300 RCM holds its own with the .300 WSM and .300 Winchester Magnum; the .338 RCM comes very close to the .338 Winchester Magnum. So far neither cartridge has expanded significantly beyond the Ruger line, but in time they may because the design is sound—not just the short/fat concept, but the fact that they feed wonderfully. The real problem with so many of our brave new magnums isn't a matter of design or performance, but too many new cartridges in just a decade.

I'm writing these lines in 2015. During the last few years new cartridge development has slowed dramatically. In part this is because of the glut we've talked about, but it's also because, in a time of nationwide ammo shortages and round-the-clock shifts at all the plants, there has been little point in introducing new cartridges. There is plenty of development in new cartridges to fit the amazingly popular AR frame, but these are based not so much on accuracy or velocity, but on trying to cram more performance into an action that has sharp limits on the cartridge dimensions it will accept.

We all have our favorites, and of all the new magnums, the .270 WSM is the one I have used the most. Although it shoots only slightly flatter than the .270 Winchester, it churns up more energy and seems to hit harder. I've used it for quite a bit of mountain hunting, including on this Siberian ibex in Mongolia.

Again, given a good barrel, good action, and good ammo you can get tiny groups from almost any cartridge. But if you wanted to invest in a really good barrel, and your goal was to get the very best accuracy possible, then you might—I say again, *might* want to consider cartridge design as a criterion.

On the other hand, it's fairly rare for us to consider either accuracy or case design as the only criteria for choosing a cartridge. Usually we have some performance characteristics in mind. For instance, if you are interested in a light, versatile mountain rifle, then you might consider one of the short magnums, whether a WSM or an RSAUM. It could be in .270, 7mm, or .30-caliber persuasion, depending on your preference. It could be housed in a short action, and would approach full velocity in a 22-inch barrel, saving bulk as well as weight.

Perfect choices, right? Maybe! Let's hold on just a second and make sure we all know what we're getting . . . and not getting. One thing that is seductive and a bit misleading about the entire class of short and fat cartridges is that, compared to standard cartridges and belted magnums of like caliber, they perform best with *standard bullet weights*: in .270, 130 to 150 grains; in 7mm, 140 to 150 grains; in .30 caliber, 150 to 180 grains. Above this point, case capacity starts to be problematic. Since the short, fat cartridges are designed to fit into short actions, bullets that are heavier and thus longer must be seated deeper into the case, and that starts to rob powder capacity. This doesn't apply so much to the .270, since the 160-grain Nosler Partition is one of very few heavier bullets available in that bullet diameter. It applies big time to the 7mms and .300s, though: Standard 7mm bullets go up to 175 grains, Berger offers a 180-grain bullet, and there are even heavier bullets for long-range and match purposes. Standard .30-caliber bullets go to at least 200 grains, and there are 220-grain bullets intended for larger game. Berger offers a 230-grain long-range match bullet, and there are .30-caliber bullets as heavy as 250 grains.

The .375 Ruger has probably been the most successful large-caliber American cartridge. Although it's a bit faster, it won't do anything the .375 H&H won't do . . . but it fits into a standard-length action and can be built into a lighter, handier rifle. I've used it for quite a bit of African game, including this Zimbabwe Cape buffalo.

The .375 Ruger (right) is an unbelted cartridge using the .532-inch rim and the belt diameter of the .375 H&H. The case was shortened to create the .338 Ruger Compact Magnum (left) and its companion .300 RCM . . . and it was also necked up to create the .416 Ruger.

Is it important to be able to use the heavier bullets? Probably not, if your intention is to hunt the deer/sheep/goat class of animals at normal ranges and you have no desire to enter long-range competition. However, in the case of hunting bullets, heavier bullets tend to penetrate better and deliver a heavier blow. Extra-heavy match bullets designed for aerodynamics hold velocity better and resist wind better. The short, fat cartridges will definitely handle these bullets, but velocity starts to fall off quickly as bullet length eats into powder capacity. So if you have interest in hunting larger and tougher game—for instance, bears—you may not want to limit yourself to the lighter bullets. The same is true if you're really serious about extreme-range shooting. The benefits of short, fat cartridges are real, but they aren't everything.

The .300 Winchester Magnum is the world's most popular "magnum" cartridge. From a design standpoint, it has two accuracy-robbing problems. First, it's a belted cartridge offering headspace on the belt. We've discussed this, but we haven't mentioned its second issue: It has a very short, .264-inch neck. Longstanding cartridge design wisdom holds that a cartridge should have at least a "full-caliber" neck (in this case .308-inch) in order to properly grip the bullet. When the .300 Winchester Magnum was introduced in 1963 there were immediate howls about its too-short neck, theoretically robbing accuracy. It is true that the .300 Winchester Magnum has rarely been used as a match cartridge, but it's also true that it is now commonly used in military sniping communities, and these extremely picky marksmen have no issues with its accuracy.

We could argue that the longer, belted .300 Weatherby Magnum is faster, and that .300 RUM, with its rimless design and fatter case, is also faster and might be, on average, more accurate—but once again the people have spoken, and at this writing the .300 Winchester Magnum is the most popular of the fast .30-caliber cartridges, as well as being the most popular cartridge that wears the "magnum" suffix. Popularity doesn't necessarily mean it has the flattest trajectory, best terminal performance, or best design for accuracy.

Popularity isn't always a pure reflection of merit. The .223 Remington is the most popular .22 centerfire, even though the old .222 Remington is more accurate and the .22-250 is much faster.

Because of the huge popularity of the AR platforms, much current cartridge design centers around developing cartridges that will fit the frame. This AR-10 is chambered to the .300 RSAUM. It's tight but it works, while the more popular .300 WSM won't quite fit.

Popularity does, however, suggest that there will be a wider assortment of factory loads . . . and, for handloaders, a richer legacy of proven load data. In the search for accuracy, these things can be every bit as important as accuracy-enhancing cartridge design features.

FACTORY AMMO

CHAPTER 6

My dad grew up in eastern Kansas in a time when there were no deer in the state. So he and his dad, my grandfather, were serious bird hunters, like many good Kansans of their day. Dad was one of the fastest and deadliest shots on quail and pheasant that I ever saw, but I don't think he ever fired a centerfire rifle until he became fascinated with them when I was about eleven years old. We learned together, but we weren't exactly self-

A centerfire cartridge consists of four components: the propellant charge, primer, case, and projectile. Choices in factory loads are more varied than ever before, but it must still be kept in mind that all of these components can be varied almost endlessly, and a factory load is just one combination.

taught. Dad had a friend, Jack Pohl, who owned the old Bishop gunstock firm in Warsaw, Missouri. Reinhart Fajen was there too, and a sign on the outskirts of town proclaimed Warsaw "Gunstock Capital of the World."

Pohl did some big-game hunting, but he was primarily a benchrest shooter and woodchuck hunter. So our initiation included learning benchrest techniques that I still use today, and hunting woodchucks in the rolling Ozark hills. A graduation exercise would be a pronghorn hunt in Wyoming. There were, however, rules to the training regimen, and one of those rules was that before we actually started shooting, I would learn how to handload. We started with Jack's equipment, using original Hodgdon reclaimed military powder stored in age-darkened jars. Then we got an RCBS press that I still have.

Not only was learning to handload, carefully and methodically, a really good exercise for a too-eager kid, but also, in those days, there were significant reasons. Cost was certainly a factor; Lord knows we shot enough to quickly amortize the equipment, probably in the first couple of years. But there was

Available choices are far greater in popular cartridges. Because of its larger caliber and limited purposes, the .375 H&H, though a standard, doesn't sell nearly as well as many smaller cartridges. Even so, these are just a few of the many factory offerings in .375 H&H.

Hornady's "American Whitetail" series is an inexpensive load, but it is obviously good ammo. Although there's no telling what load a given rifle will shoot best, this particular .270, a Kimber Mountain Ascent, really liked this 130-grain American Whitetail load!

another rationale. In those days factory ammo was OK, but bullet selection was pretty much limited to factory bullets: Federal's Hi-Shok, Remington's Core-Lokt and Bronze Point, Winchester's Power Point and the old Silvertip. These, too, were OK (and some of them are still OK today), but the main problem was that in those days factory ammo was very much a mass-produced commodity. It was an article of faith that if one really wanted accuracy, or to tailor a load for a specific rifle and purpose, handloading was the only way to go. This was undoubtedly not always true, but I was indoctrinated to believe it, and my faith was unshakable for nearly thirty years.

Today I am not so sure. It remains true that you can assemble a more perfect cartridge than you can buy, and certainly you can tailor a load to a given rifle, not only choosing the bullet you most want to use (to be addressed in chapter eight), but also experimenting endlessly with propellants, powder charges, primers, bullets, seating depths, and more. In the next chapter my young friend Phil Massaro will make a guest appearance and tell us about handloading for accuracy. He is more astute and diligent on the subject than I am, and also much more up-to-date on the most current techniques and tools for loading the most precise ammo possible.

You see, although I've now handloaded for fully fifty years, I realize that I was always a lazy handloader. Mind you, I did a bit of postgraduate stuff with a couple of wildcat cartridges, and back in the 1980s, when fresh ammo for the old Nitro Express cartridges was virtually unavailable, I worked with the old Berdan primers and figured out safe loads for cartridges like the .470 and .450/.400. Of course I always worked up loads, checking accuracy and pressure, but my goal was usually to find a good load that would beat any factory load I'd tried. Back in the day that wasn't so difficult, and when I got there I usually figured it was good enough, and quit experimenting.

Over time things changed, and today factory ammo is a lot harder to beat. It was nearly forty years ago that Federal started the race with its Federal Premium line. From the start, and today, it was and is pretty good stuff, but

How many factory loads should you try? As many as you can! These two .300 Winchester Magnum rifles, a LAW M704 (top) and a Jarrett Ridge Walker (bottom) are both extremely accurate rifles . . . but group sizes vary quite a bit from load to load.

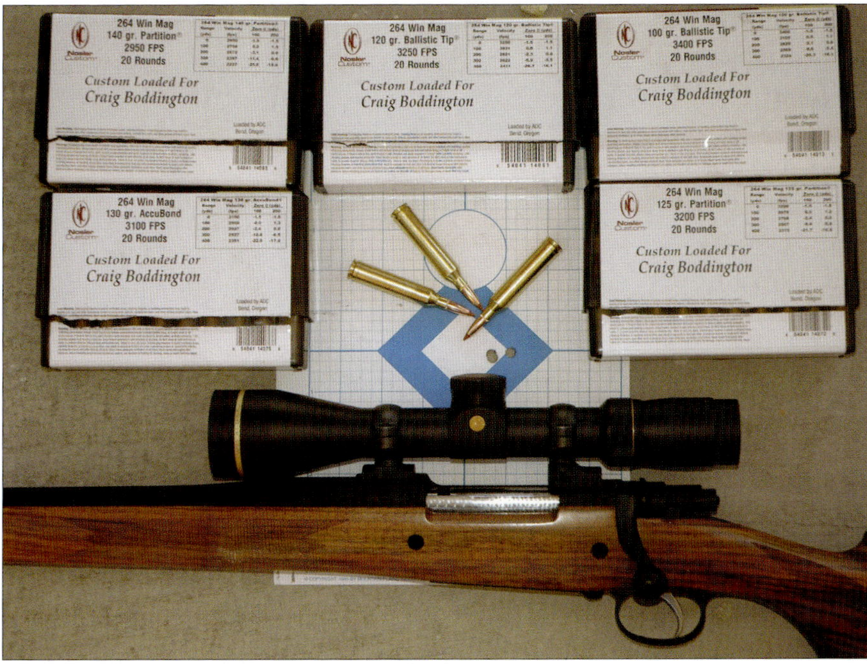

Smaller ammo companies have really stepped into the gap with certain cartridges that have a following but are not popular enough to interest the largest manufacturers. Uniquely, Nosler offers a robust selection of loads for the unloved .264 Winchester Magnum—which happens to be an old favorite of mine.

what was different about it was that it announced the use of "name" bullets previously available only to handloaders. It started with Nosler Partitions, at that time the premier hunting bullet, and Sierra boattails, at that time (and still) a premium bullet for accuracy. Federal Premium has continued to expand and offer more choices, now including Barnes, Woodleigh, and others among its offerings.

In the same period, Hornady, formerly a bullet company and reloading equipment firm, started offering loaded ammo. Initially they had Frontier, later Custom . . . and today they have several diverse lines running up and down the caliber scale. Of course their ammo features only Hornady bullets, but that line, too, has expanded. Barnes, formerly a bullet company, now has its own line of VOR-TX ammo featuring Barnes bullets. Likewise, Nosler offers loaded ammo with its own bullets, Nosler Custom, and more.

The remaining majors, Remington and Winchester, have not been complacent. While the Core-Lokt and Power Point remain important parts of their respective lines, both have continued to increase offerings in their own production bullets, and both companies also use "name" bullets from other manufacturers. Winchester has a longstanding partnership with Nosler in which both firms have collaborated on "Combined Technology" bullets—bullets that are not all Nosler, and not all Winchester. Remington has been a primary partner of Swift Bullets, offering both the Swift A-Frame and Swift Scirocco in selected cartridges.

There are also some great offshore ammunition lines, some of which are rarely seen in this country, such as Germany's RWS. Perhaps the best-known European brand, Norma, has recently made a decided push to be on the shelves in the United States. I don't think any domestic firm offers quite as many bullet choices as Norma under a single brand. Norma has produced Weatherby's branded ammo for decades, and it is good stuff.

Then there are the smaller firms that, in the wake of the last few years of ammo shortages, aren't so small anymore. Black Hills ammunition has been around for years, and today they're a major player. Their cartridge offerings are not huge and are generally restricted to the more popular cartridges, but they use "name" bullets and make really good ammo. Smaller firms such as Double Tap have concentrated on some cartridges that the majors have neglected, such as 8mm Remington Magnum, .358 Winchester, and .35 Whelen, along with popular numbers.

Then there are custom and semicustom loading firms. Perhaps the best known of these is Superior Ammunition, but there are many. In his Massaro Ballistics Laboratories, my friend Phil Massaro produces custom-loaded ammo, as does Dave Dunn's Trop Gun Shop in Pennsylvania. Such firms offer a source for hard-to-find cartridges, and for those who don't handload, custom loaders offer an opportunity to specify the bullet you want at an approximate (attainable) velocity.

This is good news. It may take some digging, you might have to plan ahead, and rare cartridges will always be more expensive than popular ones, but there is almost no such thing as unavailable ammunition. More good news is that factory ammo really is a whole lot better than it used to be.

Though not a large company, Double Tap offers some interesting loads for a number of marginally popular cartridges. I needed an "unleaded" .35 Whelen load to hunt pigs in California's "Condor Zone," and they had a fast load with Barnes X-Bullets—perfect!

There is, however, a cloud around this silver lining. No matter what case, primer, propellant, or bullet is used, a factory load is just that: One load recipe out of thousands of potential variations. Some rifles are finicky and others are not, but no rifle shoots all loads with equal accuracy, and some rifles vary significantly in group size from one load to another. So when you take one factory load and fire it in one rifle you quickly learn what accuracy your rifle produces *with that load*. What you cannot know is if that accuracy is average, awesome, or just plain terrible in relation to what the rifle is capable of producing.

Now, whether you care or not is up to you. Maybe you're a lazy shooter like I'm a lazy handloader, and good enough is good enough, but it depends on your purposes, too. If all you need to do is sit on a deer stand and wait for an eighty-yard shot, then group size isn't critical. If you want to really see what your rifle will do—or if the ultimate purpose is punching paper, prairie dogs, deer, or sheep at longer ranges—then you've got some work ahead.

I find factory ammo frighteningly expensive these days. Cost is a major drawback to shooting it. Some (few) brands are available in boxes of ten, but most commonly with rifle ammo you have to purchase a box of twenty. If it's really terrible in your rifle you'll know that in just a few shots . . . and then you have a partial box that will sit on your shelves for ages, gathering dust (as I do in my garage). The obvious advantage to handloading is that you can work up just the right amount of ammo to test a load, and have no waste. If it appears hopeless you can always stop where you are, go back to the bench, pull the bullets, recover the propellant, and start over another day.

Five-shot groups used to be the norm for accuracy testing, but three-shot groups are more common today. Statistically it's a matter of *shots*, not groups, so you can fire three five-shot groups or five three-shot groups (letting the barrel cool between groups). Measure them, and record the load and the average. This,

Left to right: .358 Winchester, .356 Winchester, .35 Whelen, .350 Remington Magnum, .358 Norma Magnum. Though hard-hitting and useful, the .35s just aren't very popular. Except for the .35 Whelen, factory load selection is almost nil; consequently, users of these cartridges need to either handload or seek out smaller, semicustom loading firms.

I took this Mozambique buffalo with a Turnbull Model 1886 in .475 Turnbull.

Sometimes handloading is the only choice. There is no other lever-action cartridge with the capability of the .475 Turnbull, but you're going to have to load your own (or get someone to load it for you).

of course, isn't a firm rule. Some folks fire more groups, throwing out the high or low, and for sure if you wobble and have a called flier, you should throw out that shot. The reason you take an *average* is that groups can be flukes, both good and bad. In evaluating a load, *consistency* is what matters. Keep your rifle consistent, too. We'll talk about break-in and cleaning later, but if you're shooting groups you probably want to clean the barrel at least every fifteen shots (whether you're shooting three five-shot groups or five three-shot groups).

This is not a one-day project, and you don't want it to be. Shooting groups is hard work that takes a lot of concentration. The larger the caliber, the harder it is. We all have a recoil threshold, and you can't shoot decent groups if you go beyond your limit. So think of it as a long-term project. If you have a deadline, such as getting a rifle ready for a special hunt, plan multiple range sessions. You have the data, so you can try a different load or perhaps two (rarely more than two, especially with heavier rifles) at every session. This also spreads out

It takes time to test loads properly for accuracy, and it probably takes multiple range sessions. Take your time, and don't be too ambitious. You're looking for averages, not good flukes or bad flukes, so two or three loads in one session are probably the limit.

To keep the playing field level, you need to take your time and allow the barrel to cool between groups. You should probably clean your rifle frequently while shooting for accuracy, and that means at least after every fifteen shots or so.

the cost of ammo and helps ensure you're getting real results rather than groups exaggerated by fatigue.

With popular cartridges you will probably never get through all the available factory loads. Bob Forker's excellent *Ammo & Ballistics*, now in its sixth edition, lists well over a hundred factory loads for the .308. Other popular cartridges such as the .223, .22-250, .270 Winchester, .30-06, and .300 Winchester Magnum offer a similarly large selection. You will never get through all of them, but you can concentrate on the bullet weights that suit your needs best, and the bullets that offer the performance characteristics you're looking for. Over time you will usually discover that almost any decent rifle shoots OK with quite a few loads, abysmally with some, and that group sizes are below average with a handful of loads. As we'll discuss in chapter eight, accuracy may not be your primary goal; the terminal performance of a given bullet for certain game or conditions may be more important. So you can make compromises, but it's both comforting and confidence-building to know the accuracy

The great old .300 H&H is still very capable, but it's no longer popular. Factory loads exist, but selection is limited and velocity is modest. We worked up a good load and gave it to Superior to duplicate. I used a Superior load with a 200-grain Sierra to take this excellent free-range sambar in New Zealand.

your rifle is capable of, and the only way to know that is to try, over time, as many loads as possible.

What if only a small selection of factory loads is available? Remember the adage "Beware the one-gun man?" There's a corollary to that: "Beware the one-load cartridge!" In order for a cartridge to be loaded by multiple firms, it must have a significant level of popularity. These days no manufacturer offers everything, of course. Remington loads a lot of Winchester-introduced cartridges, and Winchester loads a lot of Remington-introduced cartridges. Federal, Hornady, and Norma offer a good selection from both, along with their own cartridges. Just because a certain cartridge has only a few loads available does not mean it is a bad cartridge. Bad things happen to good people, and some good cartridges never catch on. Also, there are some good cartridges that were once quite popular, but their stars rose and set.

Under the heading of championing lost causes, there are several unpopular cartridges that I like very much. These include the .264 Winchester Magnum, once very popular but no longer, and now offered in one load only by Winchester and Remington, but in several flavors in Nosler Custom . . . thank you, Bob Nosler. Another favorite of mine is the 8mm Remington Magnum, but it was never really popular, and Remington now has just one load. Double Tap has another good one, but that's about it. I'm also a fan of several .35-caliber cartridges: .358 Winchester, .350 Remington Magnum, .35 Whelen. The selection for the .35 Whelen isn't too bad, but of the majors only Winchester loads the .358 and only Remington loads the .350 Remington Magnum. Double Tap has some good loads for several .35s, but the overall selection is still limited.

Hornady has been amazingly aggressive in introducing new (and resurrecting old) cartridges in recent years. Although hardly a small company, they pride themselves on being agile, and they produce an awesome selection. But some of their cartridges are only available in their own brand. It's good ammo, so that's not a huge problem, but is it possible to know how well your rifle shoots if there are only a couple of choices of loads? No, it is not. With good, modern ammunition you will probably realize adequate accuracy for most purposes, but you'll never really know if that's as good as it gets. Obviously you can go the custom ammo route, but here's where handloaders do have a tremendous advantage: As long as there are cases and bullets, you can try an almost endless array of loads and find out what your rifle is really capable of.

How many loads do you need, and how many should you try? Well, I can't put a number on either. As a gunwriter, I spend a lot of range time shooting groups with different rifles and loads. Sometimes you hit pay dirt with the first load; other times the project seems hopeless . . . and then a shining star (which can be any load in any cartridge in any rifle) appears. Unless you're a handloader or have a buddy who is, I strongly recommend against choosing a cartridge for which there are just a couple of factory loads available. You might get lucky with accuracy and for most purposes you will probably find enough accuracy to get the job(s) done. But here's the deal: There isn't always a good reason why unpopular cartridges don't sell well, but the converse doesn't apply. Popular cartridges are usually popular for good reason: They tend to shoot well.

For any hunting or shooting application, there are popular cartridges that will probably fill the bill. If you want to be contrary, different, or make a fashion statement with your cartridge, be my guest. Factory ammo today is so good that, as long as two or three loads are available, you will probably do just fine. But if you're not a handloader, I suggest that you might be better off choosing a popular cartridge that is offered in a wide selection of loads. Not only can you continue to experiment until you find the best load with the best accuracy, but you can also find ammo much more easily.

HANDLOADING FOR ACCURACY

CHAPTER 7

by Phil Massaro

Author's Note: I am now going to do something I have never done in one of my own books: I am going to turn this important chapter over to another writer, my good friend Phil Massaro. There are two reasons for this. First, back in 1979, when Bob Petersen took pity on my flailing efforts as a freelancer and gave me a job, I was very much the new kid on the block, not in all ways less experienced than my seniors, but definitely green and probably the youngest guy in the business. Decades passed, and I still seemed the youngest! Fortunately (for the future of the business) that is finally changing. We have a few great young guys coming up in the gunwriting trade, and Phil Massaro is one of them. He is energetic, enthusiastic, a knowledgeable gun guy and a dedicated hunter, and in many ways he reminds me of me quite some years back. There is a second reason: In the subject matter of this chapter, Phil is far more knowledgeable than I; his Massaro Ballistic Laboratories has cooked up some great loads for me. He is technically proficient, and, unlike me, Phil is not a lazy handloader!

First of all, thank you, Craig; it's an honor to be here, and I appreciate the kind words. At Massaro Ballistic Laboratories I've been fortunate enough to load for many different cartridges, with different bullets, for a wide array of purposes. However, there is a common thread among my clients: They want the most accurate ammunition available. The accuracy required for long-range shooting is on a different level altogether than most regular hunting or shooting situations; the tolerances of the rifle and its ammunition must be held to the highest standards.

Serious benchrest shooters already know about the tricks and techniques I discuss,but with the growing interest in long-range accuracy, many shooters interested in expanding their range envelope may not. However, accuracy is accuracy, so whether your interest is shooting the tiniest groups you can or reaching out for targets or game, these techniques remain sound.

While it is undeniable that the ammunition produced by the major factories is the best it has ever been, there are instances where handloading is required. Maybe your chosen caliber isn't available with the bullet you'd like to use, or perhaps the harmonics generated by the factory ammunition don't quite agree with your rifle barrel. Reloading can solve quite a few problems and offer the shooter a consistent source of ammunition, even if the factories decide to change the loading from year to year.

There are also many steps the reloader can take that cannot be performed with factory-assembled ammunition, and those subtle differences can have a dramatic effect on the rifle's performance. Some of the ideas I'll discuss may sound obvious, and others eye-opening, but they have made the difference between rifles of mediocre accuracy and those I cherish as tack drivers. Let us first assume that your rifle, trigger, and optics are up to snuff, so we can take those factors out of the accuracy equation.

First things first: Consistency is paramount, whether we're discussing trigger squeeze, cheek weld, or breathing, and the same can be said when as-

Phil Massaro is about to unleash a .338 Lapua at 1,000 yards. (Photo courtesy of Phil Massaro)

Phil Massaro at home in Africa with a Heym .404 Jeffery. You're unlikely to use a big gun at long range, but extra accuracy leads to confidence. (Photo courtesy of Phil Massaro)

sembling ammunition. What we're after is repeatability. Consistent ammunition, constructed uniformly, will make the shooter the weak link in the chain. That is the goal: to have gear that (without the influence of human error) will send the bullet to the same point of impact out to our chosen distances. So we want to keep things consistent. Brass cases should be of the best quality

Weighing the projectiles can result in a much more uniform end product, and when segregated into lots, you will find improved long-range accuracy. (Photo courtesy of Phil Massaro)

you can afford, and you should do your best not only to be consistent in your brand of brass, but also to try to use cases from the same lot. Match brass, say from Hornady, Norma, or Lapua, is my first instinct, but I've made accurate ammunition from standard-grade brass by being picky and employing the following techniques.

First, weigh your brass. It may sound strange, but weighing the cases and separating them into consistent lots, say within a grain or two, will give you uniform combustion chambers. This will help to keep the powder charge to a consistent level of compaction, if you're employing compressed or near maximum capacity loads. Cases that weigh more, or less, will have a slightly varying degree of wall thickness, since the overall length will be uniform (more about trimming momentarily), and a combustion chamber of a different size will directly affect the pressure generated. Vary the pressure, vary the velocity, and that will change the point of impact. It's not a big deal at 100 yards, or maybe even 200, but out past 400 that small difference can easily be magnified, and may result in a shot out of the bull's-eye (which will only hurt your feelings) or a wounded game animal (a result that no one wants).

Next, weigh the projectiles. The bullets of today are amazing, giving us hunters the construction necessary to make quick, humane kills; and for the target crowd, match bullets have been engineered to have the best gravity and wind-defying characteristics we've ever seen, some with ogives that use a combination of secant and tangent geometric curves. Still, we want to be as consistent as possible, so by weighing the projectiles and segregating them into lots that vary by 0.1 grains, we will best take advantage of the newest features. This especially holds true in the hunting bullet realm. Nosler's famous Partition

Weighing the cases and using the most uniform ones will give a consistent combustion chamber. This will help to keep pressures and therefore velocities more consistent. (Photo courtesy of Phil Massaro)

has a wonderful reputation for field performance once it hits fur, but has long been described as "not the most accurate bullet available." By weighing and segregating them, I've personally shot fantastic groups with the Partition. I'm aware that the Partition, with its flat base, isn't considered a true long-range bullet, but I've placed some accurate long-range shots out to 400 yards with it and its beefier cousin the Swift A-Frame, and I've done it with some cartridges you wouldn't think would perform well at those ranges.

With the brass and bullets sorted into acceptable lots, let's form our cases into the proper shape by sizing and trimming. Whether you're using spent brass or new brass, make sure cases have a uniform shape. Some shooters achieve better accuracy by fire-forming the brass first, so that it becomes a mirror image of the rifle's chamber, and then resize only the neck portion of the case to allow the cartridge to better align the bullet to the bore. That decision is up to you, but should you opt for this procedure you'll need a special neck-sizing die for your caliber. Please realize that if you are using neck-sized brass, it will be a bit more difficult to close the bolt of a bolt-action rifle. In the target world this is no big deal, but in a hunting situation it may slow down the cycling time for a second shot. Neck sizing is best left for bolt actions only; in other action types, especially autoloaders, it can cause feeding jams.

Whether sizing the neck or the entire case body, the process is similar. The case is lubricated and pressed into the resizing die. This die, which is a simple forcing cone in the shape of the SAAMI-specified dimensions of the cartridge case, shrinks the neck to an inside diameter dimension 0.003-inch to 0.004-inch smaller than bullet diameter, and then the case, upon the downstroke of the ram, is drawn over a caliber-specific expander ball. This ball is 0.001-inch to 0.002-inch smaller than caliber diameter. The smaller-than-caliber dimension allows for good neck tension when the bullet is pressed into the case, but can overwork the case neck, depending on the thickness of the case wall in that area.

This process has benefitted from several new tools, tools the handloader can use to improve his or her accuracy and extend the life of brass cases. Redding, in its Competition Die series, has come up with an ingenious system. The resizing die comes with a set of bushings of varying thicknesses to help minimize brass fatigue. Unlike iron, brass becomes brittle when worked repeatedly, and the

Using the best cases you can afford will help improve accuracy. The consistency of good brass, such as the Norma .300 Winchester Magnum shown here, helps keep things uniform. (Photo courtesy of Phil Massaro)

Accurate ammunition for long-range shooting starts with the best components. (Photo courtesy of Phil Massaro)

stretching and resizing of the brass can cause the neck to split. To extend the useful life of the brass that you are going to use for long-range loads, you want to avoid overworking the case neck and mouth area. The Redding system requires you to accurately measure the outside dimension of your case, loaded with a bullet of proper diameter, to assess the wall thickness of the case neck. (The bullet diameter cannot change, but the case thickness can vary.) To avoid overworking the case neck, the bushing inside the resizing die shrinks the case neck only to a dimension small enough to be brought back to shape by the expander ball. This results in brass that won't have to "spring" back and forth as much, which means it will maintain its concentricity better and will last much longer.

The brass must be trimmed to a uniform length. Some loaders prefer to trim to 0.010-inch below the specified case length to allow the brass to stretch, but I like to maintain the SAAMI spec on all my brass to keep the neck tension consistent and to minimize changes should I need to use new brass.

I like to use automated trimmers such as the RCBS Case Prep Station, as they are every bit as accurate as hand trimmers. The Case Prep Station has a

I like quality gear when it comes to assembling good ammunition. The Redding T7 turret press and Redding Competition dies are among the best you can buy. (Photo courtesy of Phil Massaro)

graduated adjustment knob allowing for precise trimming adjustments; it gives me the consistent results I'm after. This same machine gives me a chamfering and deburring tool on the top, so my bullets will seat easily into the cases and chamber smoothly.

When priming the cases, I use the best primers I can get my hands on, especially for the long-range stuff that requires the level of attention we're after. Hands-down, my favorite primers are the Federal Gold Medal Match primers. Whether or not they are the hottest-burning primers can be debated, but I've

One of the author's favorite long-range rounds, the 6.5-284 Norma, is shown here loaded with Berger 140-grain Match bullets, ready for the range. (Photo courtesy of Phil Massaro)

*Good primers, seated by hand, will give consistent ignition. The Lyman hand primer will keep the primer seating depth uniform, and the Federal Gold Medal Match primers have given excellent results. (*Photo courtesy of Phil Massaro)

found them to be reliable, lot to lot, year after year. I like to seat them by hand, so I can get a consistent feel and seating depth, and usually seat my primers just slightly recessed. My Lyman Hand Priming Tool is easy to use, and will seat the primers quickly and consistently.

That brings us to loading the bullet. The choice of bullet style will be dealt with elsewhere within the covers of this book, but if you have chosen a bullet with a ballistic coefficient (BC) on the higher side of the scale, that means the

The RCBS Case Prep station is a good tool to trim your brass accurately to length. The graduated dial allows the reloader to set the length exactly where he or she wants it. (Photo courtesy of Phil Massaro)

bullet will probably be on the longer side of bullet choices within your caliber. Seating depth is a topic that could fill the remaining pages of this book, but I'll try to be brief. In a hunting rifle, you'll want to keep your cartridge overall length (COL) to a length that will function properly through the magazine (if you have one; the Ruger No. 1 and other falling-block actions are exempt from this caveat, as feeding isn't an issue). This can pose a problem in some cartridges, such as the .300 Winchester Magnum. The engineers at Winchester designed the case for maximum capacity from a "standard" or .30-06-length receiver, shortening the neck to .264-inch, shorter than the one-caliber-minimum length that most folks want to see. The end result is this: The longer bullets that give the best long-range results have to be seated very deep in the case in order to function through the magazine of my Winchester Model 70.

Here is some .300 Winchester Magnum brass, all trimmed up and ready for loading. (Photo courtesy of Phil Massaro)

Some bullets just don't like this seating depth, as they shoot more accurately if they are a little closer to the lands and grooves. This leaves me with a dilemma: I either use the rifle as a single-shot, or choose a bullet that functions well when seated at standard depths. I do both. When I ordered my Savage Model 116 in 6.5-284 Norma from the Savage Custom Shop, I purposely had it built on the longer 116 action to accommodate the long, lean 6.5mm bullets. That way they could be seated out as far as I'd like without hitting the lands and grooves.

I can't give you a definitive rule regarding seating depth. The proper depth is that which the rifle likes, and it usually depends on the combination of bullet and particular rifle. I can offer the following (very general) observations. Barnes bullets, and quite a few of the other homogenous alloy bullets, like to be pretty close to the lands and grooves. They don't like "bullet jump." Try seating them 0.015-inch off the lands, and back the depth off in 0.010-inch increments, and observe the changes in accuracy. These bullets have been known to be very sensitive to small changes in seating depth, so some experimentation is warranted. The same can be said of the Berger match bullets.

The Swift Scirocco II, the Nosler AccuBond, and other similar polymer-tipped, bonded-core bullets seem to like a lot of bullet jump. They shoot most accurately at a seating depth at or near to the SAAMI-specified COL, so they work for hunting purposes without too much issue.

It'll take some work at the bench, and some range time, to nail down the depth that your rifle likes best. I know that spending more time at the range, shooting your favorite rifle, may seem like a chore, but you seem the type of person who is up to the task . . .

Those Redding Competition dies that I mentioned? They are designed to seat the bullet in just about the most concentric method available, and the seating die comes with a micrometer-adjustable dial that allows you to precisely adjust the seating depth by increments of 0.001-inch. And, as my 6.5-284 Norma can attest, they make a difference in bullet runout and overall accuracy. I find them to be a very worthwhile investment for the loader who has decided to make the best ammo for precision work.

Propellant choice will depend on the cartridge you're shooting, but some powders and cartridges go together like peanut butter and jelly: the .22-250 and H380, the .308 Winchester and IMR 4064, the .375 H&H Magnum and

One of the author's favorite long-range rifles is a custom Savage Model 116 in 6.5-284 Norma. (Photo courtesy of Phil Massaro)

Reloder 15. These are time-proven observations, but aren't carved in stone. Again, the basic premise here is that for long-range work, we want our ammunition to be repeatable and consistent, so that the amount of error magnified by the long distances is minimal. Powder choice is important, but even more important is the standard deviation (SD) of your velocities. A dramatic variation in velocities can result in inaccurate shots. Temperature fluctuation can also pose a problem, as modern nitrocellulose-based powders can produce lower velocities in the colder extremes, and higher velocities in the heat of summer, or in the tropics. The variations may be enough to cause a miss at long ranges. Hodgdon has a line of Extreme rifle powders, including VARGET and H4831SC, which help minimize the effects of temperature fluctuation, and Alliant has introduced Reloder 23 and Reloder 26 with the same thought in mind. As much as I love and use tried-and-true powders like IMR 4350 and Reloder 19, they have been noted to be susceptible to temperature influence. With the longer, target-style bullets, which eat up case capacity quickly, take a look at ball powders such as

H380, H414, and Winchester 748, as they occupy less space in the case than the stick powders, and can often be problem-solvers.

The use of a good chronograph is the easiest way to measure the standard deviation of your handloads. You can figure SD mathematically, but an advanced chronograph like the Oehler will give you your SD on the screen or in a printout. It is not the same as the "average velocity," and it is at least as valuable. In any case, chronographs are much simpler and less expensive than they used to be. A chronograph is an essential tool, as you must know the precise velocity of *your* loads in *your* rifle to ascertain the downrange trajectory. You should be looking for loads with a velocity variance of less than 30 feet per second or so, in addition to watching the accuracy.

Diligence will pay off when it comes to handloading for your long-range rig. Pay close attention to the bullet recommendations that Craig Boddington is about to make; you can get them to shoot well by tailoring the loads to the rifle. Remember, each rifle is different, so you may have to go back to the drawing board for every rifle. Now, I've got to get back to the loading bench.

BULLETS: ACCURACY OR PERFORMANCE?

CHAPTER 8

Whether you shoot factory ammo or handloads, you will quickly find very few rifles shoot all loads equally. Actually, no rifle shoots all loads equally. However, some are very tolerant and shoot a variety of loads reasonably well; others are downright finicky, producing awful accuracy with some loads, but shooting well with certain loads the rifle likes.

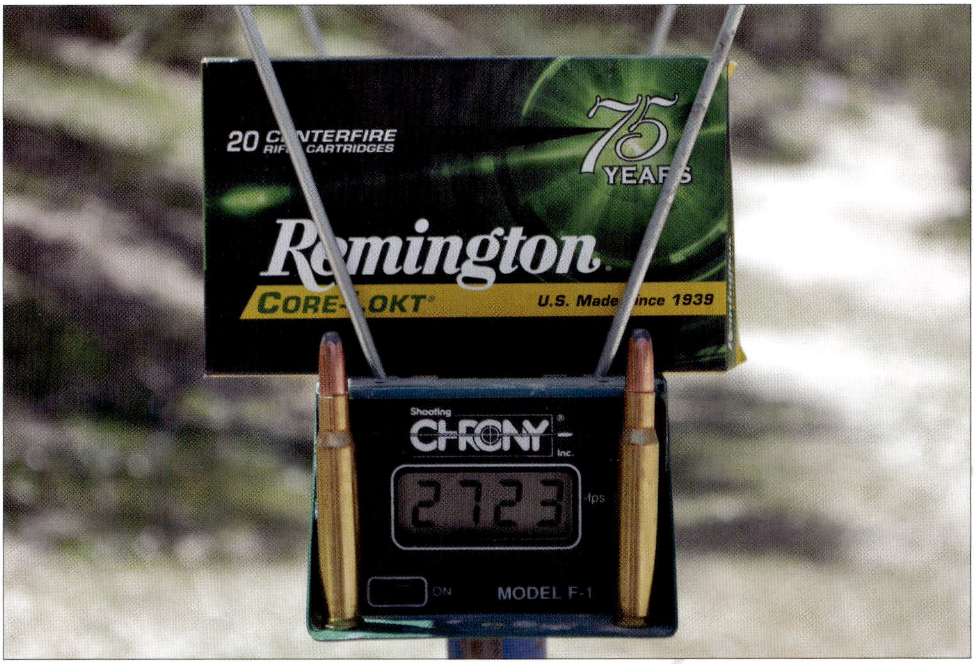

Let's not be knocking plain old bullets! This packaging announced Remington's 75th anniversary of the Core-Lokt bullet, a 180-grain .30-06 and right on the money for velocity and still a great game getter. By the way, for close-range knockdown, don't overlook a round-nosed bullet!

There are four components in a self-contained metallic cartridge: case, primer, propellant, and bullet. With factory ammo, about all you can do is switch brands and bullets, but in handloading you can switch from one case manufacturer to another, and you can try different brands and "strengths" of primers (standard, magnum, match, etc.). Usually these differences will be subtle. Propellants, however, can make a major difference not only in velocity but also accuracy, and bullets probably make the biggest difference of all.

On the range this poses no problem. You can choose whatever bullet you like—or that your rifle likes best—and punch paper or ring steel to your heart's content. If you're considering hunting ammo, however, you often have a dilemma. Regardless of what you're planning to hunt, you probably have some preconceived notion of the bullet you would like to use, or at least the performance characteristics you think are needed for the job at hand. Sometimes there is serendipitous coincidence: The bullet you wish to shoot produces groups you're happy with (or at least can live with). Other times, well, here's

There's a bewildering array of "designer" bullets on the market, but for a whole lot of hunting purposes, don't overlook the good old "cup-and-core" lead-tipped bullets. Accuracy is often exceptional with simple bullets such as these.

Component bullets are available in a huge selection of weights and styles. It's almost impossible to try them all, but based on your performance criteria for the hunting or shooting you intend to do, there are usually a lot of great choices.

the real problem: There is absolutely no telling what load or bullet a given rifle will shoot best.

Sure, there are trends. Match bullets are so named because they are made to exacting standards and designed to be conducive to the highest level of accuracy. Berger and Sierra match bullets are legendary, and Hornady's much newer match line is also very good. If I wanted to punch the tightest groups my rifle was capable of, these are the bullets I would start with. The problem is that match bullets are *not intended as hunting bullets.* Yes, I know, some folks use them. At long range, where velocities have dropped, hollowpoint match bullets can perform very well. However, match bullets are designed for accuracy, not for performance on game.

A full-metal jacket (FMJ) bullet, whether military, match, or a "solid" intended for elephant, will not expand, and is generally illegal for hunting in most North American jurisdictions. A hollowpoint match bullet may expand and perform nicely, especially at longer ranges and lower velocities, but in my experience they are erratic. I have seen them splatter at close range, and at longer

Left: 7mm-08 Remington. Right: 7mm Remington Ultra Mag. There is a huge difference in velocity between these two 7mm cartridges. A bullet that performs perfectly in the 7mm-08 may expand too quickly in the 7mm RUM . . . especially at closer ranges.

Clear back in 1981 I used the then-new 300-grain Sierra .375 to take this huge brown bear . . . and I've used the same bullet to take several Cape buffaloes. This is not a "tough" bullet, but with plenty of bullet weight and not too much velocity, extremely tough bullets aren't always needed.

ranges I've seen them act like solids, passing straight through without doing much damage. Remember, they are not intended for use on game, so this is no indictment whatsoever. Rather, it's a simple matter that if you use bullets for purposes other than what they were intended for, you are taking a risk.

So for hunting we generally use hunting bullets. These vary from very frangible varmint bullets to quick-expanding big-game bullets to very tough, controlled-expansion bullets intended for the largest and toughest game. Perhaps the quickest expanding hunting bullets are traditional cup-and-core bullets like the Berger VLD (a hollowpoint) and Sierra's GameKing (a traditional bullet with exposed lead tip) along with the polymer-tipped bullets that have limited additional design features to retard or control expansion. These include the Nosler Ballistic Tip and Hornady SST.

The tipped bullets are seductive; they look sexy and, unlike conventional lead-tipped bullets, the polymer tip won't flatten or batter in the magazine, and it also won't burn off at high velocity. However, it must also be understood that, upon impact, the polymer trip is driven down into the bullet, thus initiating and tending to expedite expansion. The bullets just mentioned all tend to be extremely accurate, but they will expand quickly . . . and the higher the velocity, the quicker they will expand. This is not necessarily a bad thing; I like all of these bullets for the deer/pronghorn/sheep class of game, but close shots at extremely high velocity can be messy.

I have one important comment: Bullet weight cures a lot of problems. In terms of accuracy this may not be helpful, as some rifles group better with heavier bullets, and other rifles vice versa. But in, say, .30-caliber, a 180-grain bullet will generally not expand as quickly as a 150-grain bullet of the same design. In some measure this is because the heavier bullet will be a bit slower, but it's also because you simply have more bullet. So one of these bullets that happens to offer fantastic accuracy in your rifle may be a perfectly good choice for deer-size game . . . and you might be able to move it up to elk-size game simply by adding more weight.

Almost every manufacturer now offers polymer-tipped bullets. They don't batter in the magazine and they retain their shape in flight. Just remember that, across the board, on impact the tip drives down into the bullet and initiates expansion.

Swift offers two bonded-core bullets. Left, the Scirocco is one of the tougher "tipped and bonded" bullets, but it's going to lose a bit of weight during expansion and penetration. Right, the dual-core A-Frame with bonded front core is one of the toughest of all lead-core bullets.

I had a .300 H&H that just loved the Sierra GameKing. In 150-grain weight it worked wonderfully on sheep and deer, but for heavier game I bypassed the 180-grain bullet altogether and moved up to a 200-grain Sierra. The Sierra has a reputation, not altogether earned, as a "soft" bullet. It's not a hard bullet, for sure, but when you step up to a heavy-for-caliber bullet, the game changes considerably. The 200-grain Sierra has worked well for me on elk and African plains game up to kudu, wildebeest, and zebra, and I've taken several buffaloes with a .375-caliber 300-grain Sierra GameKing with no problems.

While simple cup-and-core bullets often tend to be accurate, a problem they often have is not necessarily splattering (expanding prematurely or coming apart) but jacket and core separation. This is somewhat exaggerated by a boattail design, which has a greater tendency to squirt the lead core out of the jacket. This is often not as bad as some folks make it out to be. With simple bullets, especially boattails, it is not uncommon to find jacket and core

Choice of bullet can sometimes make a huge difference. I wasn't planning on hunting lion when a "problem lion" permit became available. The rifle I had was a .300 Remington Ultra Mag, but since I was shooting 200-grain Swift A-Frames, I had no problems.

separated against the hide on the far side. This doesn't worry me much, as the lodgment suggests that this happened at the very end of penetration, when the bullet was slowing to a stop and probably tumbled.

Obviously a bullet that comes completely unglued and fragments is a bad deal—on one shot it may drop game like lightning, but on another shot it may fail to penetrate and cause a nasty surface wound. Even this may not suggest a bad bullet, but simply a bullet that impacted at higher velocity than it was designed to withstand. There are some bullets, for instance, that perform wonderfully in a 7x57 or 7mm-08, but should not be used on game in a 7mm Remington Ultra Mag.

Design features such as a thicker jacket and less core exposed at the nose tend to retard expansion, and there are some bullets with mechanical features that do the same, such as Remington's Core-Lokt and Hornady's InterLock, that have raised bands in the jacket that tend to grip the core. These are not hard or tough bullets, but the Core-Lokt is more than seventy-five years old and the InterLock not far behind. There is no telling how many millions of deer and other game have fallen to these bullets! Again, bullet weight makes a difference, as does velocity. One of my favorite loads is a 180-grain Hornady InterLock in the .30-06; it's accounted for a wide assortment of African plains game of all sizes and at all ranges. I've had equally good results with a 180-grain InterLock in the .300 Weatherby Magnum, but I've generally used it on sheep and goats. This means the range has usually been farther, so at impact the bullets are pretty much back down to .30-06 velocities.

Chemically bonding the core to the jacket is a significant step up in toughness. Bill Steiger's legendary Bitterroot bullet was probably the first bonded-core bullet that was effectively marketed, followed by Jack Carter's Trophy Bonded Bearclaw. Core-bonding absolutely keeps the jacket and core together, allowing for fairly dramatic expansion without the core and

Top: These are homogenous alloy bullets, all showing almost complete weight retention, except for the one at far right with its petals broken off.
Below: This is a selection of bonded core bullets, and all are beautiful. If you want penetration, the homogenous alloy bullets are hard to beat. If you want expansion and *weight retention, you'll love bonded core bullets . . . but they cannot penetrate as much because expansion always limits penetration.*

I used a 185-grain Berger VLD in .300 Winchester Magnum to take this zebra at a bit over 400 yards. The Berger bullet is legendary for accuracy, and their VLD hunting bullet is a good choice for long-range hunting.

jacket separating or even very much of the exposed lead wiping away during penetration. A further development has been adding a polymer tip to a bonded-core bullet. Nosler's AccuBond was probably the first, but now we also have Hornady's InterBond and Swift's Scirocco (and the improved Scirocco II). The most recent is Federal's update of the Bearclaw, the Trophy Bonded Tip. These are all great hunting bullets. The Scirocco is probably the toughest of the group, almost always maintaining about 90 percent of its weight, but I have used all four of these bullets and like them all. Even with enhanced weight retention, however, they are not what I think of as "penetrating" bullets because they offer radical expansion. This is not a bad thing, as expansion creates a larger wound channel and does more damage to vital organs. Just understand that expansion is the enemy of penetration. When a bullet expands, it creates more frontal area, meaning more friction and more resistance. You cannot have expansion and penetration in equal measure.

If you want more penetration you can go to a heavier bullet, or you can step up to bullet designs that are tougher still. John Nosler introduced the Nosler Partition back in 1948. It was essentially the first "premium hunting bullet"—and it's still a pretty good one. The Partition is essentially two bullets in one, a dual-core bullet with the two cores separated by a wall or "partition" of jacket material. The front part expands fairly quickly on impact, and in fact it isn't uncommon for much of the front core to be wiped away. Partitions often lose a fair amount of weight during penetration, but this doesn't really matter because the back core, protected by the partition, continues to drive almost like a mini-solid.

The Swift A-Frame borrows the dual-core concept of the Partition, but takes it a step farther in that the front core is bonded to the jacket. Thus that front part doesn't wipe away; the A-Frame will often retain as much as 97 or 98 percent of its original weight, and since it expands fairly radically it isn't uncommon to recover an A-Frame from game, usually in beautiful shape. The Partition is a more expensive bullet than many, and the A-Frame is one of the

A 180-grain Hornady SST from a .300 Winchester Magnum dropped this whitetail right in its tracks. Like the Nosler AccuTip, the SST expands quickly, but on deer-size game that isn't a bad thing—and the effects are dramatic!

Except for the homogenous alloy GMX at left, these recovered bullets aren't especially pretty, but all did their job. Jacket and core separation doesn't bother me too much when the jacket and core are found against the hide on the far side, suggesting that this only happened when the bullet tumbled at its very limit of penetration.

most expensive of all lead-core bullets. (You get what you pay for.) A bigger drawback, however, is that neither are the most aerodynamic bullets, nor are they usually the most accurate. Of course, this is where some rifles will always make a liar out of you. I've seen awesome accuracy from both Partitions and A-Frames, but neither is a bullet I would think of first if superb accuracy was my goal.

The homogenous alloy bullets are tougher yet. Made of copper or copper alloy, these bullets are essentially hollowpoints in that a skived nose surrounds a nose cavity. Upon impact, the nose peels back in petals, with the limit of expansion determined by the depth of the cavity. Unless a petal breaks off, which happens occasionally, it is almost impossible for this type of bullet to lose weight; retention often reaches 99 percent. The drawback, which is not really a drawback if that's what you want, is that expansion is limited . . . so these are "penetrating" bullets. Recovered bullets are rare on deer-size game, and exit wounds (which many hunters prefer) are perhaps more common than on any other expanding bullets I know of.

The Barnes X was the first successful expanding bullet of this type. Although it worked wonderfully, it was known to cause rapid copper fouling and accuracy was a bit finicky. Driving bands at the base greatly reduced fouling and also seemed to improve accuracy; the version with driving bands is called the Triple Shock Expanding (TSX), and there is now a tipped version, the TTSX.

There's a back story. The copper bullet works and provides fantastic penetration, but Barnes had a monopoly on this type of homogenous alloy bullet for years. It wasn't because it was patented; this type of bullet has been around for years, so it wasn't really patentable. Rather, other manufacturers were nervous about crossing the bridge into "unleaded" bullets. The creation of lead-free hunting zones here and there made this a moot point. I've lived in one of them for years, California's "Condor Zone," where we are obligated to use lead-free bullets for all hunting. With such restrictions increasing, other manufacturers had little choice but to join in. So now we have Hornady's GMX, Nosler's E-Tip, and other homogenous alloy bullets from both large and small manufacturers. Some expand more than others; that depends on the depth of the cavity. However, all are pretty much penetrating bullets rather than bullets that offer radical expansion. They do expand over a considerable velocity range, but, inevitably, as velocity drops, expansion is reduced.

As for accuracy, generally speaking I wouldn't consider any of them the most accurate bullets out there . . . but you never know. Many rifles shoot them well, and some shoot them extremely well. And that's really the sticky part. As I said,

My wife, Donna, used a 180-grain Hornady Interlock in .30-06 to flatten this big Mozambique sable. Although not a complex bullet, the Interlock is accurate and works very well, especially at .30-06 velocities.

there are trends, but as in high school debate class, one of the things you must avoid is the glittering generality. There is simply no telling exactly which bullet any given rifle is going to shoot the very best. Depending on the game you are hunting and performance characteristics you like, you must make choices. For instance, are you one of those who wants an exit wound, or do you prefer a bullet that stays inside the animal and expends all of its energy? Both viewpoints have merit, so there isn't a right or wrong answer, but depending on which you prefer you will gravitate to one type of bullet or another. Then you're going to have to find out what your rifle shoots best. In choosing a hunting load, you will often have to make compromises between performance and accuracy, but the choices often won't lie between a bad choice and a good choice, but between good, better, and best.

Obviously it depends on what you're doing. If you're shooting prairie dogs, then accuracy is most important and bullet performance doesn't matter much at

I also shoot a lot of 180-grain Hornady Interlocks in my .300 Weatherby Magnum, but generally I'm using this cartridge at somewhat longer ranges for sheep and goats, so velocity has dropped off a bit. This excellent Blanford urial was taken from about 275 yards.

Norma's Oryx bullet is yet another very good bonded-core factory bullet. Expansion is radical, weight retention is pretty good, and terminal effects are impressive!

all. If you're hunting open country and expecting long shooting, then you want as much accuracy as you can get . . . and you probably want a fairly soft bullet that will continue to expand reliably as velocity drops. If you're going up against an Alaskan brown bear or a Cape buffalo, you can sacrifice a bit of accuracy and even aerodynamics: The target is big, and nobody shoots dangerous game at long range. Terminal performance, however, becomes paramount because you may be betting your life on it.

The good news: No matter what your purpose, there are almost certainly a whole bunch of suitable choices. Somewhere among them you will probably find a bullet accurate enough in your rifle for your purposes, and offering a close approximation of the terminal performance you want. It may take some time at the range to figure it out, but that's not a bad thing at all.

Break-In, Cleaning, and Heat

CHAPTER 9

So you have a new rifle with a bright, shiny bore. Take a look at it through a good magnifying borescope. I had the opportunity to try out a really good one, the Hawkeye Precision Borescope from Gradient Lens Corporation. I looked at some of my barrels, and I was absolutely horrified. Up close, that smooth, shiny surface wasn't so smooth after all. Relatively new barrels showed all manner of tool marks and rough spots; older barrels showed fouling that I thought I'd cleaned out, throat erosion, and, in a couple of cases, some minor pitting.

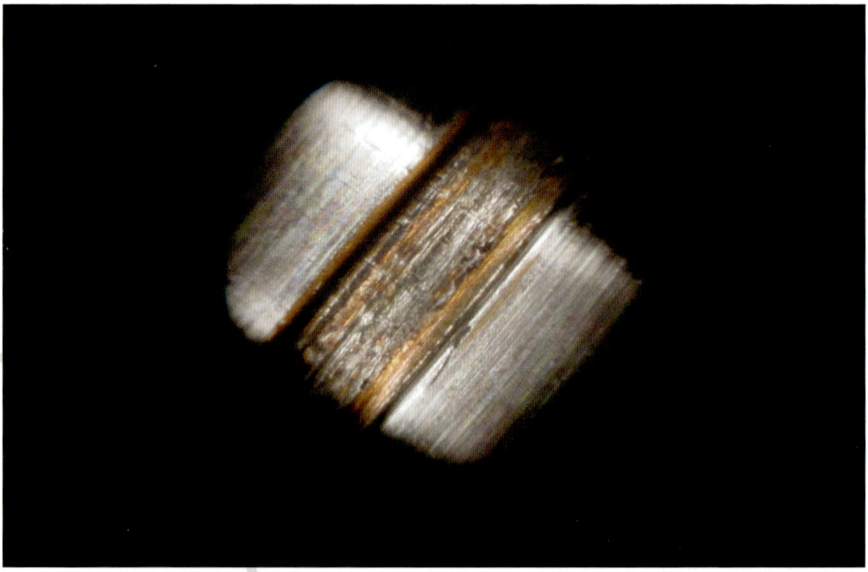

This is copper fouling, captured by the Hawkeye borescope. Fouling essentially reduces the interior diameter of a barrel, so it obviously and inexorably impacts accuracy.

I probably should have bought the Hawkeye, but I didn't on the premise that there are some things you're better off not knowing. That depends on how finicky you are, but you can pretty much take as a given that, viewed microscopically, that bright, shiny bore probably isn't as smooth or as perfect as you think it is. This is not as serious as it sounds; it's just the way it is: If you look close enough, nothing made by man is quite as perfect as it may look from a distance. As we discussed in chapter one, some barrels (especially new barrels or badly maintained older barrels) actually look rough to the naked eye . . . but appearances can be deceiving, and there is no telling in what condition a given barrel might shoot its best. Some barrels that appear quite rough shoot well right out of the box, and some older barrels that show throat erosion and minor pitting may still shoot very well.

However, a rough barrel is likely to shoot better after it smooths out. It will also foul much less. All those rough edges and tool marks collect copper and powder residue, so fouling is more rapid and also much more difficult to remove. Also, while some barrels will make a lie of any assumption, a smooth barrel will generally shoot better, or at least more consistently. *Lapping* is actually a process in which a finished barrel is polished and smoothed. It is not something you want to overdo, as you are actually removing barrel steel, but with a good barrel, lapping is a fairly standard procedure, and it can help smooth a factory barrel (which, typically and understandably, will have more tool marks and inconsistencies than a match-grade barrel).

We hear a lot about "breaking in" a barrel. Lapping, one way or another, is essentially part of the process. There are two primary ways to do it: Hand-lapping and fire-lapping. In hand-lapping you are essentially polishing the bore by hand, using a very fine abrasive. Note that some top-quality finished barrels are advertised as "hand-lapped," and most custom rifles have already received this process. Most factory barrels and inexpensive replacement barrels have not, but that doesn't mean they won't shoot. There are a number of lapping compounds on the market, but my longtime favorite is J-B Bore Cleaner, a cleaning paste that is actually a very mild abrasive. One hundred passes of J-B on a tight felt patch will make a difference.

Fire-lapping is polishing by shooting bullets coated with a mild abrasive. Both Wheeler Engineering and NECO offer kits with descending levels of

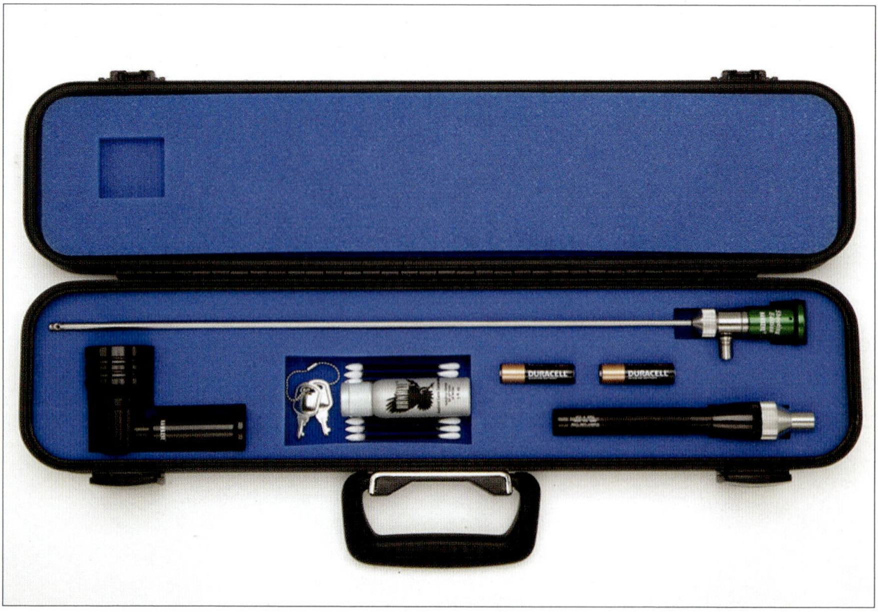

A good borescope is a very sophisticated tool, probably not essential for everyone . . . but you'll be surprised at what it will reveal. This is the Hawkeye borescope from the Gradient Lens Corporation.

grits that you can coat bullets with, most abrasive first and finest last. You do want to be careful with this, as you are removing barrel steel. Another, more prepackaged, option is David Tubb's FinalFinish. David is America's (and the world's) most accomplished rifleman, with a record eleven National High Power championships at Camp Perry, two Wimbledon cups, thirty NRA Silhouette titles, and a whole lot more. Nobody knows more about rifle accuracy.

Tubb's FinalFinish, available in most popular bullet diameters, is a numbered series of abrasive-coated bullets, Number One through Five, with One being the most abrasive and Five the least. His recommended regimen for barrel break-in is simple: Fire ten shots with Number One, clean the barrel. Fire ten shots with Number Two, clean the barrel, and so on until ten shots with Number Five; clean the barrel, and you're done. At this point Tubb reckons you have removed about 0.0003-inch (three ten-thousandths) of an inch of barrel steel, smoothing and evening the internal surfaces in the process. For a time Tubb was offering his FinalFinish kit in loaded ammo, but only for a few select calibers. At this point, according to his website, FinalFinish is coated bullets only (fifty bullets with ten of each grit), but he also has a custom reloading service, so if you aren't a handloader I suspect his company could load up a kit for you.

A system like this essentially accomplishes both lapping and barrel break-in; although both processes seek to smooth the barrel and remove imperfections, they are not exactly the same process. Whether the barrel is lapped or not, serious riflemen are finicky about breaking in a new barrel. The problem is that every accuracy freak has his or her own system. Some are perhaps better than others, but all are based on shooting and cleaning, shooting and cleaning . . . and more shooting and cleaning. One guy wrote in a chat room that he fires one shot, cleans, fires another shot, cleans, and so on up to ten shots, then fires groups, cleaning after each group until fifty shots are fired.

That is undoubtedly effective, but perhaps extreme. The main points are to fire a few shots, clean thoroughly, and repeat, and *don't let the barrel get hot!* I have used Tubb's FinalFinish kit on a couple of factory rifles, and can honestly

I do a lot of my gun cleaning at the range, especially when I'm testing loads or shooting for accuracy. There are lots of different systems, but I generally clean after about fifteen shots . . . and more frequently when breaking in a new barrel.

say that I've seen measurable improvement in groups between start and finish. But I've also seen improvement the way I usually do it, sort of the old-fashioned way: firing a couple of groups (cooling in between), cleaning thoroughly, firing a couple more groups, cleaning thoroughly, and so forth.

Just recently I've been "breaking in" a .300 Winchester Magnum Ridge Walker by Kenny Jarrett. Jarrett is famous for accuracy, and one of the finickiest accuracy freaks I know. Unlike most custom makers, he doesn't source barrels; he makes his own. Of course this barrel came to me lapped, but even so I'm being very careful with it, firing a couple groups, cleaning thoroughly, repeating the process. This is a time-consuming process that takes multiple range sessions. Although the rifle initially shot just fine, after about fifty rounds the groups started to tighten up noticeably.

Mind you, while we all develop our own protocols for break-in and cleaning, there are no rules. Some barrels shoot as well as they ever will right out of the box (producing groups that may be great, mediocre, or awful). We'll talk about this in greater detail much later, but it is extremely unlikely, if not impossible, to turn awful groups into great groups. No matter what you do, improvement is likely to be incremental and only very rarely exponential. However, the need to break-in a barrel is real, so it's probably better to not try to assess the actual accuracy of any given rifle until it has at least fifty bullets down the barrel, and some say as many as a hundred. Just take your time, don't let it get uncomfortably hot to the touch, and clean it frequently.

So let's turn to cleaning. I am admittedly one of the worst about this. Too many years in the Marines, where, at the end of a long day on the range or a longer week in the field, our weapons would have to pass inspection before being accepted back into the armory. I freely admit that I do not clean a barrel every time I put a bullet down it, although I certainly admire those who are still anal enough to do so. I am cognizant, however, that reasonably frequent cleaning is important for both maintenance and accuracy. Also, it depends on your climate. If you are in high humidity or, especially, coastal salt air, then you must clean more frequently than in a dry climate, and, even more important, keep the bore lightly oiled. Obviously all fingerprints should be wiped clean with oil or a silicone cloth every time a firearm is touched, and any grit or dust removed from moving parts to ensure future functioning.

This is a Jarrett Ridge Walker in .300 Winchester Magnum, with groups at the midpoint of the barrel break-in period. At this point it was averaging a bit less than one MOA. Now, with about 80 rounds down the barrel, it's about one-half MOA with loads it likes.

This CZ 550 in .30-06 is a midpriced factory rifle with a barrel that certainly wasn't lapped . . . and it also needed break-in. These are initial groups with factory ammo (left) and the first groups with David Tubb's FinalFinish system. So far not impressive!

The last group with FinalFinish fired from a CZ 550 .30-06 was spectacular. This kind of improvement cannot be expected . . . but is clearly possible.

This volume, however, is primarily about accuracy, not field preparation. As part of my job I do a lot of "testing." That's in quotes, because I'm not H. P. White or any other approved laboratory, but I do shoot a lot of groups with rifles I plan to write about. Typically I haul my Tipton cleaning kit to the range, and I clean in progress. Rifles foul at different rates, and if you spend a lot of time with a given rifle you will learn how often it needs to be cleaned in order to keep accuracy from deteriorating. Something else you will learn, which is vexing, is that some barrels only shoot their best groups when freshly cleaned. Most shoot best when slightly fouled, maybe after five or ten shots, and a very few barrels keep shooting well, and even more rarely, shoot their best when really dirty.

If I'm interested in trying to evaluate accuracy, whether the average accuracy of a certain rifle or which load a particular rifle shoots best, then I generally clean *at the range* after about fifteen shots. Depending on rifle, caliber, and purpose, that could be after three five-shot groups or five three-shot groups, but the fifteen-shot rule has become my protocol. Mind you, that's just a random number. Some prefer ten, some figure twenty; fifteen is just my number if I'm shooting for accuracy. Now, if you're trying to wring the tightest groups possible you should probably vary the routine once or twice . . . try cleaning after every group, and then fire twenty rounds without cleaning.

In the Marines we started with a solvent-soaked patch, then scrubbed with a bore brush, then followed with dry patches until they come out clean. Actually, that's pretty much the same way Dad started me; like many gun-struck kids, I was given the, *er, pleasure* (as I thought of it then!) of cleaning Dad's guns long before I was allowed to shoot them. I still do it pretty much the same way. There are so many good commercial cleaning products, and I don't want to make this book a catalog, but there's still good old Hoppe's No. 9 and Outers, and I've been very pleased with a newer product called Force Field. If copper fouling seems to be an issue, then Sweet's 7.62 or Barnes CR-10 copper solvent is great . . . and J-B will take out about anything if you apply some elbow grease.

Anyway, on the range I start with solvent. Then I switch to a properly fitting copper brush (not with copper solvent!) and give it twenty passes, always cleaning from the breech if possible to avoid damage to the muzzle crown. This is not possible on lever actions, slide actions, and many semiautos, so if you must clean from the muzzle be careful, and preferably use a rod guide. I finish with dry flannel patches. I'm too lazy to keep at it until they come out spotless, but I keep at it until they come out reasonably clean.

It is probably impossible to get all the solvent out of the barrel with patches, so before I go back to shooting groups I fire a couple of fouling shots downrange. I've done this on targets, and all too frequently the first shot (sometimes two) from a freshly cleaned barrel will change point of impact by an inch or more. So I fire the fouling shots, let the barrel cool, and then go back to shooting groups. Come to think of it, I didn't count those fouling shots, so properly I guess my habit is *seventeen* shots between cleanings!

If I'm being a good boy I clean at the range when I'm done; otherwise, I do it in the garage when I get home. However, if I'm setting up a rifle for a hunt then I *always* finish up by cleaning at the range, then I fire the fouling shots. That means when I get to the hunt and check zero, I don't have to worry about whether the first shot is off because of lubricant in the barrel, or because the scope really needs adjusting.

Field maintenance is a different subject. On a typical North American hunt in which only a couple of shots are likely to be fired I don't even think about cleaning the barrel unless there's precipitation, or I'm in a salt-air environment. Just in case, I carry a little Otis pocket cleaning kit with a pull-through rod. I also use a bore snake a lot, and I clean as the conditions dictate. Africa is a bit different: Sometimes you shoot a fair amount, and although it's usually a dry climate, there's dust to worry about. Then there's the African forest. You can watch rust form as you are taking a rest break! You have to clean the rifle inside and out daily, and if you don't the rust will surely get ahead of you. I carry the same stuff, but I use it a whole lot more frequently.

Barrel heat is another important consideration. A steel barrel expands as it heats, which impacts group size, but a barrel also tends to warp, usually "walking" the shots upward on the target. The steel also becomes softer, so throat erosion and barrel wear increases with high barrel heat. There is no precise formula for barrel wear. Stainless steel is more durable than chrome-moly steel, and, as we've discussed, barrel linings and cryogenic relief definitely extend barrel life. As a rule of thumb, cartridges like the .308, .30-06, and .223

I admit that I am not consistent about gun cleaning . . . but it makes a good rainy day project. At home and on the range I use a Tipton cleaning kit that has just about everything needed.

should give at least 3,000 rounds of barrel life, sometimes much more. Velocity, which means friction and heat, wears barrels . . . so a .22-250 will wear and lose accuracy faster than a .223, a .300 magnum will burn out faster than a .30-06, and a 7mm magnum will burn out faster than a 7x57 or 7mm-08.

Cartridges that are overbore capacity, meaning they are trying to burn a great deal of powder down a relatively small hole, accelerate barrel wear. Both the .220 Swift (1935) and the .264 Winchester (1958) were immediately very popular, but sales languished after they got reputations as "barrel burners." Primarily this means rapid throat erosion, which often won't initially impact accuracy but certainly will as it progresses. Better barrel steel has improved things, but today we have some very large-cased and very fast cartridges that burn an awful lot of powder and, yes, they're going to wear out barrels. Cartridges like the .30-.378 Weatherby Magnum, the 7mm Remington Ultra Mag, the big Lazzeroni cartridges, and probably Nosler's new .26 and .28 Nosler are going to be hard on barrels, with potential barrel life unlikely to exceed 1,000 rounds.

In the field I always have a pocket-size Otis cleaning kit handy. I don't clean every time a rifle is fired, but I use it if there's precipitation, dust, or too many shots down a barrel during the course of a hunt.

A generation ago this killed the .264, a cartridge that I happen to like, but today's shooters don't seem to be nearly as bothered by shorter barrel life. Maybe we just don't shoot as much? My old friend, the late Gary Sitton, a far better writer than I will ever be, was also very good with quick-witted one-liners. We were talking about this and he said, "Hell, when we were kids it was the kiss of death if a cartridge caused rapid barrel wear . . . today it's a badge of honor if you shoot out a barrel."

If you want to win that badge, just shoot until your barrel is too hot to touch, and then keep shooting! Most of us have better sense than that, but it's quite possible to wear out almost any barrel in one day in a prairie dog town. Both on the range and in the field you need to exercise restraint. Don't let the barrel get too hot to touch, and you will extend your barrel life. Realistically, replacing a barrel is not that big a deal. At the cost of ammo today, by the time you've worn out a barrel you've spent many times the price of a new barrel, even of the very best quality. On the other hand, a new barrel is always an unknown quantity, so if you happen to have a really accurate rifle you may want to think about rationing the rounds you pour down it. I haven't gotten attached to very many rifles—they come and go—so I've personally worn out very few barrels, but I did manage to wear out the barrel on a Model 70 in .375 H&H. That's actually quite a trick, but I can't claim full credit because it was used when I got it. Twenty years later, the groups started to go. Although I'd shot it a lot, I couldn't believe it was possible to shoot out a .375, so I cleaned it thoroughly, recut the crown, messed with the bedding, the works, but the groups were no longer there. A barrel that has seen its best days will tell you, but you need to read the signs, and once it starts to go, there's no coming back.

As for barrel heat and accuracy, this is a lot like cleaning. A horribly fouled barrel can't shoot well, nor can an overheated barrel. However, some barrels shoot their best groups when stone cold, others shoot best when slightly warm, and some (few) like it hot. From a hunter's perspective this is not important. All we really care about is the first, second, and just maybe third shot from a

At the range it's important to be patient and not let the barrel get too hot. In the summertime I spend a lot of time waiting for barrels to cool!

One of few barrels that I've managed to shoot out happened to be the original barrel on this left-hand converted 1950s-vintage Winchester Model 70 .375. I can't take credit; the rifle was well-used when I got it!

stone-cold barrel. But if you're seeking the tightest groups your rifle is capable of, then it's worth experimenting a bit. It doesn't happen often, but some rifles will consistently fire a better *second* group after a first group with no cooling period in between. These subtle differences are part of the vagaries of rifle accuracy, which makes the whole subject both fascinating and frustrating.

OPEN SIGHTS AND APERTURES

CHAPTER 10

A telescopic sight helps you see better . . . and if you can see better, you can shoot better. From a pure accuracy standpoint there is no question that the telescopic sight wins hands-down. I'd even go a step further and say that, if shooting tight groups is your goal, then the more magnification the better. It's a whole lot easier to shoot the best groups your rifle is capable of with a modern 2–12X variable turned all the way up than

This .375 wears an aperture sight, which is easier on middle-age eyes than open sights. Either way, however, you don't suddenly wake up with proficiency with iron sights. If you're going to use them, plan on plenty of practice.

A young Jack O'Connor admires a nice Coues deer. The rifle is definitely a Springfield action with aperture sights, so it's probably pre-.270! Scopes are clearly superior for this type of hunting, but a background with iron sights is a huge advantage for all rifle shooting.

with the fixed 4X scopes I started hunting with. Likewise, if you're one of many people today who try to expand their range envelope, the magnification and precision of a telescopic sight are essential.

So, on the one hand, it might seem that a chapter on iron sights is completely out of place in this book. On the other hand, while this is not a *hunting* book, it is about rifle shooting as well as rifle accuracy. Iron sights do not allow the maximum accuracy your rifle may be capable of, and in fact, if you're shooting irons you probably know how well (and how far) you can shoot, but it's almost impossible to know exactly what your rifle is really capable of. However, iron sights still play an extremely important role in rifle *shooting*, and in a number of ways.

Today we live in a scope era. I could be wrong, but I believe that a majority of our young riflemen and women, let's say those under thirty, have almost no exposure to iron sights at all. To me this is regrettable. A scope makes shooting accurately much easier, and this isn't a bad thing, but lessons learned in properly aligning iron sights are never forgotten, and are transferable to use of a scope.

The reverse is not necessarily true. Let's say you started shooting with a scope and used a scope your whole life. Someday, somewhere in middle age, you win the lottery and are able to mount the elephant safari you've long dreamed of. You've read my stuff, and you know that this is one situation where iron sights are superior to scopes, so you purchase a big double to take on the hunt. Man, you'd better practice a whole bunch, because after being spoiled by a scope for decades, you won't suddenly wake up and find yourself proficient with iron sights!

I'm as guilty as anyone. Neither of my daughters had any interest in shooting or hunting until they were about sixteen. If I were a perfect dad I would have started them with an iron-sighted .22, as all kids of my generation did. But I'm far from perfect, and with a starting date that late, we were on a crash course. So I taught them to shoot with scopes, and to this day they have little (if any) familiarity—and no comfort zone—with iron sights. This is too bad. You quickly learn that even the slightest variation in sight picture can send the bullet into left field, and you learn that the distance isn't very great before your foresight subtends (covers) most of your target, whether a tin can or a squirrel's head. You miss some, you hit others, and you learn to make it work.

I started with a single-shot Ithaca falling block .22, using a bullet trap in the basement. (We didn't know much about lead pollution back then!) The rifle had a traditional "buckhorn" rear sight and a blade front. I don't really know if it was very accurate or not, but I put thousands of rounds through that little rifle and eventually became fairly consistent. I went on to shoot smallbore in college, position shooting with aperture sights, and during my time in the Marines aperture sights were all we had. These were all extremely valuable lessons.

Unlike a lot of people my age, I started hunting with a scope. Well, that's not strictly true; I hunted rabbits and squirrels with an open-sighted .22, also

The "buckhorn" rear sight (bottom) is a traditional American open sight, but I find the "express-style" rear sight with a fairly wide "V" faster and easier to use.

invaluable training, but I began big-game hunting with a scope, and I was nearly thirty before I ever hunted big game with iron sights. Fortunately, I had history to fall back on. I understand the limitations of iron sights, but within those limits and in certain applications they're pretty hard to beat, even today.

There are essentially two types of iron sights: "open," and the aperture, or "peep," sight. The open sight consists of a front sight, which may be a blade or a bead, and a rear sight, generally affixed to the barrel. The rear sight has a notch, the idea being to center the tip of the front sight in the bottom of the notch. There are V-notches, U-notches, square notches, and combinations. I'm not sure it matters just so long as you've practiced enough so that you can center the front sight in the rear sight exactly the same way every time. For me, perhaps because I've used such sights a lot, the easiest to use and most visible are the good English "express" sights, preferably with a silver, gold, or platinum line in the center of the V.

I much prefer a bead front sight to a blade; if the tip of the sight is circular it's much easier, at least for me, to visualize exactly where the aiming point should be. The old standard was an ivory bead, but gold (color) beads are fine, and today's fiber optic front sights are even more visible. The size of the bead also makes a big difference. The smaller the bead the more precise the aim, but smaller beads are also slower to center and, as middle age advances, harder to see. There is thus a huge compromise to be made between visibility and precision.

Just last year I had a chance to hunt with one of the new Rigby Big Game Rifles. It was a beautiful rifle built on a single-square-bridge Mauser action, intended for use with iron sights. It had an "express" rear sight with one standing and two folding leaves, and a very nice front bead on a barrel-band ramp. Perfect, except the front bead was so small I could barely see it. Twenty (or perhaps even ten) years ago I would have had no trouble, but today it's a different story! We found a herd of buffalo a hundred yards away, which is probably approaching the sensible limit for open sights. The light was good, but I just couldn't see the bead against the dark animal. In position on the sticks, cheek welded to stock, I raised the rifle to the skyline once and again to make sure I had the bead centered. I guess I did it right, because the shot was good, but it was a lot more difficult than it needed to be. My preference is a front bead of about 3⁄32-inch; this bead was about half that size, very precise, but also difficult to see. Obviously if it had been my rifle I'd just have swapped out the bead, but it wasn't, so I made do and relearned an old lesson: With open sights, choose visibility over precision.

Back when scopes were still widely distrusted, we maintained that iron sights were sturdier and more reliable. This remains true of *good* iron sights, but I'm not so sure about most others today. Many factory-supplied iron sights seem present only as an afterthought, and perhaps they *are* an afterthought, with the manufacturers believing (usually correctly) that a scope will be installed and the iron sights will never be used. I've seen modern factory iron sights bend, break, and simply fall off the rifle. Useless!

On versatile large-caliber rifles, let's say from .375 to .416, I like to see a set of iron sights, and the scope set in detachable mounts. It has been a rare occurrence when I've taken a functional scope off of a rifle to use iron sights instead, but there are times and places. Most of my hunting rifles don't wear

For my eyes, a bead front sight (right) is much easier to use than the blade front sight (left). The size of the bead makes a huge difference . . . smaller is more precise while larger is faster. This is a 3⁄32-inch front bead, for me a good compromise between visibility and precision.

In 2014 I had the opportunity to hunt buffalo with Swift Bullets' Bill Hober. He used his original John Rigby .416 made in 1929; I used a brand-new English-made .416 Rigby. Both rifles are very similar, and both are equipped with "express-style" open sights.

iron sights at all . . . if I want spare sights I pack an extra scope, set in rings. So with the exception of a large-caliber rifle for dangerous game I'm not real keen on "auxiliary" iron sights—but if open sights are installed for any reason other than looks, they must be rigid, solid, dependable, and darn near bulletproof.

The real challenge with open sights is that they require the eye to focus in three planes: rear sight, front sight, and target. Younger eyes are more flexible, but at some point—somewhere in the forties or early fifties for most people—this becomes impossible. It happens about the same time that we start to need glasses to read a menu. Open sights can still be used, but the rear sight begins to "fuzz out," so precision is lost and accurate shooting distances are reduced. The aperture, or "peep," sight, however, is a whole different deal. Also called a "receiver sight" because the rear sight is usually mounted at the rear of the receiver, this system can use the same front sight as an open sight but instead of an open notch, the rear sight is a small circle or aperture that you "peep" through. (Get it?)

The aperture sight has two distinct advantages. First, it's actually an optical sight in that the eye naturally wants to center the front sight in the middle of

Although one gets better with practice, iron sights are limited in range. This was as close as we could get to these Mozambique buffalo, and the front sight of my 1886 Winchester in .475 Turnbull was covering an awful lot of hide. I made the shot fine, but a scope would have made it much easier!

the opening. Second, since you are looking *through*, not *at*, the rear sight, your eye only has to work in two focal planes: front sight and target. Mounted at the muzzle, the front sight is far enough away from the eye that it's relatively easy to resolve, and it's just a matter of superimposing it on the target. Formal rifle competitions often require aperture sights. They are extremely precise, with precision depending not only on the size of the front bead, but also the size of the aperture. Target sights have very small openings, while hunting apertures are much larger. In a pinch, go read your Hemingway; he preferred apertures over scopes to the end of his life, and several times he mentioned unscrewing the aperture so that he had a very large (and thus fast) opening to look through. This is called today a "ghost ring" aperture, very fast but not as precise as a smaller aperture.

I have done a lot of target shooting, hunting, and military shooting with aperture sights. With practice, the precision is amazing. I've shot the occasional sub-minute-of-angle (MOA) group with apertures, but they are somewhat light-dependent; light from the side and shadows can play tricks, and as light grows dim they are, at best, no better than open sights. They are also often somewhat fragile. However, many shooters can use them effectively for some years after open sights are no longer viable, and they certainly allow enough precision to shoot farther.

Years ago I joined Finn Aagaard and John Wootters, both gone now, in some speed drills where we pitted scoped rifles against iron sights. Whether open or aperture, it is a myth that iron sights are faster. With a stopwatch, *nobody* tested faster with iron sights than with a scope. That included me, in my late twenties at the time with vision and reflexes I will never have again. The difference is simple; the scope allows the eye to function in just one focal plane, at the target. The cross hairs are superimposed on the target and the trigger is pressed. Simple! Obviously the magnification must match the distance and situation, but for up-close and fast work, a low-powered scope is faster and more precise than any iron sight.

So we've seen that a scope allows more accurate shooting and is faster than iron sights. It is also vastly superior in low light. The scope actually gathers

With practice, extremely accurate shooting can be done with aperture sights—but you need good light. This R. F. Sedgely left-hand-converted Springfield, made in the 1930s, is still wonderfully accurate . . . and especially accurate for a rifle of its vintage.

light, allowing better visibility at dawn and dusk; this gives precious minutes of critical hunting time after the hunter with iron sights is all done because he can no longer see his sights. Even the military has finally accepted these things, with first the Marine Corps and then the Army *finally* shifting to the low-magnification ACOG scope.

So if these things are true, do iron sights still have a purpose? Yes, several. As I said earlier, they remain an invaluable tool for teaching sight alignment. There are also several specialized but important hunting situations where iron sights are superior. In driving rain or blizzard conditions a scope quickly becomes useless. In part this is because of droplets or snowflakes on the lens, but also because the magnifying riflescope magnifies those droplets or snowflakes. An aperture sight is almost equally useless; go back to your Hemingway and see how many times he mentions blowing droplets out of an aperture. The open sight may not have the range, but it remains viable rain or shine.

I've said before, but I will say again, iron sights are vastly superior to scopes for elephant hunting. You don't want any magnification; otherwise, at a matter of feet you'll see nothing but a wall of gray. Most serious of all, even a scope without magnification tends to cause "tunnel vision." In elephant hunting

With aperture sights, the smaller the opening, the more precise one can be . . . but the larger the opening, the faster one can acquire the target. A "ghost-ring" sight is essentially created by removing the target aperture and simply using the larger opening.

In elephant hunting I am absolutely convinced iron sights are superior to scopes. Ranges are close and the target is large. Magnification is not needed, but the larger problem is the "tunnel vision" that is almost unavoidable when using a scope . . . especially at close range.

you need full peripheral vision because the great danger comes not from the elephant you're trying to shoot, but other elephants you may not have seen. You can, and should, train yourself to shoot a scope with both eyes open, but in this most specialized pursuit of the world's largest game there is no reason to use a scope. If the brain shot is to be taken you'll be very close, well within twenty-five yards. A long shot on elephant is fifty yards, and at that distance you'll forget the brain shot and go for the heart/lung shot. The target is almost as big as a barn door; you have all the precision you need.

Although I'm sure there are more, I can think of two additional specialized situations where iron sights are superior. One is hunting with hounds, whether for pigs, bears, cats, or whatever. The shot will almost certainly be very close, but that isn't the point. It's that tunnel vision thing again. You simply must be mindful of where the dogs are when you take your shot, so it is better to be looking over iron sights rather than through a scope. Many houndsmen simply won't allow scopes anywhere near their dogs, usually because of bad experiences.

Another situation for iron sights is heavy forest and jungle hunting. In the African forests I've used both scopes and iron sights, likewise in the jungles of southern Mexico. You don't really need the precision of a scope; in really thick stuff you are often so close you are pointing the rifle like a shotgun, and the scope becomes just one more thing to snag on vines and get in the way. Iron sights are getting increasingly difficult for me to see properly, but even so I vote for iron sights in the thickest cover just as a matter of simplicity.

A couple of years ago I hunted in the Philippines, a place where you simply cannot bring rifles. We trotted down to the local gendarmerie and "checked out" a well-worn M14 and a partial belt of corroded machine-gun ammo. I trained on the M14 and have done a lot of shooting with Springfield M1As, but my hunting partner, Saso Ivanov from Macedonia, had never seen such a rifle.

There are many hunts I'd just as soon not attempt with iron sights, but they're a lot of fun to use and add a measure of challenge. On a roebuck hunt in England in 2014 I borrowed a vintage SMLE in .303, and it had original battle sights. That was fun!

Scopes are unnecessary for most jungle hunting where shooting distances are often measured in feet. In the Philippines, a place where firearms cannot be imported, we borrowed a well-worn M14 from the local military. It worked just fine!

From experience in the Yugoslav army he was plenty familiar with open sights, but had never used an aperture. He figured it out pretty quick, and it really didn't matter because in that thick cover no shot was farther than fifteen yards. Between us we took four water buffalo and four pigs, absolutely no problems. A scope could have worked, but there was no need for it.

There is one other situation where iron sights are marvelous, and that's for just plain shooting fun! With practice and concentration it's amazing what you can do with them, and it isn't a bad thing to refresh those lessons on sight alignment. Iron sights are much less forgiving than a scope. Shooting them well is a tremendous confidence builder, and when you switch back to a scope, you'll appreciate it a lot more.

Scopes and Mounts

CHAPTER 11

Telescopic sights are hardly new; they saw some use as far back as the American Civil War. Although they became both more available and more reliable in the early twentieth century, however, they were still relatively uncommon and generally distrusted until after World War II. As I've said, I learned to *shoot* with iron sights, but I learned to *hunt* with scopes, so I was a child of the first scope era. By this time, the 1960s, telescopic sights were in common use, but they weren't exactly the same as the scopes we use today.

Back then the fixed-power ruled, as it had for some time. In the 1930s my uncle, Art Popham, had a sporterized Springfield with a 2.5X Noske scope, a pretty hot setup for the day. Thirty years later the fixed 4X was the most common big-game scope. Variables were coming along, but they were still widely distrusted. There was reason for this; most of the earliest variable-power scopes shifted zero considerably as the power ring was adjusted. In those days I had a fixed 4X Unertl and later a 4X Weaver. More powerful scopes existed—at some point we had a fixed 6X on an early Ruger No. 1 .243 for prairie-dog shooting—but we didn't think we needed more than 4X magnification, and in those days the gunwriters, including Jack O'Connor, were very consistent in telling us that was all we needed.

I got my first variable-power scope in 1976, a 3–9X Redfield, mounted on a Ruger M77 .30-06. Talk about an eye-opener! Although it was true that lots of early variables had issues, it is pure bunk to say more magnification isn't useful. It isn't necessary to make things harder than they have to be; provided the image is clear and you don't have so much magnification that all you can see is a blur of hair, if you can see better, you can shoot better. With 20/10 vision and mid-20s reflexes and conditioning I could shoot very well in those days, but as

Like all shooters of my generation, I grew up reading Jack O'Connor's stuff. He was adamant that a fixed 4X was plenty of scope for any big-game hunting. I don't agree, but in O'Connor's day variables were new and not always reliable.

distances increased I quickly discovered I shot a whole lot better (and faster) with the scope turned up to 9X than I ever could with a fixed 4X.

Today I need reading glasses to see my watch, but my distance vision is hanging in at better than 20/20. As for the reflexes and conditioning, well, today I ride on the coattails of experience. I still shoot just fine, and I still believe that plenty of magnification is a very good thing—but only to a point, and only when you actually need it. For a half-century now the 3–9X and similar (meaning 2.5–8X, 3.5–10X, etc.) variable-power scopes have been the most popular American riflescopes. There is good reason for this.

Now, I want to be careful—as much as I revere Jack O'Connor, I think one of very few things he was dead wrong about is that bit about 4X being all you need. So I don't want to do the same thing and say "9X or 10X is all the magnification you need." The limitation isn't really on the upper end, but on the *lower* end. Not all shots are going to be at long range, and while high magnification is very useful way out there, it's not only useless but downright dangerous up close. So you must have a low enough setting that, in case of an unexpected close encounter, you have a clear sight picture and not just a blur. (By the way, it's always a good idea to keep the power ring turned down until you actually *need* more magnification.)

Just how low a setting you need depends a bit on you. I'm left-handed and left-eye dominant, and I shoot from the left shoulder. Normally when I shoot with a scope both eyes are open, because while I maintain depth of field and peripheral vision with my right eye, my left eye takes over and my right eye doesn't get in the way. I wrote "normally" because there was a photo published recently that showed me shooting with my right eye scrunched shut. Yep, I remember the day. Just got off a twelve-hour plane ride, no sleep, eyes red and burning, squinting into the setting sun. It happens. So, *normally* I shoot with both eyes open when using a scope. That means that I can get away with a bit more magnification for extremely close-range shooting.

Most of us will be just fine with a low setting of 3X or so, no matter how close the shot. Although more magnification can make things easier, a high magnification of 9X or 10X should make almost any sensible and reasonable shot very possible. I think Leupold was the first to come out with a 4.5–14X variable, and I freely admit that I fell in love with that class of scope. There are others; I have a Zeiss Conquest (1-inch tube) 4.5–14X and a Bushnell Elite 4–16X, and another Zeiss Victory (30mm tube) in 3.5–12X56mm, a fantastic scope.

While I wouldn't go so far to put such scopes on a .375 or a .416, for my eyes these are all extremely versatile hunting scopes. The higher magnification may not be essential, but at longer ranges the larger image builds confidence, and I believe aids more precise shot placement . . . but you can still turn the magnification down in thick stuff. Scopes in this class also bridge the gaps between target shooting, big-game hunting, and shooting varmints.

The first time I ever hunted with a variable scope was in Kenya in 1977. I had a Redfield 1–4X on a Mauser in .375 and a Redfield 3–9X on a Ruger in .30-06. Before that I had never hunted big game with more power than 4X, so the 3–9X really opened my eyes!

In recent years the technology has gotten even better. The most recent advancements in variable-power scopes have been to increase the zoom range. A 3–9X was pretty much a 3–9X because, technologically, it was difficult to go much beyond 3X zoom capability. We are way past that now! Several companies now have scopes that zoom to six times their lowest power without degrading optics or shifting zero. This allows greatly enhanced flexibility, if not actual capability. I think Swarovski was one of the first with their Z6 series; I used a Z6 (2.5–15X) and a Z6 (1–6X) on a lengthy hunt in Tanzania in 2010. Both scopes deserve comment.

On the 2.5–15X scope: There are very few shots so close that 2.5X magnification will cause a problem, and in my world there isn't anything so far away that 15X won't bring it in. So this is obviously a very versatile and useful type of scope.

The 1–6X was mounted on a Dakota .375, and perhaps this class of scope deserves a few more words. For many years we have typically mounted low-range variables on rifles intended for close-range, close-cover work. This includes not only "dangerous-game rifles," but also rifles such as a lever-action .45-70 or .358

for black bears, hogs, whatever. With the previous limitations in zoom range, the classic scope in this range has been Leupold's 1.75–5X, or the 1–4X, which almost all riflescope manufacturers make.

The new scopes with their increased zoom ranges are advantageous on an extremely versatile rifle like the .375 H&H. Typically, we mount it with something like the aforementioned 1–4X or 1.75–5X. These are great for buffalo, but what about plains game out at 200 yards and beyond? I have long thought that the versatile .375 deserves a bit more scope. I've mounted 3–9X scopes on .375s (maybe that's a bit much), and lately I've used a Leupold 2–7X33 on a .375, not bad. The new 6X zoom capability offers an excellent compromise in a 1–6X. Yes, the difference between 4X and 6X does help at medium ranges.

For many years now the 3–9X "class" of scope (including 2.5–8X and 3.5–10X) has been the most popular. The versatility is wonderful, suitable for use in hunting both up close and far away. A Leupold 3.5–10X was used on a .270 WSM to take this Stone sheep in 2003.

Low-end magnification is just as important as high-end magnification because you never know when you might get a close shot. This LAW M704 in .280 wears a Leupold VX-6 (2–12X) . . . but it was turned all the way down for a 25-yard shot in heavy timber.

Several other companies have also increased the zoom range of their riflescopes. My intent here is not to be a scope catalog, but to talk about concepts. In the last couple of years, however, I've used several of Leupold's new VX-6 scopes. Of course they have a VX-6 (1–6X) "dangerous-game scope." I haven't used that one, but I've spent a lot of time with the VX-6 (2–12X), another extremely versatile scope that will do everything without getting you into trouble at either short or long range. Just lately I put the newest model, a VX-6 (3–18X), on a .300 Winchester Magnum. I haven't actually used (or needed to use) the highest setting in the field, but it sure does look good on the range.

With the current interest in long-range shooting, a lot of people are moving toward scopes with higher magnification. This is perfectly OK, but unless you do all your shooting on the range it's important to remember that not all shots will be far . . . and, up close, too much magnification is a problem. I remember years ago, when I was guiding in eastern Colorado, a guy showed up with a long-range setup with something like a 12–36X scope on his rifle. I didn't guide him and I can't remember how it worked out, but while such a scope has its uses, it is not a suitable scope for big-game hunting. No matter what you expect, you really don't know what kind of shot you might get, so your scope needs to have magnification both high enough and low enough to handle whatever might come along.

As for accuracy, the scope or sight you mount has absolutely nothing to do with the raw accuracy of your rifle. I've shot some very tight groups with aperture sights, although no doubt the rifle could have done better. I've also shot a very few quarter-inch groups with 4X scopes. There is no doubt, however, that a good scope with lots of magnification makes it much easier to realize the accuracy potential of your rifle.

In this regard, the reticle makes a big difference. For example, when I was a kid the two-minute dot was still a popular reticle. The designation meant that the center dot subtended, or covered, two MOA, meaning essentially two inches at 100 yards, four inches at 200 yards, and so forth. Bold and visible,

I freely admit that I like magnification! In recent years I've done most of my mountain hunting with a Zeiss Victory 3.5–12X on the Blaser R8; and a Leupold VX-6 (2–12X) in Blaser mounts. Both of these excellent scopes have made longer shots seem a lot easier.

My first exposure to "six times zoom" was on a hunt in Tanzania in 2010. This Dakota M10 single shot in 7mm Remington Magnum wore a Z6i (2.5–15X) scope, a wonderfully versatile setup. I had a long, difficult shot on this sitatunga, and I had it turned all the way up.

it remains one of the fastest reticles out there for quick shooting, especially on running game, but you cannot shoot your tightest groups if the reticle is covering everything you're trying to hit. Back then we didn't have nearly as many choices, but another was the fine cross hair. This allowed for a very precise point of aim, but it wasn't fast because the fine cross hair wasn't as easy to see, and, as light failed, it became darn near invisible.

These days most of us compromise. The most popular reticle is the "plex type," so stated because most companies have their own, as in Leupold's Duplex and so forth. This type of reticle uses thick outer cross hairs, which are very visible, with a thin inner cross hair at the intersection, which allows for a fine aim. There are many other reticles today, some of which are too busy for my taste, and then we have the range-compensating reticles with additional aiming points, which we'll talk about later. It all depends on what you like or, perhaps more important, what you get used to, but in reticles we're always walking a thin line between fast target acquisition and precision of aim. If accuracy for its own sake is your primary goal, then you want the most precise aiming point possible; for this it's hard to beat the very thin cross hair (so-called because, in early scopes, they actually used strands of hair). If your goal is accuracy in preparation for field use, then you must compromise between precision and visibility.

Now let's spend a little time on scope mounts. Today's rifles are more accurate than ever before, and today's scopes are simply amazing. It's the scope mount and rings that join the two together, and sometimes it's the weakest link. I'll tell two stories on myself, one that illustrates a fairly common problem and another that was just plain stupid. Just a couple weeks ago, in preparation for a polar bear hunt, I was installing an Aimpoint sight on the new Mossberg Patriot in .375 Ruger. The Mossberg comes with Weaver bases, and this Aimpoint has

On the same 2010 safari, this Dakota M76 in .375 H&H wore a Z6i (1–6X). While magnification isn't needed on dangerous game, both the .375s and .416s might be used on plains game, and a bit more magnification can be handy. This roan antelope was taken from about 250 yards.

Often we hamper our .375s and .416s with a classic "dangerous game" scope in the 1–4X class. Recently I've been using a Leupold 2–7X33. Shooting with both eyes open, I have no trouble up close at 2X, and a bit more magnification can be handy on plains game. This is a CZ 550 in .375 H&H.

an integral Weaver mount on the bottom of the sight. In other words, nothing could be simpler, which is good, because mounting a scope is pretty much the pinnacle of my mechanical capability. Everything went together fine and groups were good, but during the second shooting session, the rifle was suddenly way out of zero. Before panicking I checked, and the base was loose. *Duh.* Easy to fix, and easy to make sure it stayed fixed with a bit of LocTite. Of course, I should have checked it before I started shooting.

Here's the dumb one. I get some number of test rifles in. I play with them and return them. That's simply part of what I do, so I don't remember what rifle this was and it doesn't matter, because it was my fault for being stupid. Anyway, it was a .375 with a low-power scope in detachable rings, and it came with a test target that looked really good. I had some other stuff to do at the range that day, so when it was that rifle's turn I put it in the Lead Sled, checked the bore (clear) and checked the bore sight (definitely on paper). I touched off a round, something hit me square in the forehead, and I went over backward onto the cement slab, out like a light. I came to a few seconds later, head hurting (both front and back) but, strangely, no blood. I assumed the rifle had blown up, so it took me a few seconds more to check myself for damage, then to screw up my courage to take a look. The rifle was fine, still in the Lead Sled. The scope was lying next to me, because the detachable mount *wasn't locked down*. In classic equal and opposite reaction, upon firing, the scope had flown back and center-punched me on the forehead. (Amazingly, the scope was undamaged, and my greatest injury was to my pride.)

Are the lessons clear? Always make sure all scope mount screws are tight: On the rifle, on the scope rings, and whatever joins the scope rings to the bases and the rifle. We'll talk about this again a little bit in chapter thirteen, because more than occasionally "accuracy problems" are caused by the scope or the mount. For now,

Leupold's newest addition to the VX-6 "six times zoom" line is a VX-6 (3–18X). The first time I used it was on an aoudad hunt in Texas, and while I haven't needed that much magnification in the field, it sure is nice on the range.

Torque wrenches are common today, and most scope-mount instructions now have a recommended torque. Read the directions! Don't overtighten, or you'll break screws—like I often do. On the other hand, make absolutely certain all base and ring screws are plenty tight.

when mounting a scope, the ego needs to be put aside. *Read the directions*, get it right, and make sure it's right. Some very good scope mounts are extremely easy to assemble, and some are the very devil. I mount a lot of scopes and switch them back and forth frequently, but I would never say I'm good at mounting scopes (or anything else mechanical!). I just go at it slowly and carefully, and try to make sure every screw is good and tight. But, obviously, there have been times when I took things for granted that I shouldn't have, and Mr. Murphy lay in wait.

As for what mounts are best, well, again, this isn't a catalog. When I was a kid the two primary choices were the old Redfield with windage-adjustable rear base, and the Weaver. Both are still with us. I am convinced today that the Redfield-type (now manufactured variously) is a long way short of being the strongest mount out there, but it is plenty strong enough for moderate recoil levels, especially if you are very careful to seat the bottom of the rear ring very squarely between the screws. The Weaver is not the sleekest or coolest-looking mount, but it's simple and strong. Today it's gained popularity because of the Picatinny rail system which, after all, is just a Weaver mount with lots of attachment points.

These days I use a lot of Weaver mounts (who doesn't?), and I use a lot of Talley rings and bases, and I use a lot of Leupold rings and bases. In the extensive Leupold line, my favorites are the dual-dovetail and their detachable system, but their new line of AR mounts for Picatinny rails is also fantastic. But there are many good mounting systems out there today. Ruger's integral base and supplied rings is still a great deal. The old Conetrol mount is light, sleek, and strong. The older Warne detachable is good, as is the new Alaska detachable.

No matter what mount you use, remember recoil is always the scope mount's great enemy. This is not just a matter of cartridge and caliber. Obviously powerful rifles kick more and need stronger mounts, but extremely light rifles also kick more, regardless of chambering, so lightweight rifles also need stronger mounts. I've written about this rifle before, but it's worth bringing up again: Many years ago I had my idea of a "swamp rifle" for buffalo, a 6-pound .416 Hoffman. It kicked like a beast, and it also went through scopes and mounts like it was eating popcorn. Now there are a few .308 and 7mm-08 rifles out there (such as Kimber's Adirondack) that weigh less than 5 pounds. Obviously

The Talley mount (bottom) is probably near the top in scope mounts, available with both screws and detachable levers. The Weaver-style mount, now made by many companies, isn't exactly sleek, but it also works extremely well.

The Picatinny rail is really just a Weaver-style mount with numerous attachment points. Leupold's Tactical mount is strong, simple, and easy to install, and it is a great mount for the popular AR platform.

they won't kick like that .416 did, but I suggest that a few extra ounces might be sacrificed in favor of a really strong scope-mounting system.

Make sure you read the directions, get it right, and get all the screws good and tight. Some mounts recommend LocTite, others don't. *Follow the directions.* Among my bad habits I occasionally overtighten and break off screws, which is a real mess. The Wheeler torque screwdriver from Brownell's is a great tool for scope mounting, but there's a fine line between good and snug and overtightening until you hear a *snap*. The directions for the Alaska detachable mount (which I read, no kidding) actually tell you how much torque to put on each screw. Wow, what a concept! In general, though, you want all the screws good and tight with hand pressure, but without really leaning into them to the breaking point.

Now, let's move on to an entirely different and relatively new type of sight.

Dots and Lights

CHAPTER 12

Whether it's hitting the mark or not (pun intended), this book is about accurate shooting. To some, accurate shooting means cloverleaf groups at a hundred yards; to others it means center-punching a bull elk at two-fifty, or ringing steel at a thousand. Accurate shooting, however, is not about *distance*; it's about putting the bullet where you want it to go at whatever distance you're shooting. Lighted sighting systems,

The Swedish Aimpoint is the granddaddy of red dot or reflex sights. Available in the U.S. for forty years, they've evolved a lot. This is a Hunter model, nonmagnifying but "scopelike" in appearance. No red-dot sight is about precision shooting, but with practice accuracy is very good.

This is a Zeiss reflex sight in action on a running boar target. Today most major optics manufacturers offer red-dot sights; though not ideal for longer ranges, they're the cat's pajamas for close, fast shooting.

whether we're speaking of a lighted scope reticle or a "red-dot" sight, are not about precision shooting in the clinical sense of sheer accuracy. They generally won't help you shoot the tightest groups possible at any range, but they can help you take an elk at medium range, or put a quick stop to an inbound buffalo (or a gunfight) at close range.

Lighted sights are about *speed*, not precision. They don't necessarily aid in target acquisition, but they offer a bright, bold aiming point that naturally and quickly draws the eye. Like a magnifying scope, they allow the eye to operate in just one focal plane, so it's a very simple matter to quickly superimpose the aiming point on the target. In failing light or heavy shadows when iron sights and scope reticles are becoming murky, they can certainly enable better shot placement, and in any situation where faster shooting is desirable, they will help.

There are two primary types of lighted sights: a lighted reticle within a more or less conventional magnifying scope, and a reflected dot or image. This last we tend to call a "red dot" sight, but I put that in quotes because green, blue, and sometimes yellow lights are also used. Red dots are most common, but both blue and green are a bit easier on the human eye. Both blue and green are thought by many in the tactical community to be better at night, but I remain convinced that red is by far the best for daylight use. These days there are a number of sights that actually give you a choice of color, so you can experiment.

Also, while we call them "red dot" sights, sometimes the aiming point is something other than a dot. Military sights often use some sort of centered V for fast combat shooting. The "red dot" sight is perhaps more properly called a "reflex sight" (as in reflective), and it is also referred to as a "holo sight" as in hologram. The point is that the dot or image isn't really there in the center of the sight; it is reflected or projected. Either type, lighted aiming point or lighted reticle, can be powered by a battery, which is most common, or by a substance such as tritium with a fiber-optic feed, as in the Trijicon system.

The granddaddy of all reflex sights is the Swedish Aimpoint, which has been available in the United States for forty years. Typically the Aimpoint is

For any age I'm convinced reflex sights are faster *than iron sights, but at some point in our middle years most of us start to have trouble aligning the irons. Though very nontraditional on a double rifle, reflex sights offer a near-perfect alternative.*

A strong advantage to the red-dot sight is that it forces one to shoot with both eyes open. This is an advantage in all situations, but it is extremely important in dangerous-game hunting where peripheral vision can save your life.

built like a small riflescope, absent magnification but with the light-gathering capabilities of lenses. I have used it off and on over the years; it's a rugged and effective sight, and the red dot is really *fast*. Improvement has continued over the years, so the Aimpoint of today certainly isn't the Aimpoint of forty years ago. Also, now just about every optics manufacturer has some kind of reflex sight. Most of them look like a flat wafer mounted on barrel or action, joined by another standing wafer that is the "screen."

In various forms, reflex sights are popular in many shooting disciplines. The Aimpoint was first adopted by the Swedish army but, to my knowledge, no reflex sight has been officially adopted by our forces. However, they mount readily on a Picatinny rail. Our troops love them for "CQB," close-quarter battle, which, in Southwest Asia, meant the deadly game of clearing buildings. Practical pistol shooters also love them. More recently I've seen a couple of reflex sights specifically designed for shotgunning—the reflected aiming point is a lighted circle, essentially depicting the *pattern*. I've used them for turkey

I used an Aimpoint Hunter on a Montana Rifles .375 when I shot this West African savanna buffalo in Burkina Faso. The first shot was good, but upon receiving the bullet, the bull ran straight toward me. Getting him stopped with the red-dot sight was fast and simple.

hunting, which is a different form of shotgunning in that, instead of swinging on a flying target, you are *aiming* at a turkey's head and neck. This is no different from aiming a rifle. I've seen some awfully good shotgunners miss turkeys because they've never aimed a shotgun at anything standing still! In my experience these sights allow much faster and more precise aiming than just squinting down the rib.

No one thinks of these nonmagnifying "red dot" sights as precision long-range sights, and indeed they are not. But for close, fast use, they're pretty awesome. Sometimes you really don't need magnification, but unless a shot is so close as to be instinctive, most of the time you do need a precise aiming point. As I mentioned earlier, most of us reach a point where our eyes have increasing trouble resolving iron sights. I'm not quite there, but I'm definitely getting there, and the reflex sight offers a solution. I know quite a few hunters, including African professional hunters, who have mounted them on big-bore rifles for dangerous game. If you simply can't resolve iron sights any more, a telescopic sight provides one answer, but if you don't need *range*, just a visual aiming point, then these sights are smaller, lighter, and solve the problem. They do look a bit strange on classic doubles. I haven't yet put one on a double rifle, but there may come a time (maybe soon) when I will.

I've spent quite a lot of time on the range with a number of reflex sights from several manufacturers, and on a variety of firearms. Like everything else, they take practice, but they work. I've done some hunting with the Aimpoint on a variety of arms as well, from a .375 for buffalo to a crossbow for whitetails. They work.

Just a year ago I shot a buffalo with the Aimpoint. The initial shot was just under a hundred yards. That is definitely not too far for that kind of sight; it was very simple, red dot on black shoulder, and I knew the shot was good. After the first shot the buffalo ran straight toward me. He was hit very well; whether he had the strength and mobility to come all the way in I have no way to know, but I couldn't very well wait to find out. So I let him come a little bit, and then I put the red dot on the center of his black chest and shot him again, this shot dropping him. It was neither a hard shot nor a rushed shot, but it was a whole lot easier and faster than it would have been with iron sights.

Just now I'm returning from a polar bear hunt. Obviously this was an important hunt as well as an expensive one, so I gave it some serious thought. There would be no long shots, although it's not impossible to need to stop a bear at a couple hundred yards to prevent it from getting into pressure ridges or an open lead. I can shoot that far with an illuminated dot. More likely is that the bear will be tracked until spotted, then a couple of sled dogs are released and it turns into a hound hunt, with the shot at close range and care needed to ensure the dogs are clear when the shot is taken. Although I don't have a problem shooting with both eyes open, the reflex sight really forces you to that. The third possibility, I understood, was that the bear may be taken at very close range when it comes into camp to kill and eat the sled dogs (or you).

I put a very compact Aimpoint Micro H2 on a Mossberg in .375 Ruger. Of course my shot was none of the three options I'd expected. A very large boar went into some pressure ridges too rough for the sled, so we circled a bit and came in on foot with two leashed dogs. I don't speak the Inuit language, but the obvious intent was to get the bear in sight and then let the dogs distract it, but maybe the dogs didn't speak Inuit either, because at a hundred yards they wanted nothing to do with this. So we closed within fifty yards, and now the bear was watching us, clearly aggressive. My two guides had the dogs, but no rifles, so when the bear started toward us I figured this had gone on long enough! The red dot was clean and bright against white fur on white snow. It was a good choice.

I hope I'm not implying that the reflex or "red dot" sight is merely a substitute for iron sights, for use when aging eyes have increasing difficulty working in multiple planes. That regrettable fact of life is what leads many of us to these sights, but that is not their only purpose. I am now pretty well convinced that they are superior to iron sights for *all* close, fast shooting, and especially in tricky light. Europeans love them for their fast driven-boar shooting, and I'm certain they have a place in almost any close-range, close-cover shooting. The only drawback is that they are another gizmo that must be

The Trijicon scope is a lighted reticle, differing from most in that it uses fiber-optic-fed tritium rather than a battery. When Trijicon came on board as a sponsor of a TV show I was involved with, I spent a lot of time with these scopes, and I became very comfortable with their use.

At first I considered the Trijicon system a short-range affair because, at distance, the lighted post covers a lot of the target. That's true, but with practice, my range envelope grew. I took this fallow deer at a bit over 300 yards, a good maximum for the system.

(securely!) attached to the rifle, and they must be zeroed. In this regard they're no worse (or better) than any scope. However, in the case of battery-operated units (by far the majority), you'd best remember to activate the sight *before* you need it. Any battery-operated device obviously has yet another failure point. In my experience battery life is very good and resistant to cold, but at some point, even if only once a year, you have to remember to change the battery.

The biggest drawback, however, is simply part of the character of this type of sight: It is not a long-range precision tool. This is not for lack of magnification; if you're a child of the scope era (like me), with practice you'll be surprised how well you can live without magnification, at least out to medium ranges. The biggest problem is the amount of target the light or "bloom" subtends, sort of like the old two-minute dot reticle. Most reflex sights today have adjustable intensity; in low light you don't need nearly as bright a bloom as you do in broad daylight. Clearly the brighter it must be, the more target it will obscure. All of these sights today have windage and elevation adjustments, but they're generally coarser than we're used to on a scope, moving one or even two minutes per click of adjustment. You probably won't shoot your tightest groups with them, and you certainly don't want them for long-range shooting . . . but for the fast, close shooting they were designed for, they offer a very good alternative.

Lighted reticles generally have the same limitations: Battery operation, subtending of the target, the need to turn them off and on. The obvious difference is that, should the battery go dead or you forget to turn it on, you still have the basic scope with its basic reticle. I don't see the utility of a lighted reticle for target shooting, whether close or far, and it probably has no benefit for shooting woodchucks or prairie dogs. In many hunting situations you may well forget to turn it on, and only realize later that you might have. However, it does very little harm to have a lighted reticle in a hunting scope, and there are many times when it pays off in spades.

Obvious situations are anything in low light, ranging from leopard hunting to a whole lot of whitetail hunting, especially in the woods where dawn comes late and dusk comes early. One thing I've noticed over the years, however, is

I used a small Aimpoint Micro H2 on a polar bear hunt in 2015. I think it would have handled any potential shot, but at forty yards on an inbound bear, the red dot on white fur was clear and fast!

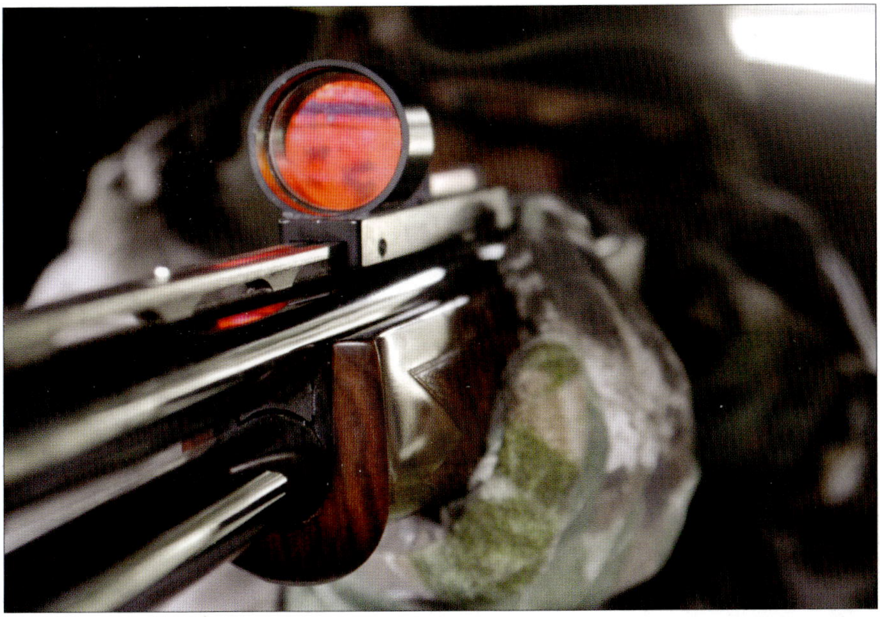

Red-dot sights are useful in many shooting disciplines, from pistol competition to close-quarters combat. This reflex sight, designed to attach to a shotgun rib, proved extremely useful in turkey hunting where the shotgun is aimed *rather than* pointed.

that dark animals tend to confound the aim, and dark animals in shadows make it worse. In this respect African buffalo are especially bad because there will be an awful lot of dark buffalo in the scope, but only a portion can be aimed at for a good hit. Wild hogs and black bears are also very dark and both are often taken in poor light and shadows.

It wasn't so long ago that I was convinced that a lighted reticle was just one more thing to worry about, more troublesome than useful. Today I know that was wrong. The lighted reticle draws the eye to the center, making target acquisition faster in any light. In really poor light, a lighted reticle allows more precise aim after the intersection of even the boldest reticle is murky. So I'm sure it allows shooting when, absent the lighted reticle, a shot might not be fast enough, even if it's possible, and I'm also sure a lighted reticle promotes better shot placement.

The issue of subtending too much target is still there, but that's getting better. The newer illuminated reticle scopes from Leupold and Swarovski (and undoubtedly others I haven't used) have, at the lowest intensity, increasingly smaller "blooms" fed by fiber optics. And of course, you don't have to turn the light on if you don't think you need it. There will be many times when you don't turn it on, but there will also be times when you're glad it's there.

To some extent, too, it's a matter of familiarity. The Trijicon system is a tritium light fed by fiber optics with an external light source gatherer. Trijicon's founder designed the ACOG scope that our troops use, but its adoption was just after my time so I never saw one in the Marines. A couple years later the company came out with its commercial scope, using a post reticle with a bold tritium tip, and then they became a sponsor of an Africa-based TV show I was involved with. I'll be honest: At first I was horrified to be saddled with what I initially considered a piece of junk. I was wrong. It took some practice to get used to it, but for African game shooting, where distances are rarely very far, it proved a good system . . . and for dark buffalo in dark shadows, it was awesome.

Lighted reticles are extremely useful in good old American deer hunting where so many shots are at first or last light. I was using a Leupold VX-6 (2–12X) with its FireDot illuminated reticle when this Georgia buck showed up just at dusk.

In my experience an illuminated reticle is extremely useful in aiding precise shot placement on dark animals. I'm convinced it saves a lot of tracking on buffaloes!

One of the things I learned, too, was that, as in most things, practice makes perfect. At the outset I figured the post reticle was limited to maybe a hundred and fifty yards; it's a bold post, and beyond that it starts to cover up a lot of the target. Yes, it does, but I learned to sight it in a couple inches high at one hundred yards, so out to two hundred yards all I needed to do was place the lighted tip of the post where I wanted to hit. Over time my range envelope continued to increase.

When the distance was such that I had to hold the post high it got tricky, because an awful lot of the animal would be hidden behind the post. Practice helped with that, too. I made several shots beyond three hundred yards with total confidence, and although I'm capable of missing with anything for any reason, I never missed a shot with the Trijicon because too much target was covered up.

Later Trijicon expanded the line to include conventional reticles with tritium-lighted centers, and (like everyone else) the company now have its own line of reflex sights as well.

Today the scopes I use for mountain hunting don't necessarily have lighted reticles. Shooting in poor light is fairly uncommon because at dawn you're still climbing the mountain, and at dusk you need to get down safely. But the scopes I use for deer hunting, African hunting, and general-purpose hunting usually

The light was growing very dim when this leopard came onto the bait. I had an illuminated reticle, and I'm certain it allowed a shot that was both faster and more precise than any conventional reticle. Today I absolutely recommend lighted reticles for leopard hunting!

have a lighted reticle. Like most people who use them, I don't remember to turn the light on all the time, but that's no harm and no foul, because it's there if you need it and you still have the standard reticle if you don't. On the other hand, there have been a lot of times, as the light grows dim on a deer stand or I'm moving through shadowed woods, when I've consciously activated the light, and there have been a few shots when I've been very glad it was there.

The illuminated reticle isn't something that you will always need or use, any more than a reflex sight is the answer for all situations. But there are some situations where it can really help you get an *accurate* shot off in the short time you often have to get on target. I wouldn't be in a leopard blind or hunt black bear over bait without one or the other, and if you choose to hunt buffalo with a magnifying scope I'm convinced a lighted reticle saves a lot of tracking. The advantage isn't really about accuracy; it's about *accuracy with speed*, and sometimes that is very, very important.

TROUBLESHOOTING FOR ACCURACY

CHAPTER 13

Unless we do really exhaustive testing with a lot of loads—and use a big scope, under good conditions, and with good benchrest technique—most of us will probably never learn exactly how accurate our rifles really are. We reach a point where we're satisfied, and unless we're really finicky, that's good enough. At that point we may even start regressing, compromising a bit of accuracy in favor of the bullet we prefer to use for a given purpose. But sometimes, that point of satisfaction is really hard to reach.

As they say, you can't make a silk purse from a sow's ear. There are quite a lot of things you can experiment with to improve accuracy, but you need to be realistic in your expectations. I am convinced that the barrel is by far the single most important component in accuracy, and everything else pretty much serves to help the barrel shoot as well as it can . . . or prevents it from shooting as well as it can. Some barrels are better than others, and, depending on what you want, some barrels just aren't good enough. If there's a genuine problem at play then a seeming miracle can be wrought, but most of the time improvements in accuracy will be incremental, and almost never exponential.

A generation ago, we figured a production rifle that produced 1.5-inch groups at 100 yards was very acceptable, and a true 1-MOA rifle was that *really good* rarity. In the next chapter we'll try to address the difficult subject of how much accuracy is really needed. Obviously that depends not only on the rifle's intended purpose, but also on you: What does it take to make you happy and give you confidence? Today rifles that produce 1-inch groups right out of the box are much more common than they used to be, but despite what you read in the magazines I write for, this kind of accuracy is not a given.

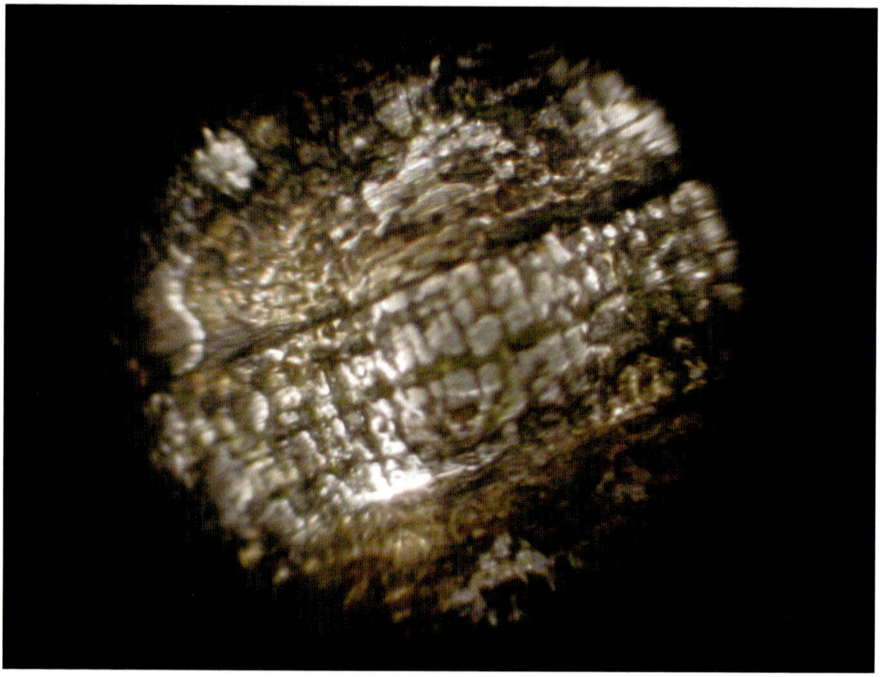

This is what throat erosion looks like, as seen and photographed through the Hawkeye borescope. This doesn't necessarily impact accuracy at this stage, although it might . . . but it will only get worse, so the time for a new barrel is drawing near.

Let's say that you start with 1.5-inch groups. Maybe you can improve on that (and maybe you can't). Maybe even, with some loads, you can achieve 1-inch groups. But you're never gonna get a half-inch rifle if your starting groups are three times larger. Not with that barrel, you're not! If your starting point is genuine 1-inch groups with some loads, then you've got a very good starting point. In fact, you're at a point where an awful lot of people would be dancing jigs and claim "mission accomplished." With some work and some fiddling, you just might get down to the occasional half-inch group with some loads. But you're never gonna get a quarter-inch rifle—not with that barrel, you're not!

From talking to lots of shooters over the years—and reading letters and emails—I get the feeling that, when accuracy isn't what a shooter wants or expects, then one of the first impulses is to start hacking on the bedding. You can do that, but it's one of the last things I consider, because once you change the bedding it's pretty hard to change it back again. There are two things

If a barrel is supposed to be free-floated, it's pretty easy to see if the stock is bearing on the barrel. Just run a piece of paper or a dollar bill between the barrel and the barrel channel, and you'll quickly find any high spots.

This Savage 110 in 7mm Remington Magnum was my first left-hand action. The stock warped and bore against the barrel on a wet caribou hunt, and just a few weeks later did the same on a deer hunt after an overnight rain. It then became my first rifle with a synthetic stock!

involving the bedding you should do, though. First, make sure the bedding isn't seriously flawed. The most common bedding technique today is free-floating. This is partly because it's the cheapest; as I mentioned, free-floating is actually absence of bedding, but it often works. Manufacturing is more precise today than ever before, so it's probably true that the average barrel today is straighter than ever. Straight barrels vibrate uniformly, and a straight barrel is very likely to shoot well when free-floated. But if the barrel is intended to be free-floated, run a piece of paper or a dollar bill down the channel and make sure there's nothing bearing on the barrel. If the barrel is not free-floated, take the barreled action out of the stock and make sure all surfaces are smooth and there aren't any irregularities.

This can actually change over time. The first left-hand action I ever owned was a walnut-stocked Savage 110. The rifle got soaked on a really wet deer hunt, and in a matter of hours the stock warped so much that one side of the barrel channel was bearing on the barrel. Some careful sanding would have fixed it, but it became the first rifle I ever owned that wore a synthetic stock. The Blaser R8 uses free-floating, not necessarily for thrift but because it's an interchangeable barrel system, so that's about the only sensible option. I've used mine since 2010, but lately I've noticed that the left side of the barrel channel is perilously close to bearing on the barrel. Since it's stocked in gorgeous walnut that I don't want to change, I've gone the sandpaper route to keep the barrel channel clear.

The second thing you can try is something I mentioned in chapter three: shimming the fore-end tip to create a bit of upward pressure. You can experiment with this almost endlessly; you can vary the pressure by using additional thicknesses of business cards, and you can alter the placement of the shims. But I wouldn't bother fine-tuning it unless you see almost immediate improve-

Here I am installing a "business card shim." You can actually use a business card, a thin piece of vinyl, or even thin brass stock. Just loosen the action screws and put it slightly behind the fore-end tip, then tighten the action screws, and see what happens. The idea is to put maybe three pounds of upward pressure on the barrel just behind the fore-end tip.

ment—and that immediate shrinkage of your group size is often amazingly dramatic. I don't want to repeat myself as we have plenty to talk about without doing so, but there's something about that little trick that apparently either dampens barrel vibrations or makes them more consistent . . . and if it doesn't work, nothing has been altered. So it's worth a try even on a rifle that is already shooting very well.

In general, however, I wouldn't immediately go after the bedding. There are other things to check out first. As mentioned in chapter eleven, a likely culprit when it comes to accuracy problems is the scope or the mount. There usually isn't such a thing as a bad scope mount, but there are plenty of mounts that weren't assembled properly. I've had a number of scopes that were slipping almost imperceptibly in the rings, especially on hard-recoiling rifles. Obviously you want to check all the mounting screws in both bases and rings, but if a scope is slipping you probably can't get the ring screws tight enough to fix it.

A bad scope can always be the culprit when accuracy takes a fall! If you don't have a spare scope, try switching the suspect scope to a rifle of known accuracy. I often use this Rifles Inc. in .300 Weatherby Magnum as a "control" for trying new scopes because its accuracy is consistent. Obviously there's nothing wrong with this Docter scope!

Action screws need to be good and snug, but hand-snug! *Overtightening can be as big a problem as loose screws because too much pressure can stress the relationship of the action to the barrel.*

What you can do, however, is shim the scope in the rings with a thickness of paper or vinyl.

While "bad" mounts are unlikely, there *is* such a thing as a bad scope. You can get a lemon out of any box or, over time, any scope can "go out." Usually you know it, but sometimes invisible internal issues manifest themselves in accuracy. This is not common, but I've seen it a couple of times. Remember, part of what I do is write about rifles and optics, so I probably shoot more rifles and use more scopes than the average guy. I'm that much more likely to run into problems, and I certainly have. If you're getting odd accuracy results, like very slight shifts in zero or uncalled "fliers" out of the group, try switching scopes. This is definitely not a "sure cure," but in large measure, troubleshooting is about eliminating variables before deciding you've got all the accuracy you're going to get (and then deciding if you can live with it or not).

I have a couple of scopes that I use as "controls"—scopes that have produced the kinds of groups that I know a couple of old favorite rifles are capable of

This is a recessed or "target" crown. Whether the crown is rounded or recessed doesn't really matter, but concentricity is essential because the crown is the last thing the bullet touches as it leaves the barrel.

producing. If I have no particular reason (whether for hunting, writing, or whatever) to start with a different scope I'll usually start with one of these. I'm certainly not advocating investing in extra optics just for this purpose, but if you have another rifle of known accuracy you can try switching scopes just to see what happens.

Action screws are another potential problem. They should be good and snug, but *hand snug*. The torque wrench is a wonderful tool, but don't overdo it. On a wooden stock, overtightening will usually just sink the screw heads into the wood, but a synthetic or laminate stock won't give, so overtightening sucks the action deeper into the stock and can actually create a bind between action and barrel. This will usually have a disastrous impact on accuracy. Loose action screws will also mess things up, but that's a little more obvious. Try the action screws, and if you can't get them to move with relative ease—hand pressure—then they're probably too tight. Unscrew them and start over.

It's easy to see if the crown has been chipped or damaged. Such damage can be caused just by resting a naked muzzle on the gritty floor of a vehicle. What is not so easy to see is if the crown is uneven or sloppily cut.

One of the biggest culprits in poor accuracy is often the crown. It really doesn't matter if the crown is rounded or if it's a recessed or target crown; it's the last thing the bullet touches as it leaves the barrel, and if the crown isn't even and perfectly square then the expanding gases don't exit evenly behind the bullet, essentially kicking the base of the bullet one way or the other as it exits.

One of my worst habits is putting a naked muzzle down on a vehicle's floor mat. In my opinion, this is the proper way to carry a long gun in a vehicle. Of course you know it's unloaded, and the action is open, but if you hit a major bump or have an accident an upright barrel is more likely to hurt somebody than an upright buttstock. However, putting a muzzle down so that it grinds against the gravel and other stuff on the mat or carpet can quickly damage a crown. A strip of electrical tape over the muzzle is great for keeping precipitation out of the barrel, but another reason for taping the muzzle is to protect the crown.

Of course, not all crowns are cut perfectly the first time. If you're wrestling with accuracy, this is not something you should take for granted, and a concentric crown is easy to check. Take common typewriter correction fluid (such as Wite-Out) to the range with you and paint the crown. It has no effect other than to make this easier to see.

Fire one shot, and then look at the blast marks, which will show very clearly on the painted crown. If the crown is OK, these blast marks will look pretty much the same at every place where a rifling groove meets the muzzle. If the blast marks are uneven, then the crown is out of kilter.

This is a very small and quick job for any gunsmith, but if you mess with a lot of rifles you might consider investing in a crown kit. I just checked Brownell's online catalog, and their Manson Precision crown refacing kit starts at $360.

As mentioned previously, most barrels need to be fairly clean in order to shoot well, but some barrels foul very quickly. So it follows that some barrels will shoot their best groups only when freshly cleaned, and a few, for reasons that I don't pretend to understand, shoot best when very dirty. Others shoot best when stone-cold, warm, or very hot. Your rifle will tell you these things, but in order to allow it to you need to vary both your cleaning and cooling regimens quite a bit.

In order to see if a crown is damaged or off-center, paint the muzzle with ordinary typewriter Wite-Out (bottom right), and then fire a shot. You will be able to see the blast marks as the gas exits adjacent to the grooves. If they aren't uniform, then the crown needs to be recut or refaced, a simple job for a gunsmith or easily done with a refacing kit (top left). This new Remington had a sloppy crown and fired the group to the right. A new crown was cut, and it fired the group at center . . . with the same load *(center).*

Perhaps the most important troubleshooting step of all is to be as relentless and exhaustive as possible in your search for the loads your rifle likes best. Now, if you don't handload and you're shooting an oddball or relatively unpopular cartridge then you may be stuck with the one or two or three factory loads available. So be it; if everything else checks out, then that's the accuracy you have available, and this is a classic (and common) case of never knowing exactly how accurate that rifle might be. If you are a handloader then the situation is exactly opposite: It is almost impossible to ever get through all the endless combinations of components that might be tried.

On the one hand it isn't necessary to try them *all*; at some point your rifle will tell you what loads it likes. On the other hand, while accuracy improvements are usually incremental, some rifles are downright finicky, and it is impossible to predict how well any given rifle may shoot. I had a Remington Model 700 Mountain Rifle in .280 Remington, and I had high expectations for it. This was years ago, and Remington was just about the only company loading for the .280. I tried every load I could get my hands on—there were probably four choices—and the accuracy was just awful. The darned rifle was shooting patterns, not groups, two inches or worse.

As I said, I'm a lazy handloader. I didn't try any of the tricks Phil Massaro suggested in chapter seven. I just loaded up some different recipes with IMR powders and Nosler Ballistic Tips. Groups instantly sank below one inch. I hunted with that rifle quite a bit, and that's what I used. Mind you, this is not to suggest that there was anything wrong with Remington's .280 factory loads—that particular rifle just didn't like them.

In factory rifles I've always had great luck with Remington Model 700s, but another model famous for out-of-the-box accuracy is the unlovely but effective and affordable Savage 110. I got a "package" left-hand .30-06, complete with inexpensive 3–9X scope, intending to use it for a TV episode, a late-season elk hunt in Colorado. Since it was for a specific TV show I knew I'd have to use a Federal load (like Savage, Federal was also a sponsor). But I was curious about what it would do, so I tried a number of loads. The first was one of my perennial favorites, a handload with a maximum—don't ask!—charge of IMR 4350 and a 180-grain Nosler Partition. This rifle didn't like it; it grouped about two inches, so much for both my favorite hunting load and Savage's vaunted accuracy.

I took this great Sonoran mule deer with a Remington Mountain Rifle in .280. This was one of the finickiest rifles I ever encountered. It was simply awful with all factory loads available at the time, but it proved a tackdriver with simple handloads. Go figure. This was one of the rare cases I've seen of exponential improvement just by changing loads.

A load with Swift's Scirocco came in just over an inch, and everything else was in between—except for Federal Premium's factory load with the 180-grain Barnes X-Bullet. This was some time ago, so the bullet was the original Barnes X, not the current TSX with driving bands, which is definitely more consistent. That load, which I was going to use anyway, grouped well under half an inch.

Over the years I've seen dozens of examples of significantly improved accuracy just by changing loads. Although I could come up with more recent examples, both of these situations have stayed with me because, although I keep saying it's unusual (and it is), in both cases the improvement really was exponential: with that .280, from a horrible 2-plus inches to very acceptable 1-MOA; with the .30-06, from a bit over 2 inches clear down to spectacular . . . *just by changing loads.*

My experience with that Savage .30-06 deserves further comment. Whether we're talking about the Barnes TSX, Hornady GMX, Nosler E-Tip, or whatever, the homogenous alloy bullets are a bit different. Since they have no lead core, they don't "squish" as they enter the rifling. They simply slam into it. Driving bands help, but acceleration is different than with lead-core bullets, and a pressure spike is unavoidable. This is neither bad nor good, it just *is*. The thing is, in many rifles this type of bullet doesn't shoot "with the pack." It may shoot a bit better, or it may shoot a bit worse, but the results will often be different from the average. That .30-06 was a classic case; in that rifle *nothing* shot as well as the Barnes X . . . it cut the previous "best group" size in half. It could just as easily have been the reverse, but this remains a case in point as to why you cannot make assumptions, and you must be as exhaustive as possible in trying different loads before you rest on the accuracy you are getting.

Although the .375 H&H is often very accurate, I don't really need awesome accuracy from a .375. I could have lived with the 2.5- to 3-inch groups I was getting (top). I tried some different loads, and obviously this rifle really liked Federal's Fusion factory load. You never know what will work best, so keep trying!

This inexpensive Savage 110 "package rifle" in .30-06 was another rare example that showed how changing loads could lead to exponential improvement. It hated some really good "premium loads" available at the time, including my own favorite handload (top right). It obviously just loved Federal Premium's load with 180-grain Barnes X (center). Needless to say, that's the load I went hunting with!

As for hacking on the bedding, this is now about all that is left. You can certainly do that. Personally, however, I'd recommend saving the time and trouble. Altering the bedding may give you some incremental reduction in group size, but if you've come this far and nothing has worked to the point where your personal accuracy goal is in sight, then I humbly suggest you have three better choices: Live with what you've got, if you can; invest in a better barrel; or pass the rifle along to someone with more tolerance.

How Much Accuracy Do You Need?

CHAPTER 14

This could be a short chapter: "How much accuracy do you need?" Easy answer: "All you can get." End of chapter. Except that isn't exactly true. What you need is enough accuracy to get the job done . . . and also enough so that you have the confidence to take the shot, which is an altogether different dynamic. So, for argument's sake, let's say that the heart/lung vital

My pet Todd Ramirez 7x57 shoots great with some loads and just OK with many. Even so, it's one of my favorite whitetail rifles . . . but I don't take it places where I might have to shoot at longer ranges.

This '98 Mauser 8x57 didn't offer much more than "pie-plate" accuracy with its original battle sights. I took it pig hunting understanding I needed to get close! One shot, one pig. Accuracy is not overrated at all, but match-grade accuracy isn't always needed.

zone on a smallish white-tailed deer is eight inches by eight inches, the size of a pie plate. Theoretically, then, if your favorite deer stand allowed no shot farther than a hundred yards, then a consistent eight-inch group at a hundred yards is all the accuracy you really need.

This may sound silly, but let's keep in mind that thousands of whitetail hunters go into the woods each fall shooting slugs in unrifled shotgun barrels. Yes, they're hoping for a closer shot, but eight-inch groups at a hundred yards are pretty good for smoothbores, and at that distance they can get the job done.

Quite different are the requirements of the serious prairie dog shooter. This rifleman is shooting at a target that, when standing on its hind feet, is no more than 3 inches across, and perhaps 8 inches top to bottom. An 8-inch group is no longer adequate. At 100 yards a 1-inch group is just fine, and at 200 yards the group will naturally spread to 2 inches. So far so good. At 300 yards the 1-MOA group will spread to 3 inches, so now we're on the margin. At 400 yards a 1-inch, 100-yard group will naturally spread to 4 inches, so now, through normal dispersion and no aiming error, some shots will miss.

Let's say, instead, that we start with 0.5-inch groups at 100 yards. Now we have natural dispersion of an inch at 200 yards, 1.5 inches at 300 yards, and so on. We are all the way out to 600 yards before the dispersion of the available accuracy falls outside of the width of a standing prairie dog.

Of course, this is purely mathematical. It is almost impossible to properly factor in human error, but let's accept that most varmints such as prairie dogs and woodchucks are taken from relatively stable rests, so human error is minimized. Most big-game animals are taken from less stable positions, where "the wobbles" play a much greater role. So an 8-inch group could work for a whitetail at 100 yards, but I submit that you're probably better off with a higher level of accuracy. You can add a rifled choke tube to a shotgun barrel and experiment with different slugs. My experience has been that groups will often shrink into the 4- to 6-inch range. Or, as many savvy Eastern hunters do today, you can replace your shotgun barrel with a rifled slug barrel.

Slug guns are beyond my area of expertise, but the fiddling I've done with them suggests that a decent rifled barrel will cut the groups in half, maybe down to the 2- to 3-inch range. Now there is enough accuracy for 200-

In the hunting world, shooting small rodents like prairie dogs is the most demanding situation for accuracy. This .91-inch group from a factory .22-250 (top left) is great for coyotes . . . but for prairie dogs it's just barely good enough. More like it is the way my Ruger No. 1 in .204 Ruger shoots, consistently close to one-half MOA. That's varmint-level accuracy!

I don't do a lot of hunting with slugs, but by local law I needed to use a shotgun on an ibex hunt in Greece. It was shotguns only—no rifled barrels and no scopes. With a rifled choke tube, this Remington 870 was shooting about four-inch groups . . . enough accuracy for this world record kri kri ibex at about 110 yards.

yard shooting, and with modern sabot slugs a fair number of slug-shooting whitetail hunters have the know-how and confidence for 200-yard shooting.

These days, in the arena of centerfire rifles, we think of 100-yard groups in the 2- to 3-inch range as horrible. This is partly because we American rifle shooters are obsessed with accuracy, and partly because, in too many current firearms publications, we are given the impression that sub-MOA out-of-the-box groups are now normal. They do occur, even (and surprisingly often) in economical bolt-action platforms from such firms as Mossberg, Remington, Ruger, Savage, Weatherby, and more . . . but they are not necessarily the norm.

A lot of factory bolt actions, including some of the pricier models, still produce out-of-the-box groups in the 1.5- to 2-inch range. With certain loads, and with a bit of work, you might get them down to the 0.75- to 1.25-inch range, but it's unlikely they will become *consistent* sub-MOA rifles, and it's almost impossible for them to consistently group in the 0.25- to 0.5-inch range. How significant this is depends entirely on what you intend to do with the rifle. Unless accuracy is the single-minded goal, it's important to keep in mind the level of accuracy genuinely needed for your purposes.

Consider that from about 1900 until after World War II, the tubular-magazine lever action and its .30-30 cartridge was by far America's most popular deer rifle. These days, sales of lever actions have finally started to wane, but there are still millions of .30-30s in the deer woods—enough that, even today, the .30-30 remains among our top-selling rifle cartridges. Realistically, most tubular-magazine lever-action rifles probably produce groups in the two- to three-inch range at a hundred yards, pretty much the same as a well-set-up slug gun with a rifled barrel.

There are reasons for this. Part of it is the rear-locking bolt and two-piece stock common to the typical .30-30. Part of it, too, is that .30-30 ammunition is a commodity. It sells into the many millions of rounds annually, but little load development has been done in decades to enhance or improve its performance. There are exceptions, such as Hornady's LeveRevolution load with the FTX (Flex Tip Expanding) sharp-pointed bullet. This load definitely expands the .30-30's capability, but it's just one load. It will group well in some rifles, but not in all.

Groups from this Remington M700 VTR in .260 Remington varied from a snappy .49-inch to a dismal 2.3 inches. The average is actually pretty good, but even with the least accurate load, no deer should be missed at the distances this cartridge is intended for.

My Winchester Model 94 "Trapper" is unusually accurate for this type of rifle. It wears an aperture sight and groups well, but, realistically, I don't know how accurate it is because it's never been scoped. It doesn't matter because I'll never use it much beyond 100 yards.

This is the only spot on my Kansas place where a longer shot is possible: The diagonal across the field is 340 yards. Even here I've never shot beyond 150 yards, so you could probably say that I have too much gun and more accuracy than I need with a .300 magnum.

In general it really doesn't matter. No one knows how many millions of deer the .30-30 has accounted for since its introduction in 1895. It still works just fine today, but I suspect the majority of .30-30 shooters still in the woods accept its relatively short-range capabilities and tend to use it in situations where ranges are close and its typical two- to three-inch 100-yard groups pose no handicap. Marlin's 336 series lever actions have always been side-eject and thus suitable for scope mounting, and it wasn't that long ago that Winchester's Model 94 was modified to "angle eject" and thus became suitable for conventional scope mounting. But the vast majority of the millions of Model 94s are top-eject. Some shooters fit them with an aperture or peep sight, and a very few have been scoped with side-mounted or forward-mounted long eye relief scopes, but I suspect the majority of 94s still in the woods are used with the factory-supplied buckhorn rear and bead-on-ramp front sight.

This means that most shooters who use these rifles have no real idea what groups their .30-30s are actually capable of. The rifle may do better, but with that sighting equipment, "pie-plate" accuracy is pretty good, and a two- to three-inch group is downright spectacular. As I've often written, when I was a kid we had no deer season in my native Kansas. Dad was a serious bird hunter, but he had no experience with centerfire rifles. He'd been a Navy fighter pilot in the war; for gunnery practice they shot skeet, but he never had any rifle training. His first centerfire was a Model 94 .30-30; my sister and I pooled our savings and bought it for him for Christmas when I was about ten, she about thirteen. We shot that rifle a lot. With its classic buckhorn sights it was pretty good out to fifty yards, but while I'm certain the rifle would do better, at a hundred yards we were hard-pressed to hold six-inch groups: "Pie-plate accuracy."

My own Winchester 94 .30-30 is a short-barrel Trapper model. I put a Lyman receiver sight on it, and for what it is, it's one of the good ones. I have no idea how accurate it actually is because it's never been scoped, but over the years, in good light and on a good day, it has produced a number of 100-yard groups hovering very close to the magical one-inch figure. On the other hand, throw in some shadows and the groups expand very quickly. With this or any other .30-30, does it really matter? Rifles in .30-30 aren't prairie dog rifles and they aren't open-country deer rifles, but within a hundred yards or so they are deer-killing machines, just like their millions of lever-action cousins.

Kansas opened its first modern deer season about fifty years ago, and it has become a top destination for trophy whitetail hunting. The image is wide-open country with big fields bounded by brushy hedgerows and winding riverine cover, but that does not describe my part of Kansas. Down in the southeast corner we have thick, oak-covered ridges with limited agriculture. Over the last several deer seasons my neighbor, Chuck Herbel, and I have pooled our properties in order to outfit on a very small basis. Although numbers and locations change, I think we have about two dozen tree stands between our places. Only one, a Texas-style tower blind on my major food plot, offers a potential shot with any distance. Diagonally across the field, a 350-yard shot is possible. I can't think of another stand that offers a shot much beyond a hundred yards; our woods are just too thick.

In other words, except for that one stand we call the "Taj Mahal," a .30-30 Winchester would be perfectly suitable. Now, even from the "Taj," nobody has ever pushed the range envelope. I think Donna has taken the longest shot from

Nice surprises can come from most brands. These are the first eight shots out of a brand-new CZ 557 in .270. The two strays are fouling shots. The next three, high and right, are the first group, and then there's an awesome group after adjusting the scope and letting the barrel cool. Don't expect this kind of accuracy from any standard factory rifle . . . but rejoice when you get it!

that stand, over halfway across the field and thus probably two hundred and change. My own longest shot on the place was taken there, maybe one-fifty. Most of my deer have been taken in the woods, twenty to sixty yards. And yet, as much as I love my light, handy .30-30, I've never used it there. Although Chuck and I describe our deer hunting as "thick timber, close and sometimes fast shooting," none of our hunters has yet brought a lever-action .30-30. Nor has any hunter brought an iron-sighted rifle. Come to think of it, though I have several lever actions that I like and have confidence in, most with aperture sights, in Kansas I have never used anything but a scope-sighted rifle.

So, although this is a tiny microcosm of hunting culture, the message seems obvious. Even though in the main we are in ".30-30 country," most of our hunters—including me—want more range and more practical accuracy, whether we really need it or not. This is treading perilously close to our next subject, confidence, but accuracy does produce confidence, so at some level you really do want all (or at least most) of the accuracy you can get, whether you really need it or not.

Perhaps a better question is how much accuracy can reasonably be expected. Again, I have no idea how accurate either my Model 94 or my dad's really are, since neither has ever worn a scope. Absent a good scope you will never know, and if you choose to use iron sights or a red-dot sight, then it doesn't matter; you have made your choice. Your accuracy expectations are limited, but you have what you need. There have been numerous applications when I've chosen an iron-sighted lever action or, for that matter, an iron-sighted big-bore rifle, understanding and accepting the limitations placed on its capabilities, if not raw accuracy. But in Kansas I suppose my default setting has been to use a versatile, accurate scoped rifle, and clearly this has been the default setting of the hunters who have joined us during rifle season.

At the other end of the spectrum, no matter what optics and loads you use, not all rifles are capable of satisfying our obsessive demands for a high level of accuracy. It's good to be hopeful, and it's worth the effort to discover how much accuracy your rifle is truly capable of. If you've spent the money on a higher-grade rifle or a really good barrel this is almost an obligation, but hidden away in the trappings of even a plain-Jane production rifle (of almost any make and model) there are super-accurate anomalies awaiting discovery.

Left to right: .222 Remington, .223 Remington, .220 Swift, .22-250. The .222 is probably the most accurate .222 centerfire, but it's no longer popular. The .223 and .22-250 are probably equal in accuracy, while the faster Swift is now hampered by a limited load selection.

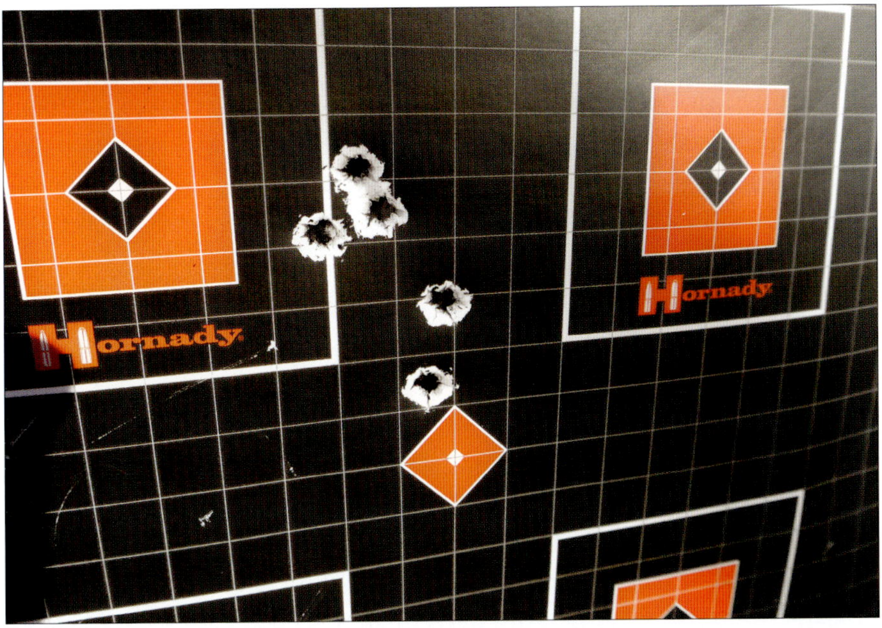

I used the brand-new .26 Nosler with 140-grain AccuBond on an ibex hunt in Turkey and had perfect performance. The top group is the first group out of the rifle; the two lower shots are after scope adjustments. I was pretty sure I had all the accuracy I needed!

Don't get your hopes up, but do your due diligence. Start with good optics and good ammo, although, as we've seen, these offer no guarantee! Nor do certain cartridges, although there are surely trends. As discussed, cartridge design is not nearly as important a component of accuracy as other factors, but it's out there. If you want a deer rifle that is most likely to be accurate, think about a .308 Winchester. Yeah, I know, I personally prefer the .30-06 for its tradition, and for its extra 100 feet per second. But I concede the .308 is the more accurate cartridge. If I wanted a flatter trajectory curve, I'd choose a .30-caliber magnum, but these are compromises. The .308 Winchester is probably the most accurate .30-caliber hunting cartridge.

There are other choices for accurate cartridges, some obvious and others not so. The .222 Remington, designed as a benchrest cartridge, is probably the most accurate .22 centerfire, but it's kind of a rare bird today. The popular numbers, the .223 and .22-250, are probably about even in accuracy and both are good, so that choice can be made based on platform (rifle), or level of velocity desired. In 6mm the 6mm Remington is faster, but the .243 Winchester with its shorter case is probably the most accurate choice. I am not enough of a .25-caliber fan to have a real opinion, but the .25-06 is the only really popular cartridge, not only with the widest selection of loads but also the greatest flexibility in bullet weights.

I do have opinions on both 6.5mm and 7mm cartridges. The 6.5s are a problem simply because the .264-inch bullet diameter has never been popular in North America. Actually, I have gotten adequate accuracy out of the .264 Winchester Magnum, but I would never consider it, on average, among the most accurate cartridges. The .260 Remington is a great little cartridge, sometimes touted as the very best cartridge based on the .308 Winchester case, but I've been through a bunch of them, and accuracy has never been anything but pedestrian, and very much not up to my expectations. Part of this is the curse of the 6.5mm: Limited popularity means limited attention to barrels, bullets, and loads. Interest by 1,000-yard shooters in efficient, mild-recoiling 6.5s like the 6.5-.284 Norma and Hornady's 6.5mm Creedmoor are changing this, and the .26 Nosler may change it more. For accuracy these are the three 6.5mm cartridges I would lean toward.

Cartridge choices in .270, bullet diameter .277-inch, are very limited, but there are no bad choices. I have gotten excellent accuracy out of the .270

In my experience the 7mm-08 Remington is one of the most accurate 7mm cartridges, probably followed by the 7mm Remington Magnum. Despite a very light barrel and light overall weight, this Kimber Adirondack in 7mm-08 is a real tack driver!

Winchester, .270 Winchester Short Magnum, *and* .270 Weatherby Magnum. Obviously the .270 Winchester offers the most choices in both factory loads and rifles, but for accuracy potential I can't state a preference.

There are a whole passel of 7mm cartridges, bullet diameter .284. Among the milder 7mms I love the old 7x57, easily my favorite whitetail cartridge, but I have to admit that I have never owned (or seen) a 7x57 that was consistently a genuine tack driver. Since I only use it at moderate range that has never been an issue for me, but without question the ballistically similar and more modern 7mm-08 Remington is a more accurate choice. Two of the .260 Remington rifles I gave up on wound up rebarreled to 7mm-08. Among the faster 7mm cartridges the .280 Remington, though not popular, tends toward accuracy, but so does the much more popular 7mm Remington Magnum. There are several faster 7mms, but they are overbore capacity, so they will be finicky. In 7mm, for accuracy I'd go with the crowd: 7mm-08 in a mild, efficient, light-recoiling cartridge; 7mm Remington Magnum if higher velocity is needed.

The Blaser R8 with a .300 Weatherby Magnum barrel has been my favorite for mountain hunting the last few years. It's consistently an MOA rifle and will cut that in half when I do my part (bottom). I used it in Russia in 2014 to take this mid-Caucasian tur.

I've already mentioned the .30-caliber, but it's probably worth saying a bit more about the fast .30s. The short magnums, whether .300 RSAUM, .300 RCM, or .300 WSM, are probably inherently more accurate than any of the longer, faster .300 magnums, but the selection of loads is more limited, so unless you handload you may not realize accuracy gains. Among the faster .30s, the .300 RUM is probably the soundest design for accuracy, but (again) unless you handload, limited load selection creates the same problem.

Personally, among the fast .30s I have long been a big fan of the .300 Weatherby Magnum. Although no one has ever claimed it to be a super-accurate cartridge, in a good rifle I have always found it accurate enough, and I like its velocity and understand its trajectory. After all, I started using a Weatherby Mark V in .300 Weatherby some thirty-five years ago! Since the mid-1990s I have used a Rifles Inc. chambered to .300 Weatherby Magnum a great deal. Based on a rare left-hand Model 70 action, it's been a favorite rifle for serious mountain hunts. More recently I've been using a Blaser R8 with a .300 Weatherby Magnum barrel, my choice on my last several Asian mountain hunts.

Realistically, a .300 Winchester Magnum would offer a greater choice and availability of ammo and, all things being equal, shrink the group sizes a bit at a very tiny cost in velocity. This was brought home to me this year. South Carolina accuracy legend Kenny Jarrett is a good friend as well as one of my heroes. I hadn't messed with one of his rifles for a long time, but he now has his own action in left-hand, so he wanted to send a rifle for me to play with. Of course he suggested his proprietary .300 Jarrett, similar in velocity to the .300 RUM or Weatherby, his concept of the most accurate fast .30. I demurred. Ammo availability concerned me, and as a writer I have business reasons to stick with factory chamberings. So, with some grumbling, he agreed to put together a .300 Weatherby Magnum, or so I thought. When the rifle arrived, it was a .300 Winchester Magnum.

With our newer propellants, my chronograph tells me the .300 Winchester Magnum is now much closer in velocity to the .300 Weatherby and RUM than ever before. And with its popularity and resultant availability, it is by far the most available fast .30. Of course I've used it over the years. The .300 Weatherby has been my most frequent choice, but I've used the .300 RUM quite a bit, and I

All of the fast .30s are extremely versatile, and all can be very accurate. Because of availability, the .300 Winchester Magnum is a great choice. My Jarrett Ridge Walker in .300 Winchester Magnum flattened this fine Eastern Cape kudu from about 300 yards.

actually like the old .300 H&H for its accuracy and smooth feeding. But among fast .30s the .300 Winchester Magnum is easily the most common choice, and uncommon accuracy seems to be a common virtue. So, my new Jarrett rifle is a .300 Winchester Magnum, and I'm learning to love it!

Above .30-caliber you start to run into popularity issues. This is changing a bit; for example, thanks to the .338 Lapua Magnum, there are extra-accurate .33-caliber barrels available. However, above .30-caliber, demand drops off and, with some exceptions (like the .338 Lapua), as recoil increases, accuracy expectations seem to decrease. This is unfortunate because, given equal quality in barrels, bullets, and so forth, larger calibers tend to be very accurate. There is a simple reason for this. A few ten-thousandths of fouling, a bit of bore roughness, or even an imperfection in a bullet's base or a slight difference in weight are much more critical in a .22-caliber than issues of the same dimension or magnitude would be in, say, a .416 with a bore nearly twice the diameter and a bullet eight times heavier.

Big bores are often extremely accurate if you can handle them. This Rigby Big Game in .416 Rigby is both accurate and tolerant: These 100-yard groups are a mix of Hornady and Swift expanding bullets and solids (bottom)! This was probably more accuracy than I needed for a twelve-yard encounter with this Caprivi elephant, but for sure I had plenty of confidence!

It is clearly much more difficult to shoot a big gun well. Even if we can, only rarely do we insist on match-quality barrels on our big bores, and only rarely do we mount the optics that would allow the utmost in accuracy. This makes perfect sense because, after all, we almost never use .375s or larger bores beyond very medium ranges, and our primary concern is terminal performance on very large targets, not the utmost in precision. It is an unfortunate irony, however, that while a lot of rifles chambered to versatile, high-velocity cartridges will prove disappointing in accuracy, a lot of big-bore rifles will actually have more accuracy than is needed.

You need enough accuracy not only to get the job at hand done, but also enough so that, mentally, you can take the shot without hesitation, knowing that your rifle and cartridge will perform. Only you can decide what this level of accuracy is. It depends not only on your targets, whether live or inanimate, but also the ranges at which you wish to engage them.

Much earlier in this discussion we talked about the 8-inch or pie-plate-size vital zone of deer-size game. From a clinical perspective, one could theorize that 1-MOA, or 1-inch groups at 100 yards, would allow shooting out to 800 yards at an 8-inch target. Theoretically, yes. On the range, yes. As a sniper, maybe, since any hit counts. As a hunter, no. At least a bit of human error needs to be factored in, because hits outside that 8-inch vital zone are not acceptable.

Sure, you could err a bit high and break the spine, but, percentagewise, you are three times more likely to err too low, too far back, or too far forward and have an unacceptable wounding shot. For hunting, a buffer zone is needed against a less-than-perfect position, a bit of excitement, and a shot presentation that may not be perceived exactly as it is. I respectfully submit, as a theory, that hunters should actually *want* about twice as much accuracy as we really *need.* So the 1-MOA group that we strive for is plenty of accuracy for 400-yard shooting, but maybe not a whole lot more. And if we're serious about 800-yard shooting on game (I hope very few of us really are), we'd better start with *consistent* half-MOA groups. These levels are certainly attainable today . . . but in all rifles, all cartridges, and with a wide variety of loads? Never!

THE "C" FACTOR

CHAPTER 15

The "C" is for *confidence*. Accuracy is an important component of confidence, but it's only one aspect. Confidence to make a shot accurately when presented, whatever the target, comes from confidence in your rifle, and also in yourself. The former is based on total faith in whatever bullet-launching platform you have chosen: It will function properly and get the job done. The latter is based on self-knowledge: You know you can make this shot; you just have to do what you already know how to do.

Both paths are smoothed by experience. If the rifle is an old friend you already know it intimately; you have utmost confidence in its capabilities, and you know its limitations. If you're an experienced hand, there are few shots you haven't been faced with. While every trigger press is a new experience, you know pretty much how to handle the situation. As riflemen, though, even the most experienced among us are likely to try out new toys somewhere along the way, or perhaps, for new and unfamiliar situations, we will need a rifle with different capabilities than our old friends.

On the other side, not all of us are experienced. Everybody has to start somewhere, and to some extent even old hands are trapped by their own experience. The veteran Eastern whitetail hunter may be a master at close shooting in the timber, but daunted the first time he hunts elk or sheep in the high country, and vice versa. There is really no way to become familiar with all the situations one might encounter in the wide world of riflery. But you can *try*. Experience can only be acquired over the years and there are no real shortcuts, but I submit respectfully that the only pathway to confidence, both in yourself and the rifle, lies in *practice*, not only acquiring proficiency and confidence in your chosen rifle, but also in yourself. Now let's address these two subjects separately: confidence in the rifle, and confidence in yourself.

"Beware the one-gun man." Grancel Fitz, shown with a nice mule deer, was the first person known to take all varieties of North American big game. He did it all with a .30-06, easily the most common choice in his day.

As for the rifle, never forget the adage, "Beware the one-gun man." I assume that many reading this book are, like me, serious rifle nuts. We ponder things to death, trying to pick the perfect rifle for the job at hand. So we switch around, searching for the perfect match of cartridge and caliber to target and range. This is perfectly OK, to a point (and I'll get to that point in a bit), but at some level the actual platform and load chosen isn't nearly as important as the shooter's knowledge of it and his or her ability to use it well.

It really doesn't matter whether we're addressing a target at 1,000 yards, a ram at half that distance, or a white-tailed buck or buffalo bull in the thick stuff at bayonet range. Pick a task and there are plenty of rifles and cartridges that will get the job done. Some may be more ideal than others, but ultimately it's the shooter's knowledge of the rifle and its capabilities that tells the tale.

Some of us are students of the rifle. We love our campfire arguments and we ponder the imponderables, trying to find the right solution. For others the rifle is simply a tool, of little more intrinsic interest than a shovel or a hoe. Provided you know how to use your rifle, it matters not which of these describes you.

For many years now I've served on the board of the Weatherby Foundation, which, among other things, annually presents the Weatherby Hunting and Conservation Award as a lifetime achievement award for international hunting. I must admit that I'm a student of that award, and although I may never win it, at this writing I've been a nominee for several years. Going back decades, I have noticed that most of the winners of this award, though accomplished riflemen (and now two women), are not rifle *aficionados*. Most tend to have just a couple of rifles that they have used almost everywhere, for almost every game animal imaginable.

Many of them have been fans of the .300 Weatherby Magnum, including Herb Klein, Elgin Gates, C. J. McElroy, Renee Snider, and undoubtedly others. I don't think this was in deference to Roy Weatherby or to gain brownie points to win the award, but simply a reflection that a fast .30 is pretty hard to beat. My friend Bob Anderson, chief archiver of the mountain hunting culture, did a grassroots survey among serious mountain hunters while working on his latest book. He found that the current preferred choice was the .300 Remington Ultra Mag. A rimless cartridge with a larger case capacity, it is probably a "better" cartridge than the older Weatherby, if it is

My friend J. Y. Jones sets up for a shot at a tahr in Nepal's Himalayas. Jones also took all the North American game with a .30-06, but when he started hunting elsewhere, he switched to a Remington M700 in 7mm Remington Ultra Mag. It worked well for him!

loaded right. My friend Bruce Keller, a recent Weatherby winner, is a disciple of Kenny Jarrett; he uses the proprietary .300 Jarrett for almost everything.

All three of these cartridges are ballistically similar, casting strong votes for the versatility of the fast .30. But this is not a discussion of cartridges and calibers. Rather, it is proof that long-term familiarity breeds not contempt but confidence.

Jack O'Connor discovered the .270 Winchester shortly after its introduction in 1925. He used larger calibers for larger game, but remained a staunch .270 fan for the next half-century. O'Connor was the longtime shooting editor at *Outdoor Life*. His opposite number at *Field & Stream*, Warren Page, was a fan of the fast 7mm. Bert Klineburger, arguably the world's most experienced living hunter, is also a lifelong fan of the magnum 7mm. Stepping back a generation, outfitter and desert rat Charlie Ren, who guided my uncle and Jack O'Connor on their first sheep hunt in 1934, figured his .25-35 was all the gun he needed.

Then there's the case of my buddy and, for the last few years, my cohost on *Guns & Ammo TV*, Kyle Lamb. Kyle is a retired sergeant major in the special operations community. His Viking Tactics caters to the tactical community, not only with products but with marksmanship training. Although he's busier than ever, in his "retirement" he has time to do a lot more hunting. The bolt-action sporter is an unfamiliar platform to him, although he uses it when he must (as when hunting in countries that do not allow semiautomatic rifles). Given a choice, however, he sticks with an AR-10 variant in his familiar 7.62mm NATO or .308 Winchester. I could argue all day that a heavy, accessorized AR in .308 isn't an ideal choice for Alaska moose hunting, but for Kyle Lamb, this is the platform he has the most familiarity with and the most confidence in.

The point is this: A lot of highly successful rifle shooters in multiple venues find what they like, are most familiar with, and have the most confidence in, and they stick with it. I, on the other hand, am a rifle nut. I would not go so far

My dad was mostly a shotgunner, but for big-game hunting this is the only rifle he used: a Bishop-stocked Winchester Model 70 Featherweight in .308. I doubt the rifle had been fired in twenty years when I shot these groups. No wonder he had confidence in it.

My uncle, Art Popham (left), and Charlie Ren on a sheep hunt in Sonora in 1934. Uncle Art used a .30-06 but later moved to a .300 H&H Improved for the majority of his sheep hunting. Charlie Ren, a famous guide at the time, used a .25-35 and thought it was just fine.

as to say that, in a hunting context, the rifle used is more important than the hunt itself, but some of us do go that far. Ideally, I like to conjure up the perfect rifle for a given task, and then implement it. Sometimes I'm exactly right, and sometimes I'm not quite right. Fortunately, the parameters are broad enough that it's hard to make a huge mistake.

Even so, I have made that huge mistake at least once. My most classic misread of a situation: When I hunted Sitka deer on Kodiak Island in 1992 I envisioned thick alders, and I was concerned about bears. I chose a .35 Whelen as an ideal compromise. I suppose I'd have come out OK if I'd had a genuine incident with a bear, but I didn't understand that in November the cover is beaten down by snow and wind, and the deer are concentrated. A shot within 250 yards was unlikely, and my rifle with its low-range variable scope was totally outclassed. My partner was kind enough to share his .300 Winchester Magnum—again, thank God for the fast .30!

So in searching for the ideal rifle I've made mistakes, not just in caliber but by using too little scope when I should have had more, or too much scope when iron sights would have worked. My situation is complicated by the fact that I'm a gunwriter. Part of what I do is try out new rifles and cartridges, and of course

Retired Special Ops Sergeant Major Kyle Lamb is most familiar with the AR platform and prefers to hunt with an AR whenever he can . . . and often with this V-Tac S&W in .308. It looks a little awkward on the horse, but his carbine-carry worked fine in Afghanistan. . . .

For most hunting situations there are lots of good choices and few bad ones. This time I really got it wrong! It was a late-season deer hunt on Kodiak Island, the cover was beaten down, and the deer concentrated. My .35 Whelen with low-range variable just didn't have the reach I needed.

there are situations where I'm obligated to use an advertiser's rifle or the product of a TV show sponsor. Usually this works OK because there is a broad range of suitability for any given application, but all too often I'm forced into the uncomfortable situation of being obligated to use a rifle that I have had limited time to become familiar with.

Here, too, experience counts. My situation is not ideal for consistently good shooting, but I'm used to it and can usually make things work. And sometimes I get lucky. In 2008 I drew a once-in-a-lifetime Arizona desert sheep tag. I thought it would be appropriate and sensible to film it for *Petersen's Hunting Adventures*, which meant I would have to use a sponsor's rifle. No problem. The sponsor was CZ, and their rifles are just fine. My own left-hand CZ in .375 is a "three-quarter-inch" rifle all day long, far more accurate than I need a .375 to be. Other CZs have been equal or better.

For this hunt, however, I drew a .270 that, with another sponsor's ammo that I was obligated to use, grouped no better than 1.5 inches at a hundred yards. This meant that, in practical terms, I didn't really have as much accuracy as I needed. Since it had taken thirty years to draw this tag, I was worried! Realistically, I couldn't shoot much farther than 250 yards. This is not the feeling of confidence one should have. But, hey, it's better to be lucky than good. On the fourth day a very nice ram presented himself at 250 yards, and I rested the rifle over the backpack and flattened him.

In recent years I've been doing a fair amount of mountain hunting in Asia. There, the high mountains are big and open, with close stalks not always possible. This is complicated by the fact that you often have an entourage on the mountain: guides, interpreters, and "helpers." Two people are bad enough, but when you have a crowd you aren't going to get close. Back in the 1990s I started hunting with a super-accurate long-barreled 8mm Remington Magnum that I had great confidence in, but I abandoned it because the rifle was just too heavy and that much power wasn't needed. I tried the .270, and it worked fine. The fast 6.5mms have also worked fine, but most of the time I want a bit more energy and bullet weight at longer distances. So I went to the .300 Weatherby Magnum, a cartridge I have long familiarity with and know intimately. And, of course, it works.

I wrote about this in a magazine article recently, and a reader suggested (very politely) that I should probably learn to shoot better, and then I would realize that O'Connor was correct and the .270 is all that is needed. True, but it's really about confidence. Some Asian sheep and goats are fairly large, but many are not. With a 120-pound urial sheep, you may not need a lot of power, but you do need something that you can be confident will handle the distance and wind. I assume this is why hunters bring .270s and .300 magnums to my place in Kansas when a .30-30 would suffice. And this is why I have come to use the fast .30 in the Asian mountains. The reader was undoubtedly correct: I should learn to shoot better, as should we all. But confidence begets success, and it's been twenty years and perhaps twenty hunts since I've missed a mountain animal in Asia.

This isn't to say I don't miss. I have, and I do. Guys in my profession are somewhat notorious for shooting better with their word processors than with their rifles, and I am among the few writers who recount their misses in print. Misses do happen. When I write about a miss (or misses) I am sure to get letters from readers stating that they have never missed, and if I'm truly such a bad shot I should consider another occupation. Well, maybe, but my suspicion is that anyone who claims to have never missed a shot either has very selective

Confidence in your rifle is essential . . . but it's also good to double-check. On the first day at altitude in Nepal I got all set up and fired one shot to check zero (top). The shot was perfect . . . that quiet smile is about all you'll get from veteran outfitter Mahesh Busnyat (bottom). Me, I kept my mouth shut!

memory, or simply doesn't have much experience. If you haven't missed, stick around. It will happen.

When it happens (not *if*), it is devastating to the confidence. Three things are important. First, without beating yourself up, try to think it through objectively and understand why and how the shot was missed. The reasons are legion and sometimes almost unavoidable: The target moved, the bullet hit an unseen stick, whatever. Most common is the obvious: The cross hairs or sights weren't in the right place when the trigger broke. But is it an anomaly, or the manifestation of a bad habit? If you genuinely don't understand why you missed, then that's a good time to stop everything and check the sights. Although it's painful, you need to know whether a miss was your fault and had nothing to do with the rifle.

Second, get back on the horse and keep riding. In the hunting context there may not be another chance, so getting back on the horse may mean going back to the range and practicing some more. Note that practice doesn't have to be painful or expensive. Shooting is shooting, and while familiarity with your chosen rifle is important, meaningful practice for the basics of positions,

One of the challenges of being a gunwriter is, all too often, I'm obligated to use a rifle that I've had limited range time with. This CZ 550 in .270 with a good Zeiss scope was a great choice for an Arizona desert sheep . . . except, with the specific loads I needed to use, groups were 1.5 inches. Obviously it all worked out!

There are several cartridges that I have tremendous confidence in. One is the .270 Winchester, and another is the .30-06. I was carrying a Savage .30-06 on this Montana elk hunt, and 350 yards was as close as I could get. No worries; that's a cartridge I know well enough in order to make the shot.

breath control, trigger press, and sight alignment can be done perfectly well with a .22, an airgun, or even dry-firing without ammunition.

Third, and this applies to both before a shot and afterward, while confidence is king, overconfidence is a knave. Professional guides live in fear of the guy who comes in saying, "Just show 'em to me . . . I can hit 'em." I guess I'm superstitious, but this is tempting fate. You can, and should, feel free to divulge the range envelope you are comfortable with, but in general keep your mouth shut and above all don't boast, no matter how confident you are. There will be enough pressure on the shot without adding to it. And if you make a good shot, take the congratulations politely, learn from it, and keep your mouth shut. The next one may not be so good.

It is impossible to say how much practice is appropriate before you take a rifle out for serious shooting. This depends a bit on your experience, and how familiar or unfamiliar the platform might be compared to what you're used to. For dangerous game, where your life may be on the line, fifty rounds is probably minimal and a couple hundred is much better. Considering hunting is always a life or death matter to the game, perhaps this is a good rule of thumb across the board. Certainly you want to shoot enough so that all mechanical functions are assured, and the rifle has become as familiar as an old friend. This is not an exam you can cram for. Nobody can effectively burn a hundred rounds of centerfire ammo at one sitting and learn much of anything from it. Spread it out over multiple range sessions, and especially as recoil increases, ration the cartridges you fire at a sitting. At .375 level or above, a dozen rounds can be too many in one sitting. This doesn't mean your precious range time needs to be wasted. Take a .22, preferably with similar action and sighting equipment, and intersperse big-bore groups with lots of low-cost, low-noise, low-recoil shooting.

As for gaining confidence in yourself, well, this is what practice is all about. The more the better . . . and you're never done. It's an ongoing process that continues every time you go to the range. It's also a matter of thought process. Unfounded confidence is bad, as this will lead you to taking shots you shouldn't attempt. But you should spend quiet time imagining yourself in shooting situations, mentally putting yourself through the steps and, of course, culminating in a mentally successful shot. Sports psychologists call this *visualization*, and it applies to shooting as well as almost all other sports disciplines.

In order to properly visualize, to imagine success—and to actually be successful when it counts—you must have some basis in what you are visualizing. While there is no real substitute for hands-on experience, practice is the next best thing. In order to shoot accurately, you have to get steady. The degree required depends a lot on the range and the size of the target, but I am convinced that in large measure confidence comes from knowing, if not the *best* way, at least a *good* way to get steady for the shot at hand. In other words, putting practice into play. In the next few chapters we will turn our attention to shooting skills, including practice regimens that will help give you the confidence to buckle down and shoot straight when you must.

Secrets from the Bench

CHAPTER 16

Plinking tin cans as kids is the beginning of rifle marksmanship for most of us. If we're lucky, we learn well from skilled mentors. If we're not so lucky, we probably pick up bad habits that, absent good instruction to correct them, may last a lifetime. I was fairly lucky. Dad was a very fine shotgunner, and I had great instruction in breaking clays. Dad was not a rifleman, but he knew some good riflemen who helped us along. I was

This picture illustrates a good benchrest position using a traditional adjustable fore-end rest and sandbag for the butt. The real trick is getting the rifle secure and steady so that all the shooter need do is concentrate on breathing control and trigger press.

The important part of the bench itself is that it be as rock-steady as possible. Cement rests are most common on formal ranges, but an old picnic table can work just fine if it's heavy enough.

further helped by pretty good coaching in a Boy Scout era that still believed rifle marksmanship was a normal, wholesome, and beneficial skill. I was helped even more by a great coach when I shot smallbore in college, and later by Marine Corps instructors.

Today, genuine marksmanship training in the Boy Scouts or Girl Scouts is rare, as are collegiate shooting programs, and an increasingly smaller percentage of our population has the benefit (and pain) of military marksmanship training. Plinking at tin cans remains a good way to start, and casual shooting with a .22 isn't a bad way to retain proficiency for shooters of all ages. Absent formal instruction, however, it seems to me that the benchrest provides the baseline starting point for accurate rifle shooting.

The standard venue for public shooting ranges is a long row of shooting benches. Their use is strongly encouraged or even required, lest an errant bullet speed somewhere into the atmosphere instead of toward the backstop. This is OK; there is much to be learned from the bench, provided it is understood that rifle proficiency doesn't stop there. For shooters fascinated by pure accuracy, the bench is essential. Benchrest competition has never been my game, but it is the most precise form of riflery. As such it has yielded many of the options we have today. Synthetic stocks, laminated stocks, short and fat cartridges, faster lock times, extra-accurate bullets, and more all originated with the super-demanding benchrest crowd. Benchrest shooters (who usually engage in other types of rifle shooting as well) spend much of their lives at the bench, trying to shoot the tiniest groups possible.

For many of us, however, the bench becomes a crutch. We have to use it to test loads and establish zero, and on many ranges we're obligated to use it. While the bench is the proper venue to determine raw and pure rifle accuracy, it's important that we not construe that benchrest shooting offers meaningful practice for field shooting or any other dynamic shooting events. Too many of us get lazy and spend too much time at the bench, and this is not good. There are no benches in game fields or tactical situations.

If accuracy is of interest it is necessary to spend time at the bench, but don't get married to it. It will prepare your *rifle* for any type of shooting. As you learn what level of accuracy you have available, the bench will also give you confidence in your rifle. The bench, unfortunately, will not prepare *you* for field shooting, and will not give you the confidence you need in yourself when you have to get steady—*fast*—and figure out a difficult shot. So use the bench as much as you need or as much as you want, but make sure you spend plenty of practice time *away* from the bench.

While you're at the bench, learn what it can teach you, which is actually much more than just the accuracy of your rifle. The point of benchrest shooting is to remove not just as much human error as possible, but to entirely remove human involvement up to the point of the trigger press. The rifle is rested steadily and solidly, with the scope or sights already aligned on the target. All that is necessary to send the bullet on its way is to press the trigger. The size of the group is already established by the alignment of the rifle and the accuracy team of action, barrel, and load. It's your group to mess up through poor technique.

The Caldwell Lead Sled is a marvelous tool for painless shooting off the bench. It harnesses the rifle and essentially adds its own weight . . . fifty pounds of lead removes most of the kick!

Here's the secret to benchrest shooting: While it offers minimal position practice for field marksmanship, it is perhaps the best place to work on the most basic principles of accurate shooting. These are encapsulated by the good old Marine Corps BRASS rule: Breathe, Relax, Aim, Sight alignment, trigger Squeeze. On the bench you are not fighting an uncomfortable position, you are not muscling the rifle onto the target, and you are not racing against time, trying to get the shot off before the animal moves or the bad guy shoots first. So you can concentrate on these basics, and you should every time you shoot from the bench.

We'll come back to BRASS, but let's start with the bench and build up from there. First off, it needs to be rock-solid. On formal ranges benches are often poured concrete, as solid as it gets. Although that's good, it is far from the only option. A heavy, old-fashioned picnic table isn't bad. There are also portable benches designed to serve the varmint-shooting market, but it's pretty hard for these to replicate the rock-solid stability of a heavy, permanent bench. In any case, the platform needs to be as solid as possible. You need to get it level, and it needs to be the right height for you. One of the portable rests I use has four extending legs with adjustable bases for leveling, and the seat is easily adjusted for height. Seated, you should be at a height so all you need to do is lean forward slightly and comfortably to bring the shoulder to stock and cheek to comb to get a proper sight picture. No straining, no stretching, no scrunching.

The rest itself can be sandbags, a formal adjustable affair like a Ransom or Redding rest, or a recoil-absorbing device like a Caldwell Lead Sled. There are two essential criteria. First, both buttstock and fore-end must be rested securely, and never on anything solid. Sandbags, though basic, are thus very good, but well-padded store-bought rests are fine. We will use the phrase again with various shooting positions, but now that you have a solid bench, a seat of the proper height, and both front and rear rests for the rifle, you can start to "build your house."

Regardless of the type of rest I'm using, I keep my supporting hand off the fore-end, instead using it to snug the butt into my shoulder.

Even a relatively light-recoiling rifle can deliver plenty kick off the bench because the body has little give and soaks it all up. Really watch this with youngsters! Here is daughter Caroline with her hot pink 7mm-08, using the Lead Sled.

Put the rifle on the rests, and then, in shooting position but with no ammo, adjust the height so that the sights or scope are perfectly aligned on the target. Check stability by backing off the rifle, then coming back. You should still be perfectly on target. Now, on the gun, close your eyes for a few seconds and open them. You should *still* be on the target. Try a couple of dry fires and make sure there is no movement.

Now let's look at your shooting position. Feet planted squarely, about forty-five degrees apart at a forty-five-degree angle to the target. Bent slightly forward from the waist, you should comfortably nestle the stock into your shoulder and your cheek comfortably to the comb of the stock. So far, so good, but here's a major dilemma in benchrest technique: What do you do with your supporting hand? In all things riflery you must ultimately do what works for you, but remember the idea here is to remove as much of the human element as possible. Many of us are compelled to hold the fore-end with the supporting hand, as we would in most rifle-shooting positions. This is not ideal on the bench. Instead, take that supporting hand and use it to push the rear sandbag (under the toe of the stock) or the buttstock itself securely into the shoulder. There is simply nothing to be gained by holding onto the fore-end of a securely rested rifle, but there is an advantage in nestling the butt into the shoulder.

A digression is important. This is the same technique I often use in the field. Shooting prone over a bipod, I curl my supporting hand (in my case my right hand) under the toe of the stock, using it to adjust elevation as well as securing the butt into my shoulder. If possible, I will do exactly the same thing when resting the rifle over a pack, whether prone, lying over a boulder, or whatever. There is just one caveat, which applies at the bench and in these "benchlike" field positions: Make sure the rifle is securely rested! A couple of years ago I was hunting Columbia whitetails in Oregon for the *Petersen's Hunting Adventures* TV show. My old friend Conrad Evarts was on the camera

This very good group was fired off the bench using Nosler's then-new Match Grade ammo in .308 Winchester. The proper way to measure a group, especially a really tight one like this, is to measure the outside, then subtract the bullet diameter (in this case .308-inch).

There are quite a few portable rests on the market, but few are as steady as a solid bench. Designed for prairie dog shooters, this portable rest from RCBS is truly excellent; it's very adjustable and almost as steady as the real thing.

and I was on the rifle. At that point we had filmed together for nearly ten years, and he had never seen me miss. That isn't to suggest I went a decade without a miss, but together we seemed charmed.

We got on a nice buck, not an easy shot at maybe 275 yards, but certainly doable. We'd pitched up behind a brushy tree, so I crawled to the right to get clear, dragging my pack, and set up in sort of a high prone position over the pack. From that position it was a "gimme" shot, rifle steady, butt tight to shoulder, but just as the trigger broke, the rifle slipped off the pack! I felt it happening but couldn't stop the trigger break, and I saw the dust about three feet to the right of the buck. I will never forget the look of abject horror on Conrad's face as he asked (a bit more profanely), "What just happened?" I could recount misses forever, but that's the only time I've ever had a rifle slip off a rest like that. Obviously it wouldn't have happened if I'd kept my supporting hand on the fore-end, so perhaps my system doesn't translate perfectly from bench to field.

Here I am on the bench with a .375. Even with a Lead Sled, it's a good idea to ration how much you shoot large-caliber rifles at a single sitting. Once you start worrying about recoil, your shooting is bound to go downhill!

But with that one caveat in mind, from a steady rest I believe the supporting hand does more good at the rear of the stock than on the fore-end.

OK, now the rifle is perfectly steady and you're on it. When it is safe to shoot, load one cartridge, get back on the gun, and check position again. The rifle is perfectly aligned with the target and you don't have to "muscle it" or adjust to keep it there. Now for BRASS.[1] First is Breathe. The best benchrest shooters (and snipers) can consciously slow their heart rate at this point. I cannot, but we can all take two or three deep breaths, exhale half of the last one, and Relax our bodies as completely as possible before you Aim.

Seconds are passing, and you cannot wait until you go into oxygen deprivation. If you can't finish the trigger press, Breathe again, and start over. In those seconds you must check Scope or Sight alignment one more time. Still on

[1]BRASS stands for Breathe, Relax, Aim, Sight alignment, trigger Squeeze.

target with no conscious adjustment? Perfect! Now comes the most important part, the Squeeze or, as we prefer to call it in this volume, the trigger press.

Your hand has long since been comfortably and naturally curled around the pistol grip. Your finger is now on the trigger, as horizontal and centered as possible. As discussed much earlier, exactly where your finger makes contact isn't so important, provided it's neither tip nor joint, but a comfortable spot in-between. On a two-stage or trigger-safety trigger, you have taken up the slack or pushed the trigger bar back until your finger contacts the trigger. Now begins the press until the trigger breaks, and it continues steadily through the limit of the trigger's travel.

No matter the position, the concepts of breath control and trigger control are almost universal in riflery. As in English, there are exceptions to every rule, and a quick running shot is probably one of them, but that is not by nature *accurate* shooting, although hopefully accurate *enough*. Otherwise, the good old BRASS rule applies, and there is really no better place to both learn and practice these principles than on the bench because if the position is steady and proper, you really don't have anything else to worry about.

That's Donna's trigger finger on her Blaser. She has much smaller hands than mine, so her finger is going to contact the trigger closer to the fingertip. Exactly where doesn't matter, but contact needs to be consistent, and it should not be at the tip or joint but somewhere in-between.

As far as shooting protocols, we've pretty much covered that in previous chapters. Three-shot and five-shot groups are equally valid. It just takes more three-shot groups for validity, but three-shot groups are easier to hold, and certainly more appropriate for light-barreled sporters. In general you don't want to let a rifle get too hot, as in too hot to touch the barrel, but without going overboard it can be useful, at least for knowledge, to see if you have one of those odd barrels that shoots best hot. If you're trying that you probably want to concentrate on getting your shots off fairly quickly, as a hot chamber will heat the cartridge, increasing pressure and velocity and potentially changing point of impact. If your breathing and squeezing isn't right and you have to start over, which is very common, take the cartridge out and chamber another one.

Ideally, it's best to shoot from a barrel that is at least cool, if not stone-cold, and this definitely applies to light sporter barrels that heat up very quickly. How long you should wait between groups depends on barrel diameter, velocity,

Two-stage military triggers and modern "trigger safety" triggers like this one on a Ruger American allow you to position your finger and take up the slack . . . you know by feel exactly when the actual trigger press begins.

Conrad Evarts and I pose with a nice Columbian whitetail taken near Roseburg, Oregon. The back story: Two hours earlier I was shooting at a bigger buck when my rifle slipped off the pack. When shooting over a rest in the field, I use my supporting hand to snug the butt, but that time it got me. Make sure the fore-end is securely *rested!*

ambient temperature, and breeze. On hot summer days you'll spend a whole lot more time waiting for barrels to cool than actually shooting. It's a pain, but something that needs to be factored into your range time.

If your position is good and the sight picture is proper when the trigger breaks you should know it, and you should also know it if you "pull" a shot one way or another. In grouping for accuracy you can and should throw out "called fliers"—shots you knew were bad. In establishing an average you can probably also throw out your worst group if you want to. Maybe you had a bad cartridge or a bad bullet? But flukes can be good as well as bad, so be as wary of the unusually good group as you are horrified by the really awful group. Ideally, if you throw the worst group out of your average you should probably also throw out the best group. (But do any of us really do that?)

I think the best group I ever shot was with my long-barreled 8mm Remington Magnum, a three-shot one-hole cluster measuring, as best I could tell with a micrometer, .052-inch, just over a twentieth of an inch. That rifle has produced a number of quarter-inch groups, and I reckon at worst it's a sub-half-

MOA rifle, but it's never again come close to that one spectacular group. On that day were the conditions just right, and was my blood pressure abnormally low? Or did three good bullets just happen to land in the same place? I've done plenty of bragging about that group and that rifle, and for sure it's a very accurate rifle that I've always had great confidence in, but try as I might, I've never been able to come close to that one stellar group. So flukes can be good as well as bad, but are probably not indicative of accuracy you can count on.

A word about recoil: The only thing I know of that accentuates recoil worse than a benchrest is the prone position. In both situations the body has nowhere to go and simply must take the pounding. Prone is a bit worse because it places your head in an unnatural position. Prone is bad for scope cuts! But the bench is nasty because, from a proper benchrest position, the rifle is essentially in free recoil. How much recoil it takes to hurt depends on the person, and of course it depends hugely on gun weight. I've noticed that even a

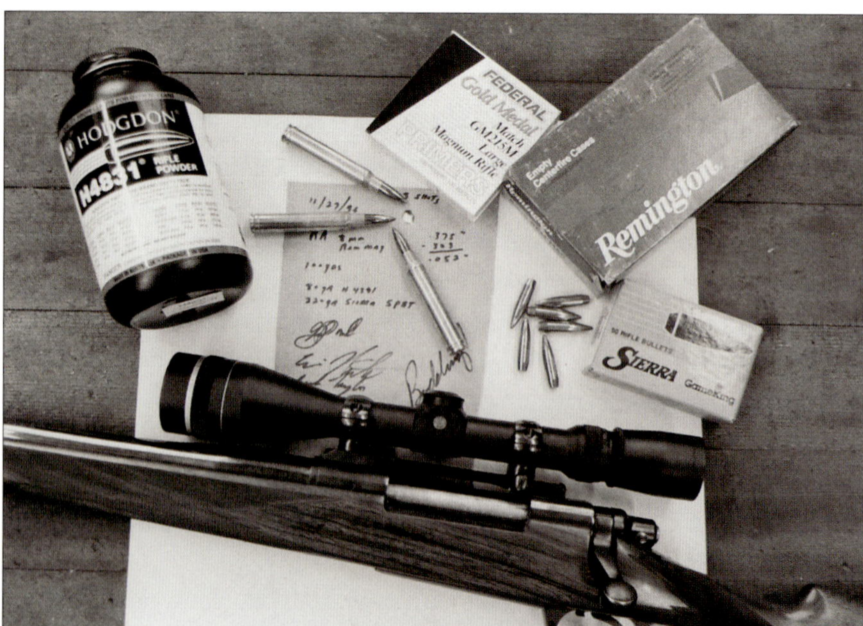

This is the tightest group I've ever fired, three shots with an 8mm Remington Magnum measuring .052-inch. This rifle is extremely accurate and has produced many great groups . . . but nothing even close to this. So flukes can be good as well as bad!

.260 Remington or 7mm-08 bounces my daughters pretty badly on the bench, so don't underestimate the recoil factor.

You cannot sit calmly behind the rifle and press the trigger if you know it's going to hurt you, so I recommend being a wimp. I keep a PAST recoil shield in my kit. I always use it when shooting rifles above the .30-06 level, and I insist that Donna and my daughters strap it on at much lower levels than that. You can also fold up a towel and put it in your shoulder. For more severe recoil I use a Caldwell Lead Sled. This is really a clever concept. The fore-end rests in a typical padded rest, while the butt is securely held in a web harness. Depending on model, either the front or both front and rear are height-adjustable. Underneath there's a tray where you can put a couple of twenty-five-pound bags of lead shot. This essentially adds fifty pounds to the rifle, going a long way toward taming even the most obnoxious beast of a rifle.

Obviously muzzle brakes also work and are essential on fast blasters such as the .338 Lapua Magnum. But they're noisy. My hearing loss is now so profound that I can't spare any more decibels, so I steer clear of muzzle brakes as much as I can. However, provided you make a commitment to use good hearing protection—even in the field—a good muzzle brake provides another sound option for taming recoil to manageable levels.

The primary values of the benchrest are determining the accuracy of your rifle (and loads), and building confidence in your rifle. But as you go on to other positions, the goal is always to achieve a stable platform as close to that rock-solid benchrest as possible. As we'll discuss, you can "build your house" with shooting aids such as bipods and tripods. There are multiple uses for a daypack, and even a light rice-filled sandbag or a shooting glove can be carried along to scrunch under the butt. Even though there are no benchrests away from the shooting range, the intent is always to come as close as you can to that degree of stability. That is why some shooters, when preparing for a difficult or long shot, will say, "It's time to 'bench up.'"

Position Shooting

CHAPTER 17

The benchrest provides a baseline for stability, but for all other rifle shooting I believe there's another baseline: The standard NRA competition positions of prone, sitting, kneeling, and standing (formerly called offhand). In the old days, before computers and TV, and when there was a lot less big-game hunting than there is today, most gunwriters at least dabbled in High-Power competition, and their writing is full of references to these basic positions. I shot a bit of service rifle competition in the Marines, but most of

I am in the kneeling position with a hasty sling. A tight sling helps in almost all positions, and with practice you can make an almost instantaneous sling. This is the position I used to take a Shiras moose on a snowy hillside in Colorado.

Here I am prone, with a hasty sling. Randy Babala and I had been crawling down a slope toward a Stone ram, and at this point we ran completely out of cover. Prone is the easiest position to learn and the steadiest . . . but all too often terrain and vegetation won't allow it.

my formal experience with position shooting goes back to smallbore competition. Though the targets were only fifty feet away, this is an extremely exacting and precise discipline in which the center bull is smaller than the .22-caliber bullet, and the "X-Ring" is just a dot.

It was a very good background that serves me well to this day. Mind you, I was no champion. In fact, my worst position was prone, the easiest but most precise, mostly for lack of attention span. From a competitive standpoint I was better at sitting and kneeling, and my best position was standing. This carried through to my Marine Corps shooting, which, in my day, used all four positions at varying ranges. Although I was occasionally the high shooter in my company or battalion, I never set any range records, but I earned the Marine Corps Expert badge every year until I got too senior to be worth the ammo expended. The Expert qualification wasn't so difficult—220 out of a possible 250 points—but you never knew what the conditions might be like on qualification day. Draw a gusty day and sometimes it came down to the wire. I could usually do well in the standing position and at 500 yards slow fire. The

500-yard target was huge, the position prone, but with the 5.56mm you had to get the wind right on the first shot.

OK, enough bragging. This was just to say that I do have formal experience with the four NRA positions. And I should add that I still practice them on the range and use them in the field. In the field, when possible, I augment them with a natural rest, a backpack, or a shooting aid (bipod, sticks, etc.). I also typically use a hasty sling, which is neither NRA nor Marine Corps approved. No matter. The intent is to hit the target. There will be times, however, when there are no natural rests to be found and no option but to set up and shoot. So I believe it is critical to the accurate rifleman or woman that he or she be well-grounded in the four basic shooting positions, and practice them with some regularity. Once you have them down it's easy to augment them with any other stability you can achieve, but it is best to start with the basics.

The general rule of thumb is that the closer you can get to solid ground the steadier you will be, so in terms of stability and accuracy the positions, in descending order of stability, are prone, sitting, kneeling, and standing. We'll start with the use of the sling, which is a tremendous aid to all four positions. Then we'll take a look at each position, and finish with some tips on practicing. As a side note, the specific photos used to illustrate the positions will show me demonstrating them *right-handed*, for the benefit of the majority, although I normally shoot left-handed.

The Sling

These days there are many kinds of sling arrangements and different protocols for using slings. Any way you do it, use of a sling is pretty much a matter of enhanced isometrics in that the sling is pulling against you, tightening your position and enhancing stability. The formal target sling actually doesn't attach to the rear sling swivel, but instead loops around your supporting arm above the bicep; you wrap into it with your supporting hand. The old-style military sling also serves as a carrying strap, but for formal range work it is detached from the rear swivel and doubles as a loop sling.

For many years I used a two-claw military sling, and on occasion (as Jack O'Connor recommended) I actually detached it from the rear swivel and used it as a loop sling. The last time I did this was some years ago in west Texas. I

Use of a "target sling" is almost a lost art, but there are times when it's useful. I was stuck without cover or a natural rest when I spied this fine west Texas pronghorn, so I unhooked the rear sling swivel and got into a crossed-leg sitting position with a tight sling.

had what turned out to be the best pronghorn I've ever shot working toward me through some yuccas, and I was completely stuck with no natural rest available. While the buck was behind a thick patch I detached the sling from my rear swivel, made a loop, and got into a formal crossed-leg sitting position. When the buck came clear I shot him at 250 yards.

Formal use of a target sling is very rare in the field today. Most of us use a much simpler carrying strap. For years now my favorite has been Trader Keith's canvas web sling, comfortable yet flexible, but almost any sling can be used as a "hasty sling." Here's how you do it:

With the rifle more or less horizontal, let the sling hang down (attached front and rear). Thrust your supporting arm between rifle and sling and wrap your hand around it, clockwise for a right-hander, counterclockwise for a lefty. With the sling wrapped around your forearm, grasp the fore-end behind the sling swivel stud. You need to play with the length of the sling a bit, but as you raise the rifle to your shoulder the strap now tightens against your chest, creating that isometric pressure that pays dividends in almost all shooting positions.

Prone

Prone is very steady and fairly easy to master. Unfortunately it's one of the least likely positions to use in the field because so often there's too much low brush in the way. But if prone is possible, it should be a default position because it is so steady. You simply lie down behind the rifle, and you must determine what is most comfortable for you. In my youth prone was taught with the legs apart and the body at about a 45-degree angle from the rifle butt. The only problem with this is it places the rifle butt on the outside of the shoulder, which is not ideal. Today it's much more common to lie more directly behind the rifle, often with shooting-side leg cocked. In this fashion the rifle butt can be easily and firmly snugged into the pocket of the shoulder, where it really belongs.

Prone is far the best with a hasty or even target sling, but positioning of the elbows is extremely important. Both elbows must be well-grounded, with the shooting elbow out at a slight angle. This will seem natural. The trick, however, is to get the supporting elbow *under the rifle*, not out to the side. This takes a bit of stretching and is not especially comfortable, but it works much better.

The modern prone position puts the shooter behind the rifle so that the rifle butt can be snugged into the center of the shoulder. The only real trick is to get the supporting arm as directly underneath *the rifle as possible, not out to the side.*

The prone position is easily augmented with shooting aids such as bipod or pack. If the fore-end is securely rested, then it's best to use the supporting hand to snug the butt into the shoulder.

In all of these positions you need to find what the Marine instructors called "good body alignment," which means the body is naturally pointing the rifle at the target. Get into position with an empty rifle, action open, and aim at a target. Then relax your hands, and have a buddy come around and gently kick the muzzle from the front. The rifle should remain on target. If it doesn't, you need to move your body a bit left or right or change your angle until you achieve that natural alignment.

Although vegetation will often preclude shooting prone in actual field situations, it is one of the best and easiest positions to augment with a bipod or by resting over a low log or a backpack. For AR shooters, if you can get your body low enough, the magazine (especially a 30-round magazine) can often be grounded for extra stability.

Sitting

The sitting position is not quite as steady as prone, but with practice it can be *very* steady. The disadvantage is that, done properly, the sitting position is difficult to master and without question the most difficult to get into. To do it right you have to be fairly limber and you can't have a whole lot of extra girth around your midsection. On the other hand, the sitting position is extremely useful, and if you practice enough to make it comfortable you will find there are quite a few opportunities to use it. It will get you above low brush and is a whole lot steadier than kneeling.

There are really two sitting positions: bent knee and crossed leg. The bent-knee sitting position is faster and doesn't require as much gymnastics, and also gets the line of sight a bit higher. Some shooters, especially folks my age, will find the crossed-leg sitting position almost impossible to get into, but the bent-knee sitting position is not nearly as steady.

For the simpler, faster bent-knee position, just plop your butt down with the axis of your body at about a 135-degree angle from the target. If it's easier to visualize, that's about 45 degrees left of the rifle-target line for right-handers; 45 degrees right of the rifle-target line if you're left-handed. Spread your thighs about 45 degrees, bend your knees with calves more or less vertical, and plant your feet solidly on the ground. Then lean forward from the waist so you can rest your elbows *over* your knees. The tendency is to put the elbows on top of the knees, because this doesn't take as much bending and stretching. You can do that, but there will be a tendency for the elbows to slip off the knees (sometimes at the wrong instant). So here's the tricky part: Try to lean a bit farther forward and get your elbows over your knees. This will lower your line of sight a bit, but is much steadier and more secure. Sitting can be done with or without a tight sling (either hasty or target), but it is much steadier with a sling.

As with all the positions, you must find your own natural body alignment, but you should practice it in the same way. Get into position and on target with an empty rifle, action open, and aim in. Get a partner to come around in front of you. As he/she pushes on the muzzle close your eyes. When you open them you should still be on target. If you aren't then you need to shift your butt and your feet to change the angle. Practice a bit and you will get it right naturally; the rifle will come to shoulder on target and stay there.

The crossed-leg sitting position takes a whole lot more gymnastics and will not be possible for everyone, but it is steadier, and is a good thing to have in your bag of tricks if you can do it. Same deal: Plant your butt with the axis of your body at about the same angle. Draw your legs in and cross your ankles.

The crossed-leg sitting position takes a lot of practice to get into quickly—and you'd better be limber! It is much steadier than the bent-knee sitting position, but also lower, so there will be times when vegetation won't allow it. The big secret is to bend forward far enough so that the elbows are over the knees, not on top of them. This will preclude an elbow slipping at the wrong moment!

This picture illustrates the bent-knee sitting position on a rocky hillside (in Spain). As with the crossed-leg sitting position, get the elbows forward over the knees rather than on top of them. This position is not as steady as crossed-leg sitting, but it is faster to assume and gets the muzzle several inches higher to clear obstructions.

Your thighs are nearly horizontal to the ground, and the *sides* of your feet are on the ground. Most properly, when you cross your ankles your support or weak side leg is out and your shooting side leg is in, but we are not talking formal competition here, so whatever you can make work is fair game. Get your ankles as tight in to your body as you can. Like I said, this one takes some gymnastics, and isn't far from a proper yoga position when you're done!

Now bend forward from the waist and, once again, try to put your elbows *over* your knees rather than directly on top of them. Your back will be bent way forward and the position will probably not be comfortable, but it's very steady. You can work on adjusting your position in the same way, but if you don't have any background in the formal positions it will take some practice and some stretching before you can get into the crossed-leg sitting position easily and quickly. A tight sling will help tremendously.

The kneeling position is not nearly as steady as sitting, but it's much faster, and with practice, you can essentially wrap into the hasty sling, drop to one knee, and shoot almost instantly. As with sitting, a major element is getting the supporting elbow forward of the knee, not directly on top of it.

Over the years I have taken an awful lot of game from the sitting position, both the bent-knee and crossed-leg positions. The former is simply for plopping down and shooting when that seems the best option, but the crossed-leg position can be extremely useful when you have a bit of time, can't find a natural rest, and you need to get over a bit of low vegetation. On the last day of a Tanzania hunt I still had a buffalo on license, and we followed a big herd all morning, catching up just as they started to lie down. We identified a nice bull at 150 yards, a very long shot on buffalo, but he was covered up by other buffalo and we were completely stuck. We sat there in scant shade, with no water, for nearly four hours waiting for the buffalo to get up.

When they finally did, we were still stuck. Of course the bull we wanted was one of the last to get up, so we had buffalo feeding all around us with no room to maneuver. I got into the most formal crossed-leg sitting position I could and adjusted the sling good and tight. When the bull stepped out from behind a tree I pasted him on the shoulder, and that was the conclusion of that safari.

Kneeling

The kneeling position is not especially steady, but it beats the heck out of standing, and a primary advantage is that it is *fast*. As with sitting, there are two variations: Low kneeling and high kneeling. In both situations you simply put your support-side leg (left for right-handers, right for left-handers) forward, toes pointed forward, calf vertical to the ground, knee bent. For high kneeling your shooting knee goes to the ground at a 90-degree angle to the gun target line. You bend forward with the rifle so that your supporting elbow rests *over* (preferably not on) your supporting knee. In this position the sole of your shooting-side foot is as flat to the ground as you can get it.

The difference with the low kneeling is that the outside of your shooting-side foot is flat to the ground, and you actually sit on the inner surface of your shooting-side boot. This takes split-seconds longer to assume and is not as high, but it's a bit steadier. In both situations a hasty sling helps a lot, but also in both situations your shooting elbow is not supported. Practice keeping that shooting elbow out, nearly horizontal, and using your shooting hand to pull the rifle into your shoulder as you prepare to press the trigger.

Kneeling is not a long-range position, but it's ideal for medium-range encounters where you don't have time to find a steady rest, but standing is not sensible. Essentially, you simply drop to one knee and shoot.

Standing

The standing position is the court of last resort. It is the least steady by far, so in the field it should only be considered at fairly close range, and in situations where circumstances simply don't allow a steadier position. Hopefully it is the shooting position that you will use the least. However, when there are no other options that means you need to get the shot off fast and accurately. So, since standing is the least steady and most difficult to master, it is probably the position you should practice the most.

Standing unsupported is the least steady of all shooting positions; it should never be used if any steadier option exists. However, since it's the most difficult of all positions, it should be practiced at least as much as any other . . . and perhaps more. As shown, a hasty sling creates isometric pressure across the chest, which helps tremendously.

Sometimes you simply must stand up and shoot, so it's important to practice the standing position. It is useful for close-range encounters when there isn't time to find a steadier position, or the movement required would make things worse.

There are strong differences between the formal standing position and how it will most likely be assumed in the field. In all situations it is key to plant your feet about shoulder-width apart with your *supporting side* foot pointed directly at the target. In the formal standing position your shooting side foot is straight back on the gun-target line with your foot facing outward at a 90-degree angle. You thrust your supporting side hip forward and rest your supporting elbow on that hip. In competition we often use palm rests and such to make this easier. (If you're an AR shooter, the magazine makes a pretty good palm rest.) The shooting elbow is out, horizontal, and the shooting arm pulls the rifle into the shoulder. Since I have a background in competitive shooting I have occasionally used an approximation of this formal standing position in the field. Sometimes there is simply nothing firm to rest on and too much brush to get lower, but there's time to get it right.

More often, the standing position is used in a fast-breaking situation at close range, where there is really no option except to stand and shoot. This situation is a bit more like shotgunning than rifle shooting. The supporting foot *always* points toward the target; the supporting elbow is horizontal, pulling the rifle in; and both feet must be securely planted, about shoulder-width apart. The shooting foot will usually be about 45 degrees off the gun-target line (right for right-handers, left for left-handers). Just as in shotgunning, plant your feet, slip the safety as you raise the rifle, pull the rifle tight into your shoulder, find your sight picture, and press the trigger.

Even with practice, relatively few of us will be steady enough to hit our pie-plate-size target consistently at a hundred yards, but with practice most of us should be able to take a quick, accurate shot out to maybe sixty yards. At that range and closer you're in a window where you often can't risk the movement required to get steadier, so you simply must stand and shoot. You'd better know how.

Practice

The various positions need to be part of any sensible and comprehensive training program, but the good news is that, for position practice, you don't need to burn up lots of expensive ammo or withstand a lot of recoil. Perfectly meaningful position practice can be done with a .22, and that's a good thing to do on the range while you're waiting for centerfire barrels to cool. Just as good, get an air gun and set up a range in your garage, basement, or back yard. Just one thing: Try to equip your practice rifle with sights that are similar to the sights you will use in the field.

Are you a city dweller? No garage, basement, or back yard? No worries. Check your magazine and chamber, distance yourself from all ammunition, and practice your positions by dry-firing in your living room. Dry-firing, snapping on an empty chamber, is not recommended for rimfires, but does no harm whatsoever to most centerfires. The primary exception is break-open rifles, including doubles. For these, get snap caps and use them. In Marine Corps, basic training recruits spend painful hours and days dry-firing, practicing not only positions, but the BRASS basics, long before they go to the range with live ammo. Later, when "range week" is on the training schedule, there will usually be some training-day hours devoted to "snapping in." We would get in a school circle with a white barrel with miniature targets in the center, and

As with all the other positions, a standing position can be augmented and made much steadier. In Kyrgyzstan's Tien Shan Mountains I found a handy boulder to stand against for a 350-yard shot on a fine mid-Asian ibex.

Position practice doesn't have to be painful. Donna used a scoped Kimber .22 to work on her prone position with the rifle rested over a pack.

practice not just positions, but the ritual of breathing, relaxing, aiming, and squeezing. Many of us don't have ready access to a range, and range time is precious. Meaningful practice can be done by dry-firing at home, and this is perhaps the best way to practice not only shooting positions, but also the use of sticks and other shooting aids.

STICKS AND STONES

CHAPTER 18

Familiarity with the basic shooting positions is essential, but given a choice—and time—a solid rest is far preferable to any unsupported position. This means, generally, that you modify a basic shooting position with some kind of natural or unnatural support. The former could be rocks, logs, trees, fence posts, whatever—something that's already there and can be used for a solid support. The latter is something you have with you: bipod, shooting sticks, pack, whatever. The goal is to get steady, and sometimes you have to be creative. As with most things, the more experience

We carry our three-legged sticks almost everywhere! Donna used them to take this free-range fallow deer in England a couple of years ago.

Here I am setting up over a pack in Coues deer country in Arizona. This photo is more than thirty years old, so resting over a pack has been a favorite position of mine for many, many years!

The trick to using a natural rest is getting the height right. Sometimes you will sit behind it, other times you'll kneel, and once in a while you'll stand to the rest.

you have, the easier it is to figure things out. If you limit your range sessions to shooting from the bench you aren't likely to be as creative as you might be if you practice away from the bench, experimenting with a variety of positions and rests.

While it's important to expand your repertoire of shooting positions, one of the things you will learn through experimentation is what works best for you. Some shooters rely heavily on "crossed sticks," but while I do very well with an attached bipod, I have never been able to get over an up-and-down wobble when I use a freestanding two-legged arrangement. I do much better with three-legged "African shooting sticks" and carry a set often, but my own preferred technique and default setting is to find something (*anything*) I can throw my pack over to make a rest. It's good to know what your comfort level is, because that might be better for you than other options that are technically more stable, but it's also unwise to become wedded to just a couple of options.

Shots afield can come in any shape or form, and the more ways you know to get steady the more successful you will be. The options are so varied it's impossible to cover them all, but let's look at several common solutions.

Rocks and Trees

The most frequently used type of rest is probably a natural rest, an object that sticks far enough out of the ground to make a stable platform for the rifle. The rules are simple, and there are two: First, the line of the muzzle is lower than the line of the scope, so whatever is used for a rest must be high enough to clear not just the line of sight, but, more importantly, the path of the bullet. Second, no matter what else you do, the rifle must *not* be rested directly on any solid object. Any direct contact with the barrel is almost certain to send a shot wild, and, depending on the bedding system, direct contact with the fore-end can be just as bad. Even if the rifle will allow an accurate shot when directly rested, recoil will wreak havoc on the stock.

As we'll see, I almost always carry a daypack, so I have a buffer ready at hand. Not everyone does, but there are other options. My old friend Bob

Prone position, pack, and an old cement water trough in Namibia combined to make a steady setup for a 300-yard shot at a great warthog.

A rocky outcropping in the Gobi Desert offered a perfect standing rest for a shot at a nice Gobi ibex. No matter how you are able to use it, a solid natural support usually beats any unsupported shooting position.

Milek loved to scrunch up his cowboy hat under the fore-end. Gloves work, and as a last-ditch option you can simply use your hand, but if you're using a bare hand on rough bark or a craggy boulder, expect some damage!

Any horizontal rest such as a boulder, stump, or fallen log offers the very best chance to replicate a shooting bench. As you close for a shot this is an opportunity you should look for, and if a really good rest becomes available, consider stopping to take the shot rather than closing a few more yards and having a less stable position. The trick with a horizontal rest is to get the height right. You can throw a backpack or a rolled-up coat over it, and *in extremis* a hunting buddy or guide can lay over it and become a human sandbag. You'll also have to choose which formal position to modify. Sometimes you can lie behind or over a natural rest. Often you can sit behind it. Sometimes you can kneel, and occasionally you can stand against the rest.

One of the most difficult shots I've faced in years was on a Himalayan tahr in Nepal's high country. We were on a steep-sided finger above a thick draw, and a nice bull tahr came into view on the next finger, 460 yards away. With the ground sloping away in front of us there was no way to lie down, and no way to build up a tall enough rest for sitting, kneeling, or anything else. We had no place to go, but fortunately we had a bit of time.

The trees on our ridge were stunted but stout. I found a low horizontal limb that gave a decent angle, and I adjusted the height by sitting on a backpack. The position looked ridiculous, but wasn't much different than a benchrest. The animal was facing away from the downhill breeze, so I held on its rear end, used the proper stadia line, and shot it precisely behind the shoulder. The situation was about as good as it gets, but it took some quick, creative thinking to figure out the solution.

A vertical rest is almost never as steady as a horizontal rest, but can provide a very fast option that beats the heck out of any unsupported situation. Whether a tree, an outcropping, or a fence post, the rules remain the same: The rifle cannot be rested directly against a solid object, and the *closer you can get to the ground*, the more solid you will be. So, in a fast-breaking situation, if there's a tree handy, you can stand against it, resting against your supporting hand between rifle and tree. Expect to lose a bit of skin on your knuckles, but it's worth it if it's a big buck or a ranking al-Qaeda trophy.

My shot at a Himalayan tahr was a really difficult one: The tahr was 460 yards away, there was a crosswind, and, because of the steep slope, there were very few options to get steady. I used a stunted tree, sitting on a pack to get the height right.

Depending on the height and the terrain and how much time you have, maybe you can kneel, sit, or even lie down next to that tree. Remember to lean into it. For right-handers the shot is best from the right side of a vertical rest; for left-handers it will be from the left. For me a vertical rest is never optimal, but if you snuggle up and really lean into it, the stability is there.

This is something you can easily learn on almost any range: Pretend the overhead supports or the vertical legs of a benchrest are trees or fence posts. The biggest mistakes, I think, lie in not cushioning the rifle properly, and in not leaning into the rest as much as possible. Put your weight into it—the tree isn't going anywhere.

The Pack

As I've said, this is my default setting. Not everybody carries a daypack, and I'm not suggesting everyone should. I almost have to because, as an occupational thing, there's no point in me being there if I don't have a couple of cameras with me. That's the main point, but I also usually have an extra knife and knife sharpener, ammo, raingear, dry socks, extra gloves, in cool weather another layer—heck, maybe a chainsaw and pontoon bridge. I carry too much *stuff.* But in so doing I have a ready-made rest, if I can just get the angle right.

So it's almost a ritual with me. I pick a spot where I can slide the pack into position. Maybe it's the crest of a ridge or knoll, maybe it's an appropriate boulder or log. I take the pack off and drag it into position, which is sometimes not easy when I'm low-crawling with rifle and pack. But that's what I do, and that's my comfort level. It is not for everyone, but packs are extremely useful.

Please note that I said *packs*, plural. Often the shooter isn't the only person carrying a pack. Multiple packs can be piled up, creating a near-benchrest situation. This is especially common in mountain hunting, where the guide and anyone else who is along will likely have a pack. Some years ago in Alaska we had a very big black bear moving on a sidehill across from us. It took us hours to cross the valley and work up through the skunk cabbage and devil's claw, but it actually worked. A half-day later the bear was feeding a couple hundred yards below us. With the slope falling away below us, we piled up all the packs we had, eventually making a very good approximation of a benchrest. I flattened the bear, and that was that.

New Zealand outfitter Chris Bilkey demonstrates how to use a vertical rest. As he's showing, the really critical thing is to make sure the rifle isn't pressing against any solid object. Depending on height you can lie down, sit, kneel, or stand, but, generally speaking, the lower you can get, the steadier you will be.

Much more frequently I drag the pack with me to a shooting position, then push it ahead and set the rifle over it. In a guided hunt or buddy hunt situation, the other person can help. In September 2015 I was trying really hard to get my daughter Brittany a mountain goat. We had the goats in and out of sight for agonizing ages as we worked our way uphill, with the ultimate shooting position established as the last false crest below the goats (there were two billies feeding together).

When we got to the bottom of that last little ridge we crawled up, dragging packs. I set up a quick rest, Brittany slithered in, and as soon as we made certain which was the largest goat, she made a perfect shot. So simple, provided the whole scenario isn't foreign to everyone.

While actually resting over the pack(s) has been my most familiar use, there are other options. In a low sitting position, a stiff pack (with internal or external frame) can be set in front to rest the rifle, or, in kneeling, can be used to the side to stabilize the shooting elbow. Both work, and both are beneficial. To change the height, a pack can be put under your butt in a sitting position, or between butt and heel in a kneeling position. Haven't thought about these options? Then you probably won't think of them in the field, but if you have practiced them, then the options may come to mind when the need arises.

Bipods and Other Pods

According to legend, the old-time buffalo hunters often rested over crossed sticks, plinking bison after bison. They probably did. But in those days extremely heavy barrels were the norm. This is perhaps an excuse for the simple fact that, although I've tried, shooting off crossed sticks doesn't work very well for me. This is not to say they don't work; they work well for good friends of mine who I don't consider to be better rifle shooters but who are certainly better at using this particular system. It could be me. I've fought high blood pressure all my life, and when I'm trying to steady a rifle on an unattached bipod—"crossed sticks"—I cannot eliminate an up-and-down wobble. Maybe you can, so try it.

I feel pretty much the same way about monopods. Mind you, a long monopod or a tall walking staff that you lean against, whether sitting, kneeling, or standing, is probably better than shooting unsupported in any of

This was my daughter Brittany's shot, but we crawled up together, and I pushed the pack into place. She slithered in, rested the rifle, and made a perfect shot on a fine Rocky Mountain goat.

these positions. For me there are better options because I know the monopod allows both an up-and-down and a side-to-side wobble, whereas a proper sitting or kneeling position does not. But that's me; you might be different.

An attached bipod is a whole different story. There are many brands, but the granddaddy of them all from Harris Engineering remains, to me, the benchmark. Models vary, but the best ones allow the shooter to level the rifle on an uneven surface, with telescoping legs for different heights.

A bipod generally attaches via the front sling swivel, and it essentially becomes part of the rifle. With the legs grounded, you can push forward, creating isometric stability. Depending on height adjustment and length of legs, you might go from prone to sitting to kneeling.

There is, however, one major drawback: You are adding weight and bulk to the rifle. Because of this I don't use bipods all the time. They are total nightmares in saddle scabbards, and in thick cover (where their use is least likely) they are just one more thing to catch on branches and vines.

Uphill and downhill shots can really mess up what might otherwise have been a very good rest. At the range Donna is practicing getting steady for an uphill shot, combining prone with a pack and what might be, in the field, a rock or a log.

There are many good uses for a plump pack. At the SAAM shooting school Doug Pritchard shows Caroline how to use a pack to stabilize her supporting elbow—a great benefit in almost any shooting position.

In open country, however, they pay incredible dividends and are probably worth the extra weight and bulk. I use them, but I am not married to them because they will not work all the time. Just this past spring, I went on a free-range aoudad hunt in west Texas. I didn't bring a bipod, but my friend and outfitter Hunter Ross offered me one. Seemed like a good idea, so I clamped it on my rifle. When it was my turn we had a big herd below some rimrock, a couple of huge rams in the herd, and a perfect flat rock to crawl out on. I dropped the bipod legs, crawled out, and tried to set up, but it was impossible. Remember, the rams were *below* me, and with the bipod legs extended and a horizontal surface to shoot from, there was simply no way I could raise my body enough to get a sight picture.

It could have been a complete disaster, and in fact a similar situation had been for Donna a day earlier. The difference was I had a bit more time before the sheep started to mill, and a lot more years of experience in figuring such things out. I ducked back, folded the bipod legs against the barrel, and slid my daypack forward. From a much lower prone-over-backpack position, I had to make sure the muzzle was clear of the edge of my rock. It was, and I center-punched the biggest ram, a great trophy.

There have been many other situations where a bipod worked wonderfully, so I am not against them and often attach them in situations where longer shots are likely and cover is limited. No shooting solution works all the time. Be prepared for the most likely situation in the cover you have—but be flexible.

African Shooting Sticks

Two legs are steadier than one, and three legs are steadier than two. In Africa, three-legged shooting sticks are almost universal, partly because they work, and party because they fit the conditions. In Africa there is usually too much low brush to allow shooting prone, or even sitting or kneeling. Also, "long" shooting is almost unheard of. African hunters generally don't use big

Here at the SAAM shooting school, Caroline is shooting prone with a bipod. No solution fits all situations, but there are many times when an attached bipod is a wonderful asset.

One thing about an attached bipod: If you're going to use one, you should check it out at the range. It essentially becomes part of the rifle, so depending on the way the rifle is bedded, an attached bipod will occasionally change the rifle's zero.

scopes, and since a drop of blood equals a filled license (as I think is proper), folks tend to be very careful. So the deal is to get close enough to be certain, and steady enough to almost eliminate error.

The situation is different in Africa, too. It is awkward for one person to carry both rifle and three-legged shooting sticks, but in Africa one is almost never hunting alone. Usually, as I've described elsewhere, the lead tracker goes down the trail, carrying the sticks. If there's a PH he goes next; if not, the shooter goes next. Either way, if the tracker sees a great animal, such as a world-record three-toed gazork, he will point it out, set up the sticks, and fade to the side. If there's a PH, he steps up next, confirms judgment with binocular, and steps to the other side. The shooter comes forward, rests over the sticks, either makes or accepts the judgment, and takes the shot.

Now, to me, shooting sticks are so effective (and also so familiar) that I often carry them myself in all kinds of places. After breaking one or another tripod leg in rough country I now secure the three legs together—*tightly*—so I can use the whole affair as a walking staff. You can make your own sticks or use a commercial brand. My favorite has become the three-joint model from African Sporting Creations with totally over-engineered aircraft aluminum joints. They take down for storage in a gun case, and also take down for use as a tripod rest in three different heights. In a fast-breaking situation, there isn't always time to unscrew the legs to change the height, but in a hide or blind you certainly can.

You can also spread the shooting sticks low and wide and use them when sitting or kneeling. In 2009 in northern Pakistan we slogged through deep snow toward what appeared to be a really good ibex up in some cliffs above the valley. I was using my shooting sticks as a staff, but when we got as close as we could, I spread them wide and sat in the snow for a really tough uphill shot. It worked. I had much the same situation in Cameroon in 2008 with a big Derby eland, except we crawled for an hour over sunbaked ground before we set the sticks low for a sitting rest. (That worked, too.)

Three-legged shooting sticks are almost universal in Africa because they fit the situation very well. Make sure you learn how to use them before *you go!*

The two secrets for three-legged shooting sticks are getting the height right and finding the best use of the supporting hand to hold rifle and sticks together. I like them about level with my first shirt button so that I can lean into the rest. I then grip both sticks and fore-end to tie it all together.

Typically, however, the three-legged African sticks are used from the standing position, offering speed and at least some stability while getting you above low vegetation, which will almost inevitably be thorny. On your first day in Africa you will almost certainly be asked to demonstrate your proficiency off sticks. Be sure this is not your first exposure, as this is another exam you cannot cram for. Make or get a set of sticks and practice with them on the range.

From the standing position, two things are especially critical. First, the height must be right, allowing you to lean forward slightly into the sticks, putting some weight into them. Ideally, your supporting hand is actually pulling the junction of the sticks back, creating that isometric pressure we have mentioned several times. For me the right height is about the level of my first shirt button, maybe three inches below my Adam's apple. Only experience will determine the right height for you, but the position is not nearly the same as an unsupported standing position; your rest isn't perfect, but you have a rest so you must lean into it and tie it to the rifle and your body.

The next important thing is the position of your supporting hand. The most comfortable and effective answer depends much on the size of your

In Pakistan in 2009 I had a really tough uphill shot at a great Himalayan ibex. We were stuck in deep snow, so I spread the shooting sticks wide and sat behind them.

On Mozambique's open floodplains, the closest we could get was 375 yards, and there was nothing to rest on. We had two sets of shooting sticks, so we used one under the butt and one conventionally. This is almost as steady as a benchrest, and this arrangement resulted in an extra-good Lichtenstein hartebeest.

hands. I hold the intersection of the tripod with my middle, ring, and little fingers, while I hold the fore-end between thumb and fore-finger. People with smaller hands probably can't do this, and people with large hands probably have purchase to spare. You simply must figure out what works for you, and then be consistent.

An unsupported standing position should be steady enough to fifty or sixty yards, certainly on larger animals. Shooting sticks should extend stability to perhaps a hundred and fifty yards, and this will cover most shots at game in Africa. There are ways to extend this range envelope, and these are worth practicing. A partner or PH can, from the supporting side, bend over, grasp the sticks, and offer a shoulder to support the shooting elbow. Stabilizing that elbow can make a difference in almost any shooting position, but it really helps with sticks.

Another option is to use two sets of shooting sticks. The second set can be set under the rifle butt, almost creating a benchrest, or under the supporting armpit in what my friend Tim Fallon of the SAAM shooting courses calls the

Donna is practicing using short sticks as a tripod in combination with a sitting position. Height-adjustable sticks can be used in a wide variety of positions! She is wearing a PAST recoil shield, a really good idea for range work!

We almost always have a .22 on hand during range sessions, and we ran through a couple of magazines while we were waiting for centerfire barrels to cool. A .22 is a great tool for practicing from all *shooting positions!*

"chicken wing." Either way, whatever distance you are comfortable with shooting over sticks can essentially be doubled by these ploys. Last year in Mozambique we were trying to stalk a herd of Lichtenstein hartebeest on open ground. We walked, they walked. We angled, they angled. It took some work, but we finally closed to about 375 yards and set up with two sets of sticks, a complicated arrangement but essentially a standing benchrest. One shot, one big bull down—the biggest hartebeest taken in Mozambique in recent times. There are usually lots of options for enhancing stability, but you want to be as stable as possible, and when it comes to getting steady, all options are fair game.

Fast and Close

CHAPTER 19

It's a shame that columnist and novelist Robert Ruark didn't live longer. His demons caught up with him when he was just forty-nine, but in the last twelve years of his life he did a *lot* of hunting, and gave us many of the very best passages in sporting literature. I commend his work to anyone who hasn't yet discovered him. Aside from superb use of language, what I like best about his work is that, unlike many writers of his generation and my own, Ruark never claimed to be anything but a journalist. He admitted to his

My first whitetail was taken on a hound hunt in North Carolina in 1974. I was urged to use a shotgun, but I clung to my .270 and I shot this buck in midleap as he tried to clear a levee. It was a "shotgun shot" and maybe a lucky shot . . . but it worked.

That's a very young me on a quail hunt in the mid-sixties; I was fourteen or fifteen. Shotgunning does nothing for precision rifle shooting, but a strong background in shotgunning is excellent for shooting moving targets with a rifle.

mistakes and misses, and although he was not without ego (no writer is; ego is an essential tool in that you have to believe someone would actually wish to read your ramblings!), he wrote about his shooting in a self-deprecating way, and I suspect he was quite a bit better than he let on.

Although Ruark is best-known for his African writing, there are two passages from elsewhere that have long stuck in my mind. As a youngster, related in the collection of columns that gave us the superb *The Old Man and the Boy*, he talks about his first whitetail, a fine buck that, pursued by hounds, came dashing through the swamp and ran straight into the young Ruark's 16-gauge charged with buckshot. The second is from India, recounted in *The Old Man's Boy Grows Older.* A big tiger came bounding ahead of the beaters, passing Ruark in midair like a very large crossing quail. So Ruark used his .470 double like a shotgun, leading him and dropping him in midleap.

I actually have two parallels to these situations. My own first whitetail came in 1974. I was stationed at Quantico, in Virginia, but the North Carolina deer

Hound hunting for leopard is fast and exciting . . . and can be dangerous. I've seen two charges while hunting leopards with hounds, so you must be prepared for anything.

Like Jack O'Connor, my old friend Chub Eastman loved to shoot running jackrabbits with a rifle. He was completely undaunted by moving game.

season opened earlier. So on a blessedly long October weekend I drove down to Lake Mattamuskeet. This was a hound hunt, and although I was strongly advised to use a shotgun, I clung to my .270. I was standing on a levee, bored and thinking this was silly, when gradually the music of the hounds swung my way and got closer and closer. I saw the flash of antlers as the buck paused before crossing the open levee, but it was too thick to shoot. Then, with the dogs closing, the buck gathered itself and tried to clear the levee in a mighty leap. My bullet caught him at the apex of the leap, and he dropped onto the levee. It was an unusually fine, heavy-antlered buck for that era, and no further fun was made of my rifle.

Thirty years later I was in South Africa, hoping to film a leopard hunt with hounds. It was not to be my leopard, and in fact hound hunting was then illegal in that province. We had written permission from the game department to conduct a hound hunt as a test case; however, the idea was that, when we found a good track, a member of the provincial game commission would come along to observe. So, in good faith, we were baiting not far from the Kruger Park boundary when we got a call asking us to come to the game department office.

We presented ourselves and were told that one of the commissioners had gotten cold feet, and permission to hunt with hounds was rescinded. Well, we'd come a long way to do this, and we weren't happy about the reversal. So, grumpily and probably disrespectfully, we made to leave. The hapless official stopped us at the door and said, to make sure we were clear, "You may not *hunt* leopard with hounds, but if a problem cat comes out of the park we will call you, and of course if there's a *wounded* leopard, all means for recovery are acceptable. Do you understand?" We did.

Sometimes God has a sense of humor. That very night another hunter in camp, hunting over bait, wounded a leopard. We were awakened at midnight and told they would bring in the hounds at daylight, and we could accompany them and film if we would like.

At first the dogs were precautionary. It was expected that we would find the leopard dead, and the dogs were brought in because the riverine cover was thick and dangerous, and the Kruger boundary was a bit too close. After we found a patch of wet blood, things turned serious.

We worked opposite sides of a draw, one team on either side, and on my side we drew either the short straw or the long one, depending on how you look at it. The dogs went crazy in the cover ahead, and we pitched up to find a very much alive, very angry, and very large leopard fighting the dogs in a gray patch of dry cover, just movement and sound in the dust. Having lost the race to the leopard to two younger men, I was in a perfectly safe third position. PH Abie Steyn was in the lead. As he approached he made eye contact with the leopard, which immediately perceived that the dogs weren't his real problem and instantly launched a full-on charge. Abie shot him with his Krieghoff .470. It was a brilliant shot, full in the chest and maybe only an inch or two off center. The shot saved him and perhaps us, but didn't slow the leopard at all, just turned it a few degrees. It squirted past Tim Danklef close enough to touch; he fired the unfamiliar .30-06 he carried, but I'm not sure the rifle was even shouldered. Understandably, that shot missed.

Now it was my turn, but there was no real danger; the leopard had enough and was outbound. We were on the left edge of a little knoll, and as the big tom

This is an embarrassing photo! Though moving very fast, that pig is in the wide open and I'm swinging with him on sticks. I missed him three times! Nobody hits 100 percent on moving targets, but sometimes you have to try!

PH Angie Angelloz and I are all smiles. This is one of my very best buffaloes, taken with a running shot from about twenty yards. I was shooting a double, and I sort of pretended it was a quail . . . except very big and very black.

These are two of the three wolves I shot on the run in northern Alberta in 2014. I fully concede that I couldn't do that every time, but on that morning I was on autopilot.

passed me it went airborne, headed for a thick *donga* below. The shot was like a station 6 low house skeet shot. I was shooting my old .375 with a Leupold 1.75–5X scope. I got on him and swung through, and although the hit wasn't obvious I was pretty sure I saw him visibly melt in midair, and he was still when he landed.

Make no mistake, there are few comparisons to be made between Robert Ruark and me. He was a far better writer, a successful novelist, and a widely syndicated columnist. He also drank more, and perhaps as a result I've already lived quite a bit longer than he did. But we do have one thing in common: We both had very strong backgrounds in shotgunning. Shooting fast and close with a rifle is much more akin to shotgunning than the deliberate aiming required in most riflery, and the faster and closer the shot, the more similar they become.

Among my own mentors there are at least two widely divergent schools of thought regarding shooting big game on the move with a rifle. Jack O'Connor wrote that an animal is "just as big moving" as it is standing still. This is a simplistic truth, but it's a whole lot harder to hit a moving animal (properly) with a single bullet than with a shotgun pattern. O'Connor practiced what he preached, spending lots of time in the Arizona desert shooting running jackrabbits with rifles. He was also an accomplished shotgunner, an avid quail hunter when he lived in Arizona and a chukar hunter when he moved to Idaho. I hunted various birds with John Wootters a number of times, and he was also very good with a scattergun, but he took a completely opposite approach. He told me once that he wished modern hunting rifles had built-in cutoff switches so they would not fire if the target was moving. (He said the same thing about shooting offhand unsupported: "We would have a lot less wounded game if the rifle wouldn't fire unless it was solidly rested.")

Although I think the majority of today's hunters will take running shots, at least under certain conditions and within certain distances, the ethics policemen among us tend to lean toward Wootters's school of thought. At least one outdoor cable network, *The Outdoor Channel*, has a firm rule that they will not air running shots. I don't think it's quite as easy as O'Connor made it sound, but I think it's unrealistic to rule out running shots. Sometimes that's all there is, and if you know what you're doing they can be almost second-nature.

I do try to avoid them, especially at distance, and because of that I've no doubt failed to take moving shots I could have made. ("Gee, I really thought he was going to stop.") On the other hand, I've made some good ones. In western Tanzania in 1993 we were trying desperately to get a sitatunga and we were

Europeans love their driven hunts, and most shots are moving (if not actually running). They practice shooting at moving game, and as a result they tend to be better at it than most Americans. A "tableau" of game is a common feature of a large driven hunt in Germany.

I am shooting at a two-headed "running deer" target at the Bisley range in England. Most European ranges have some sort of running-game target, whether deer, moose, or boar. In some countries, hitting the running target is a prerequisite for obtaining a hunting license!

running out of time. The moon was full, the movement nocturnal, but we had fresh tracks every morning. Veteran PH Geoff Broom got the bright idea of doing mini-drives through small patches of riverine papyrus. The first time a bull came out I failed to shoot. ("Gee, I thought he was going to stop.") The second time there was no question about that. I was ahead of and to the side of the "drivers," and the bull flushed ahead of them, making twenty-foot leaps. He came right over me: station 8 skeet, high house! I could only see brown through the scope when I slapped the trigger, but we got him.

Another time, hunting with Geoff's son, Russ Broom, in Zambia, PH Angie Angelloz and I got on the tracks of a dozen buffalo bulls near the Kafue Park boundary. They were bedded when we caught up, so we waited several hours for them to get up. We had just started to crawl toward them when a stray eddy gave us away, and the group stampeded away from us. We had barely stood up in disgust when the whole group reversed and stampeded straight

This is a "running rabbit" range in Germany. It was really fun . . . and, using a red-dot sight, it was much more like shooting moving game with a rifle than with a shotgun.

toward us. I can only assume they hit another weird wall of scent. Anyway, we pulled back to a small mopane tree and let them come, figuring they would gallop past at maybe twenty yards. They were all mature, so I was focused on the lead bull when Angie, in a calm voice, said quietly, "The third bull is very big." I switched to the third animal in line and swung the .470 as if he was a big black quail, taking him inbound, on the point of the on-shoulder under the curve of the horn. All four legs collapsed in midair and he skidded on his brisket, leaving a huge rooster tail of dust. Angelloz had been correct: The horn spread was forty-seven inches, one of my two best buffalo.

Another time, on a deer drive in western Kentucky, I had a nice white-tailed buck come out to my right at full gallop. I was on a bend of a creek, so it was a shot I'd been anticipating. I was as ready as I could be. I swung with him at fifty yards, got the cross hairs even with his nose, and the 7x57 went off. The deer never broke stride, and my buddy was sure I'd missed. The thing is, given a bit of experience, when it's right you pretty much know it's right, and

I was sure I hadn't missed. We never found a drop of blood, but the deer was piled up just out of sight, shot in the center of the shoulder.

A North American animal I'd wanted for many years was a wolf, and I'd messed up a couple of good opportunities. On a fine January morning in 2013, I was sitting in a ground blind on a bluff overlooking a frozen river in northern Alberta. It was about 25 degrees below zero F. On the middle of the ice was a moose carcass, with wolf tracks going every which way. Dawn had come and gone, and I was figuring it was going to be a long, cold day when three wolves strolled down the river toward the bait.

My Blaser in .300 Weatherby Magnum was propped on shooting sticks, which were set for a sitting position. As soon as it got light I'd ranged everything in sight and practiced the scenario. The bait was 200 yards away, and in order to make the downhill shot I knew I'd need to cut the netting to get the barrel far enough out. In total disbelief about what I was seeing, I reached down,

The late Chub Eastman works a Blaser straight-pull bolt on a running boar target. Unfortunately, the only way to get good at shooting moving game is to practice, and opportunities in the United States are rare.

The next best thing to actually shooting a rifle at running game is shotgunning. All shotgunning is to the good! My own background is mostly in American trap and a little skeet, but sporting clays offers the greatest variety of shots and, thus, is probably the best preparation for field shooting.

grabbed the knife from the snow, slashed the netting, and slowly eased the barrel out. The lead wolf was a big, dark brute, and by now was almost to the bait. I didn't wait for it to stop.

It went down hard at the shot. In Alberta wolves are on the same license as coyotes, no limit, and I knew they were a problem for both livestock and game in this area. The other two wolves were already in full gear, but I didn't hesitate. With the rifle still rested on the sticks, I got ahead of the second wolf, remembering to keep the cross hairs low for the downhill angle. The bullet slapped hard in the cold, still air and this wolf rolled. The third was now streaking up the river, pushing three hundred yards but not quite straight away. Swinging the rifle, I held daylight in front of the nose, and this one, too, went down hard on the ice.

OK, enough chest-thumping. I would never guarantee I could make any of those shots every time; especially that last series! The point is running shots are very possible, but they're also easy to mess up. To keep things even, it wasn't so long ago that I emptied my rifle at a running boar at less than a hundred yards and never touched it. I was standing on sticks, in my mind swinging smoothly, and I have no idea what I was doing wrong, but something fundamental (probably stopping the swing).

Missing a pig is not serious; there are lots of pigs. In Chad in 2001 I missed running shots on two different aoudad rams. This was serious, because the animals are thinly dispersed and opportunities hard to come by. In both cases we jumped rams unexpectedly, once as we topped out on a mesa and another time when we were tracking three rams and bumped them in a draw. After the second miss I was in despair, thinking I would go home empty-handed and believing I deserved to. We kept hunting and I got a nice ram—but not because I earned it!

Any shot can be missed, and for lots of reasons. Heck, I've missed entire buffalo! But on game animals, worse than missing is not hitting quite right, and this is the great danger in attempting running shots. In general, distance is the enemy. How far is too far depends on target speed and angle, and also

If you are using a shotgun as a tool to get better at shooting moving game with a rifle, consider putting a sight on the shotgun! This is the Swedish "Red Ring" sight, one of several reflex sights specifically designed for shotguns.

If you haven't hunted elephant, it's difficult to understand how close you must often get to judge the tusks. The encounter above will result in a frontal brain shot, and it's going to be very fast and instinctive, pointing rather than aiming.

what you're shooting at and what you're shooting *with*. My 300-yard shot on that running wolf was foolish and probably should not have been attempted. I can only say that, in that moment, I was on autopilot. Mitigating distance was a shallow target angle, and I was shooting plenty of gun. But, as memorable as it is, that may be a shot I should have passed.

A stationary target is always preferable, of course, but within, say, a hundred yards, I would lean toward the O'Connor school: A target is just as big moving as it is standing still. Experienced European hunters tend to be very good at running shots because they do them a lot. The driven hunt is very common in many countries there. Wild boar, moose, and wolves—even deer and bears—are often hunted in organized drives, and the shots are always at moving game. Since this is the case, European hunters *practice* shooting moving game with a rifle a whole lot more than we do. Running boar targets are available on most ranges, and in both Finland and Sweden (and probably elsewhere) you must pass the "running moose" shooting test in order to be

Sometimes you either take the shot standing or you walk away. With practice most people should be able to place shots accurately from an unsupported standing position out to at least fifty or sixty yards . . . and most of us shouldn't try such shots at a hundred yards.

licensed. In our electronic age a new wrinkle is a "shooting theater," an indoor range where live-fire practice is done on projected images of live animals, the "score" electronically calculated.

In America running-game targets exist, but are rare. If you possibly can, seek them out and try your hand. It is almost impossible to master any shooting skill if you don't have the opportunity to practice. Jack O'Connor practiced on running jackrabbits. Legend has it that he wasn't very good at shooting groups. This may or may not be true, but I believe he was very good at field shooting, and was definitely undaunted by moving targets. I have heard of guys putting targets in old tires and rolling them down hills, which sounds like a lot of fun but extremely labor-intensive. However you can manage it, I'm sure there is no better practice for hitting moving targets with a rifle than actually shooting at a moving target with a rifle. On the other hand, I am equally convinced that the next best thing is shotgunning.

Although so far we've focused on moving targets, there are really two separate subjects here: hitting moving targets, and hitting *close* targets very fast, although both have similarities to shotgunning. Let's finish with moving targets and then we will move on to point-blank shooting.

In order to hit a moving target, you must establish your lead. This is based on the speed of the projectile and the speed and angle of the target. The first you can learn. I know, for instance, that I can tell the difference in required lead between a .45-70 at 1,800 feet per second and a .270 at 3,000 feet per second. On European running-game targets, after a few shots I could even quantify the difference between, say, a 9.3x62 and a fast .30-caliber. Actual target speed, however, is generally an unknown, and it's almost impossible to read the precise angle. (Meaning: What looks like a broadside shot usually isn't quite broadside.) The speed with which the gun is being swung—moving in relation to the target—also makes a major difference. Scientifically we can do all the calculations but, in the field, hitting moving targets thus becomes art, not science. This is why it must be kept to relatively close range, so that lead calculations don't need to be as precise.

The basics are quite simple, and really are exactly the same as shotgunning: For an offhand shot, plant your feet so that you aren't off-balance. This usually means taking a step to establish a firm stance, just as you would (or should) if a grouse or pheasant rockets up from under your feet. If shooting a moving target from a rest, make sure that gun movement is unimpeded so that the rifle can smoothly track the target.

The next essential is gun movement. In shotgunning we talk about various techniques such as the swing-through, sustained lead, and point shooting. In the swing-through you start behind the target, catch up, swing through, and slap the trigger as soon as the proper lead is established. The sustained lead is just that, more deliberate: You establish and maintain your lead, keep the gun swinging with the target, and press the trigger. Without question this is the way to pass those European shooting tests on moving targets. Point shooting is more instinctive: You pick the right spot in front of the target, mount the gun, and fire, expecting the target's movement to carry it into the pattern.

All three have their place in some form of shotgunning, but in hitting moving game with a rifle, it seems almost essential to shoot with the barrel

Much hunting in really thick cover ends up in point-blank instinctive shooting. This is in the Philippines, and there's a water buffalo right in the center of the photo, about six yards away behind those two trees.

Both of my bongos were taken in very thick cover where the rifle was really pointed rather than aimed. This is my second bongo, taken in 2004. I don't think it was more than five yards away.

moving. So the smooth, continuous swing is almost mandatory, and if you stop or slow the swing as you fire, you will almost certainly miss or hit too far back.

Although we have talked a lot about the conscious, deliberate trigger press in rifle shooting, this pretty much goes out the window when shooting at moving targets: The trigger has to go when the lead is correct. In my mind, when faced with a moving shot I subconsciously almost switch from rifle shooting to shotgunning. The result is not as precise, but as long as the shots are close, not as much precision is required.

Again, close shooting at a point target is related, but not exactly the same. Whether it's a gunfight or a close encounter with an animal, speed is of the essence, except near misses don't count. The shot must be fast because things probably aren't going to get better, but it must also be accurate. Scopes are a problem because they cause "tunnel vision," and too much magnification means that all you will see at very close range is a blur. There are relatively few field situations where a close shot, however unlikely, isn't possible, so we need to be prepared for the close-in surprise encounter even while expecting the longer shot. Much earlier, in discussion about variable scopes, I wrote about the necessity to have a low-range magnification low enough to enable close shooting. I think that's essential, but it doesn't do you much good if you wander around with the magnification turned up. Keep the magnification turned down until you need it.

Then do one more thing: Try to train yourself to shoot with both eyes open, even when shooting with a scope. If you have both eyes open you maintain peripheral vision and depth of field with your weak or nonshooting eye, and this is really essential in the fast, close encounter. At very close range it doesn't even matter if you can't perceive a proper sight picture through your scope. Your binocular vision will take over. That is, provided you have one more thing going for you, and that is *stock fit.*

Just as in shotgunning, when a properly fitting rifle is mounted the sights or scope should be roughly aligned where your eyes are looking. You can check this in your living room (first making sure your rifle is empty). With the rifle down, focus on an object and stay focused on it. Bring the rifle up, and the sights or cross hairs should be on that object. Now bring the rifle down and do the same thing, except, as you bring the rifle up, *close your eyes.* With the rifle shouldered and cheeked, open your eyes. If stock fit is truly proper for you, the sight picture should still be very close to spot-on when you open your eyes.

In thick cover the close encounter is actually fairly common. Both of my bongo were taken at a matter of feet, one with a scope and the other with open sights, but in neither case were sights particularly important. Rather, both shots were a matter of *pointing* the rifle like a shotgun rather than *aiming* it as in most rifle shooting. In today's Africa many shots at elephants are taken at less

PH Mark Haldane and I smile over a really great Livingstone suni. A lot of Africa's pygmy antelopes are best taken with shotguns, but it isn't shotgunning per se*; you are actually aiming the shotgun like a rifle . . . much like our turkey hunting.*

than ten yards, and in really thick stuff buffalo may be the same. Please don't misunderstand me: Precise shot placement remains critical. But there isn't time to ponder the finest nuances of sight alignment; the shot must be taken quickly, based to some degree on trust in the rifle's proper fit and "pointability."

Good example: I have a bad habit of flubbing the frontal brain shot on an elephant. I'm probably not alone in this; it's a far more difficult shot than it looks because the relatively small brain is buried deep within the skull, and the proper exterior spot to hit varies tremendously based on shooting distance and angle of the head. Also, deep straight-line penetration through bone is required of the bullet, so even if you do everything right there is always a chance the bullet won't get there. And no, a near-miss to the brain will not reliably "stun" an elephant. Sometimes yes, but in my experience things happen very fast after a failed brain shot.

The good news is you know it instantly. If the elephant is indeed brained the back legs collapse first, then the rest, and it happens so fast the elephant is down before the rifle comes fully out of recoil. If the brain shot fails the entire gray mass is almost instantly into motion. If it charges, you'd better try again, *fast*, and hope you're not alone. If it is a close encounter where the elephant is stationary, the normal reaction to a failed brain shot is the animal will turn away very quickly. If you're fast, the much simpler and more easily visualized side-on brain shot is momentarily opened up. Then, in split seconds, the shoulder shot, and then, in a couple more milliseconds, the going-away hip shot.

One shortcut to improving your "fast-and-close" shooting is to get training. There are several good shooting schools that offer "safari-shooting" courses as well as long-range training. This is the charging elephant target at the SAAM shooting school; instructor Chip Beaman is watching my technique.

I've done the frontal brain shot well, but I've also done it poorly on several occasions. I'm not very happy with my track record, which is why I join most experienced professional hunters in suggesting that inexperienced elephant hunters stay away from it if possible. Sometimes, especially in thick cover, there is no option. You maneuver this way and that, trying to see the tusks. Sooner or later you are "made," and the elephant, now on full alert, turns to face you. At this point you can see the ivory, and you either shoot or don't shoot. I have not been consistent on the frontal brain shot, but (touch wood) I've been consistently brilliant on the follow-up, which happens so fast there is no time to think about it. This is a shot where you are pointing instinctively, not aiming. Perhaps this is another place where a sound background in shotgunning pays dividends.

Although we never know exactly how we might react when faced with a close encounter, whether potentially dangerous or just *fast*, this is not a difficult scenario to train for. "Gun drills" are the answer, first with dry fire and then live. They do a very good job of this at the "dangerous game" courses at Tim Fallon's SAAM shooting school at FTW ranch, but you can do the same at

The effects of a very successful "gun drill" with a big double—both barrels touching. This is training you can do on your own range. Turn and fire from all possible angles, and start very close and gradually move the target out.

Make sure part of your training regimen includes learning to work the action from all shooting positions. Sometimes the first shot isn't quite enough, and this is especially true in fast, close shooting.

home (dry fire) and on the range. It's more fun if you use as a target a picture of the animal you intend to hunt, but any target will do. You start with the gun down in whatever normal and comfortable "more or less ready" carry you use. Practice with the target facing you, as if you were walking down a trail, and then with the target to your right and left, and perhaps even behind you.

The primary teaching points are: Learn to take whatever step is necessary to plant your feet as the rifle comes up; learn to snick the safety *as the rifle is raised*; and then place your first shot and at least one follow-up shot accurately and *quickly*. In concept it really is no different than "draw and fire" pistol drills, and at least initially the distances from rifle to target should be about the same—seven to ten yards. If gun fit is good, you should soon find you're able to place two shots more or less on top of each other in much less time than it takes to read half of this sentence. If you are actually preparing for a hunt for dangerous game, whether bear or buffalo, then a lot of these drills should be done with the actual rifle to be employed. However, the real purpose is to learn how to raise the rifle smoothly and quickly, get on target, and take the shot(s) *fast*. Most learning can be done with a .22, preferably one with similar sights to the hunting rifle.

With today's preoccupation with long-range shooting, to be discussed shortly, it seems to me that too many of us are forgetting that there is almost always the possibility—and sometimes the probability—of a close encounter or a moving shot. Over time experience will prove this, but I think sound training and practice should prepare the complete rifleman for all extremes, close and far, with the knowledge that, year in and year out, most shots will be presented and taken somewhere in the middle ground.

Rangefinder Revolution

Chapter 20

Optical "split image" rangefinders have been around for a long time, and many scope reticles, such as the mil-dot, can be used to estimate range as well. Although I commanded snipers and sniper units many times, I never had any formal military marksmanship training beyond the standard service rifle and pistol, and only basic familiarity training with infantry crew-served weapons, so I don't pretend to understand the mil-dot system. But I can tell you that it was created not only to serve as a consistent holdover system that shooters could train with and learn, but also as an optical rangefinding system.

These days the proliferation of accurate laser rangefinders has rendered all optical and manual rangefinding systems redundant, if not obsolete. A result is that, today, not all mil-dot systems are created equal. Properly, "mil" refers not to "military specification," but to milliradian, which is an angular measurement of one-thousandth of a circle. One milliradian subtends (covers) one meter at one thousand meters. The "mil" system was standardized within NATO in the 1950s for use (more or less) throughout the militaries of NATO signatory nations for calling and adjusting artillery fire; it was later adapted to riflescopes. One proper mil-dot in English terms covers about 3.6 inches at 100 yards, and about 36 inches at 1,000 yards. The distance from the center of 1 dot to the center of the next dot should cover 2 milliradians, so by mathematical extrapolation, this serves as a rangefinding system. If a standing 6-foot man (helmet to boots) is bracketed by 2 mil-dots, center to center, then he is 1,000 yards away.

As I admitted, I never learned the system, and have no intention of trying to learn it at this late date. Isn't it easier to mash the button on a laser range-

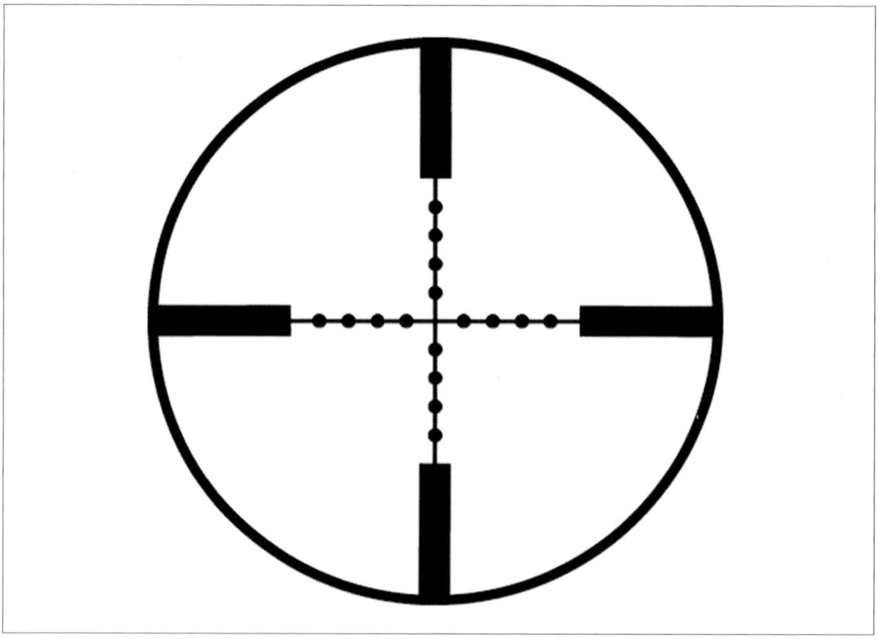

Developed for the military, the "mil-dot" reticle is actually a rangefinding and compensating reticle. A proper mil-dot subtends one milliradian, which is about 36 inches at 1,000 yards. From the center of one dot to the center of the next is two milliradians, or 72 inches at 1,000 yards . . . bracketing a standing man from helmet to boots. This is Leupold's mil-dot reticle for its tactical scopes.

finder and read the range? When I was a kid we had no rangefinders at all, so outside of a "known distance" rifle range, we had to guesstimate distance by eye. Imagine that!

Rifle trajectories have changed very little in my lifetime. In 1915 the Charles Newton-designed .250 Savage became the first commercial cartridge to break the 3,000-feet-per-second barrier. In 1935, Winchester's .220 Swift was the first to break 4,000 feet per second. The Swift remains one of very few that do; most of our flattest-shooting hunting cartridges have velocities in the low 3,000s. A few reach the mid-3,000s, but many good ones, including most of our military cartridges, have velocities in the high 2,000s. We have flattened trajectories somewhat through bullet aerodynamics, but the mechanics remain pretty much the same. In order to hit at longer ranges, unless you zero your rifle absurdly high at 100 yards, you will have to start holding over your intended point of impact at some point on the near or far side of 300 yards. At 400 yards considerable holdover is required.

For hits at longer ranges this means two things are essential. First, you must know your cartridge's trajectory. This is just a number. It doesn't really matter if your rifle is zeroed so that point of aim and point of impact coincide at 200, 250, or 300 yards. At longer ranges you simply must know what the number is. With your zero, whatever it is, how many inches is your bullet dropping at 350, 400, 450 yards, and beyond?

Second, you must know the range. When I was younger we attempted to do this by eye. Generally speaking we used the "football field" method since, at least in America, most of us have a pretty good visual of the hundred-yard football field. So, how many football fields lay between us and the deer? Note that this was not the only method. There are amazing accounts of thousand-yard sniping in the Spanish-American War by soldiers using not only .30-40 Krags but also the trapdoor Springfields in .45-70 that many of our troops

One of my favorite pictures: The end of a long day in Nevada, 1978. I don't know who is in the worse shape: me, the horse, or the deer! In those innocent pre-chronograph days, I'm pretty sure this buck was taken from about a quarter-mile, a very long shot in those days.

Although capabilities have improved significantly, compact hand-held laser rangefinders haven't changed much in size or configuration since their introduction. In the center is Leupold's top-of-line, a 1200i with True Ballistic Range. Binoculars that include a rangefinder have improved dramatically . . . I carried the big, heavy Leica Geovids (left) for years. Today there are several options that are only slightly bigger and heavier than regular binos. On the right is the Zeiss 10X45 RF rangefinding binocular.

still carried. Largely this was done through careful study of topographic maps and "registering" rifle fire much as artillery fire or mortars might be registered. Although optical artillery rangefinders saw some use, ranging by map was a primary method clear through Vietnam. Read about Carlos Hathcock, "White Feather," if you have any doubts.

Hunters, of course, weren't terribly concerned about distances of that magnitude. Back then 400 yards was rightfully considered a fairly long poke. With practice many of us got pretty good at estimating distance to that range, maybe a bit beyond. But, generally, none of us were as good at it as we thought we were. Out to a quarter-mile or so it probably didn't matter too much. We were using flat-shooting cartridges (pretty much the same flat-shooting cartridges in use today), so a fifty-yard error in range estimation wouldn't necessarily cause a miss. In recalling the few long shots I pulled off in those days, I honestly have no idea exactly how far they were! I never took time to actually pace off a shot.

Beyond a quarter-mile, all trajectory curves start to steepen and ranging errors become ever more critical. In other words, as distance increases, precise knowledge of range becomes more and more important. Honestly, not knowing any different, we didn't worry about that too much back then. If we figured the distance was 400 yards we held some daylight over the backline, and if our estimate was close, such a shot often worked. Memory being the wonderfully selective thing it is, I can remember a number of longer shots that worked in those innocent pre-laser-rangefinder days, and I have some difficulty recalling shots that didn't work.

On the last day of a tough Nevada mule deer hunt in 1978 we made a long swing through some broken country, eventually jumping two very nice bucks in a canyon. They were in thick stuff in the bottom, headed up toward the far rim. I bailed off my horse and lay down on a flat rimrock boulder. There would be no shot until they almost topped out, and I was pretty sure the distance was a bit more than 400 yards.

The laser rangefinder is a great enabler. With a storm coming in fast, I knew that this French chamois, a small target, was 400 yards away.

I was shooting a .30-06 with 180-grain Nosler Partitions handloaded to a chronographed 2,800 feet per second in my rifle, a pretty flat-shooting load. As they topped the rim they slowed to a walk, and I held a bit ahead of the larger buck with a good bit of daylight over the backline. I must have had the distance reasonably correct, because we found the buck stone-dead just inside the brush above the rim.

On another mule deer hunt, this one in Colorado, we were on a ridge looking across a snow-covered valley to a rocky knoll. On the crest of that knoll, in the lee of a boulder, a very big mule deer buck was bedded, surveying his domain. I was stuck, with no cover to get closer but also no urgency. I studied and re-studied the ground, and I was reasonably sure the distance was about 500 yards. Honest, I've been spoiled by laser rangefinders for so long now that I don't know why or how I was sure of that, but in those days we studied the ground and tried to figure it out. I was shooting a .300 Weatherby Magnum

This was my first Asian sheep, a Trans-Caspian urial I took in Turkmenistan in 1995. I was carrying the original Leica Geovids, and I remember clearly that the shot was 305 yards.

In-scope laser rangefinders are clearly the emerging technology in riflescopes, and some already come equipped with on-board computers that can adjust a shooter's hold. This is Bushnell's Yardage Pro, an extremely affordable rangefinding scope, but understandably limited in range.

with 180-grain loads, and I knew the trajectory. Some handy boulders and a backpack were made into a very close approximation of a benchrest, and while I sat there shivering, I had plenty of time to figure the shot.

After an hour or so, the buck finally stood, broadside. There was no wind at all, so I held most of the deer over the backline and fired. Amazingly, I hit the buck with my first and only shot, but I'd underestimated the range by just a bit and the hit was low in the chest. The trail was clear, and we found him piled up a couple hundred yards up the valley.

If I really stretched I could probably recall a couple more early long shots. And I could also come up with a couple of long shots that didn't even come close. Again, how many of us actually paced off our shots? In the sporting literature from the first three-quarters of the twentieth century there are lots of references to 400- and 500-yard shooting, but I think there's a fair amount of exaggeration involved. Based on hold and bullet drop, on the two recounted I can be reasonably certain of the actual distance. On that Nevada

Knowing the range is extremely comforting . . . especially when hunting in unfamiliar country for unfamiliar animals. I'm all set up over a pack in coastal Peru (top), I've used my Zeiss 10X45 RF, and I know a bedded tropical whitetail is 220 yards away. When he stands up, I take the shot.

buck, well, it was the end of a seven-day hunt, too hot with full moon, and we'd seen very little. I was desperate. With the Colorado buck it was early in the hunt, but I had lots of time to study the shot. In those days I had relatively little experience, but plenty of youthful confidence. Even so, given the same circumstances and the same rifles, I would probably try both shots today. Except that today, under the same conditions, I would have perfect knowledge of the exact distance.

By the 1980s we had very compact "coincidence" rangefinders; Ranging, Inc. was the primary supplier to the hunting market. When you looked through it at an object you saw two images; a dial moved the images together and you read the range. There were models for bow hunters, which were very accurate at closer ranges. At longer ranges there was less precision, and, as I recall, some subjectivity from one person's eyes to another's. Some shooters swore by them. I didn't; I sometimes carried one, but I don't recall ever actually using it on a long shot in the field. Better tools were coming soon.

The first laser rangefinder I ever saw was Russian military surplus, a bulky, heavy thing able to range mountains at twenty thousand meters. Obviously it was intended for artillery spotters, and it was very accurate, expensive, and monstrous. Randy Brooks of Barnes Bullets had one, and we played with it on an elk hunt in about 1990. Only a few of these got out onto the civilian market; it was soon learned that this was not an "eye-safe" laser, and I heard about some cattle being blinded while hunters were trying it out.

As I recall, Bushnell led the way with the first compact eye-safe laser rangefinder. It had neither the range nor the capability to "ping" on smaller objects like today's rangefinders, but it was a landmark achievement. The first time I used one was in eastern Colorado, when I was guiding Kevin Howard to what we were pretty sure was a hybrid whitetail-mule deer cross. The buck was with some does in really open ground, with just a couple of shallow coulees for cover. I can't remember how far the first reading was, but we needed to get closer. So we bent low, then went hands and knees in cactus and melting snow, and then low-crawled, me checking distance every time I found a bush tall enough to allow sneaking a peek. I'd never used one before and I thought it was the cat's pajamas! I think we were at 235 yards when Kevin got set up and hammered the buck.

It is extremely handy to have both rangefinder and binocular in one tool, but rangefinding binoculars are still larger, heavier, and more expensive. Thus the alternative solution—carrying both binocular and compact rangefinder—remains a valid option.

Since then, laser rangefinders have come a long way. Almost every major optics manufacturer offers them, often in several different "grades," or maximum distances. Several companies incorporate them into binoculars, and there are even a few rangefinding riflescopes, still an emerging technology. The laser rangefinder essentially works by shooting out a laser pulse or narrow beam that is reflected back to the receiver. The receiver calculates the time elapsed between sending the beam and receiving the reflection, and gives the distance. Civilian rangefinders are limited by the fact that they must be "eye safe," meaning of restricted intensity, so the instruments we have are nothing like the laser rangefinders and target designators used by the military.

Obviously rangefinders with greater range are costlier than those with more limited range, but there are plenty of inexpensive rangefinders that will read well beyond 1,000 yards, which certainly fills the bill for most civilian purposes. Although the whole concept is based on a very narrow beam, the farther it goes, the wider the beam spreads. So, with all laser rangefinders, there are limitations on "ranging" small objects like animals, and equal limitations on our ability to hold them still enough. Serious long-range shooters mount a rangefinder on a tripod, which eliminates a lot of human error, but there are still limits on what any rangefinder can range. The readout is generally digital within the viewfinder, but laser rangefinders don't "run out of numbers;" the laser beam just runs out of gas. Low light and highly reflective surfaces, like vertical rocks and dense trees, are best. So lots of times we find ourselves ranging on such landmarks *near* an animal, rather than attempting to range on the animal itself.

As I said, I've been spoiled by rangefinders for many years. Sometimes I've gotten amazing readings, such as more than 1,800 yards from a unit rated to 1,200 yards. Other times, you just can't get the darned things to read. This is consistent in any precipitation: If there is rain, snow, or even light fog, you will find rangefinders nearly useless. It is also consistent if you're excited and can't hold the unit still enough, and under all circumstances the beam must have a

This is my buddy Zack Aultman's "super stand," overlooking an endless Georgia power line. Both rangefinder and binocular are ready, but I've already ranged every landmark in sight and tried to commit general distances to memory.

Fog is still hanging over the Oklahoma sand hills behind me. This was a morning when no rangefinder could read distances, a day when guesstimating range by eye was essential. I'm pretty sure this buck was about 350 yards away when he stepped out of the fog, because that was my hold.

clear path to the object being ranged. If grass, a twig, or whatever gets in the way, forget it.

So, field conditions being as they are, the laser rangefinder is not a *panacea*. There will be times when it won't read. Against those times, I suggest you spend a lot of time playing the "how far is that?" game with your rangefinder. Whenever I'm in a blind or on a stand I range everything in sight, trying to commit to memory the distances to prominent objects. Likewise when I'm glassing from a good spot. This is useful, but take it one step further: Before you range a rock or a tree, make a guess as to how far it is. Then range it, get the true range, and look at it again. How close were you? Do this over and over, every time you use your rangefinder, and over time, you'll get a lot better at judging range by eye.

The laser rangefinder is a marvelous tool. Under normal and average conditions it eliminates one of the great variables in shooting at longer range. In this case we will define "longer range" *as any distance at which you need to hold over your target in order to hit.* Obviously this is different with a muzzleloader or .45-70 than it is with a .300 Remington Ultra Mag.

Today some laser rangefinders go quite a bit further than just giving you perfect distance. Although today's stand-alone rangefinder isn't much bigger than a smartphone, it has much of the same mini-computer capabilities. Leupold led the way with its True Ballistic Range (TBR) system, which not only measures the actual range to the target, but also measures the uphill/downhill angle and gives you your "hold" reading or "slant range." This uphill/downhill thing is one of the most vexing for riflemen. We drive ourselves insane over it, often to no purpose because angles usually aren't as severe as we think they are, and you need some combination of major angle *and* serious distance before your hold needs to be adjusted. Such shots do occur, and the most modern laser rangefinders will tell you your adjustment. They will also tell you when you need not worry about it.

Coming on fast now are hold adjustments offered by the rangefinder after adjusting it to your velocity and zero. As I said, emerging technology is now taking this a major step further with laser rangefinders built into a riflescope that make trajectory corrections for you. Although the top-of-the-line systems are still very costly, both Burris and Bushnell have amazingly affordable laser riflescopes right now, the only catch being that they are not unlimited in range.

I freely admit to having relatively little experience with this new technology. Obviously it has awesome military applications, and I have no issue at all with its sporting use in the larger sense. However, America's senior conservation and record-keeping organization, the Boone and Crockett Club, has ruled that use of on-rifle lasers disqualify trophies from inclusion in their *Records of North American Big Game.* Mind you, I don't hunt for the record books and, in my lifetime, have taken only a small handful of animals that qualify. However, I've been a professional member of B&C for thirty years, so there's a loyalty issue involved, and also the fact that, whether I agree or not, I appreciate their point of view: How much skill do we wish to take out of the equation, and at what point have we gone too far?

I'm not prepared to answer that, but so far I have shied away from on-board computers and in-scope lasers for my own use. As technology emerges these are decisions each of us must face for ourselves. There's no real right or

Even at modest distances, knowledge of range is sometimes critical. At 160 yards, this was the longest shot I've ever taken on a Cape buffalo. I studied the range and set up a good rest . . . and dropped this buffalo with a single 400-grain bullet from a .416 Rigby.

Today we can have perfect knowledge of range and we can know our trajectory, but that's still only part of the solution. These pronghorns are in range, but the wind is howling. Reading the wind remains the most difficult variable for shooting at distance.

wrong, and I make no judgments. For now, I am convinced that the laser rangefinder is a wonderful tool, under ideal conditions removing knowledge of distance as one of the great variables in rifle shooting. As we will see, there are still plenty of other variables we need to worry about.

The Long-Range Game

CHAPTER 21

"Revolution" is too strong a word, and "fad" seems too flippant and disrespectful. However you term it, the current interest in and fascination with long-range shooting is unprecedented, and actually reflects a sea change in American culture.

In the American Revolution we idolized our sharpshooters with their Pennsylvania rifles. Timothy Murphy remains one of our heroes from that

With the rifles and optics we have today, amazing accuracy is truly possible. I fired this three-inch 600-yard group with one of Kenny Jarrett's Beanfield Rifles in his wildcat .300 Jarrett. I'll take that accuracy any day, but in the field 600 yards is approaching my absolute limit.

conflict, credited with killing both Brig. Gen. Simon Fraser and Sir Francis Clerke at the Second Battle of Saratoga, 7 October 1777. History records that he climbed a tree, took a solid rest with his long rifle, and fired four shots, mortally wounding General Fraser and killing Clerke. Murphy, known to be a deadly shot, was directed to take out General Fraser, and at what was then the extremely long distance of three hundred yards, it took him three shots. Clerke, who was British General Burgoyne's aide-de-camp, rode to Fraser's assistance, and by now Murphy "had the range." He fired one more shot, killing Clerke instantly.

For the next two centuries, however, our employment of snipers was sort of a dirty little secret. There are exceptions. Buffalo hunter and U.S. Army scout Billy Dixon is still celebrated for ending the Second Battle of Adobe Walls in 1874 by knocking a Comanche off his horse at nearly a mile (current research suggests the actual distance was closer to a half-mile, still a heck of a shot). Later that year Dixon would win the Medal of Honor for bravery at the Battle of Buffalo Wallow, just one of eight civilians to be so honored in the history of the award. Fellow Medal of Honor winner Alvin York's sharpshooting exploits in World War I is also the stuff of legends (and motion pictures). Although their shooting is justifiably memorable, neither Dixon nor York were snipers. Dixon was a buffalo hunter and York was an infantryman—both happened to be gifted riflemen, and fate offered them opportunity to use their skills.

In general, all the way through Vietnam, our snipers and their tactical employment were kept in the closet. Charles Henderson's popular book, *Marine Sniper: 93 Confirmed Kills*, probably started to change things a bit. Its subject, Gunnery Sergeant Carlos Hathcock, became a cult hero, but our military never gave him the recognition he deserved. In 1969 an amphibious tractor he was riding on struck a mine. Hathcock was blown off the top and knocked out. When he came to, the vehicle was burning, with men trapped inside. Ignoring his own injuries, Hathcock walked into the flames repeatedly, bringing seven wounded men to safety. It is probable that the burns he sustained led to his early death in 1999.

In the mid-1990s a petition was circulated asking that he be considered for the Medal of Honor, not for sniping, which was simply his job, but for saving the seven men. At one point the Secretary of the Navy stated that if the

Thanks to the laser rangefinder, we now can have near-perfect knowledge of range, and thanks to the proliferation of chronographs, we can have near-perfect knowledge of our trajectories. The Oehler is the real Cadillac of rangefinders, giving a printout that includes standard deviation as well as high, low, and average. The Chrony (top left), on the other hand, is extremely economical . . . but you'll have to do some figuring by hand.

My finishing shot on this excellent Marco Polo argali was at 650 yards. That is not a shot I would normally attempt in the field, but I had hit him at 350 yards and needed to stop his escape into China.

Medal of Honor was not bestowed he would award Hathcock the Navy Cross, in my mind a minimal award for the heroism involved. Neither happened, but in 1996 the Commandant of the Marine Corps presented him with the Silver Star (the highest award he had authority to bestow). Hathcock is without question the most famous sniper from the Vietnam War, fame he never sought and wasn't comfortable with. He was actually not the highest-scoring sniper from that conflict, but we know little about most of his peers.

Stephen Hunter's excellent novels featuring former Marine sniper Bob Lee Swagger have done much to elevate and popularize the sniper in American culture, but much of this work has been done by the snipers themselves, starting with the First Gulf War and continuing to this day. Some of the sniping in Iraq, such as the Battle of Fallujah, had similarities to the sniper duels of Stalingrad. More often, however, the deserts of Iraq and mountains of Afghanistan offered perfect "sniper country." With better optics, better rifles, and effective ranging—and let's not forget really good training—incredible

Bullets for long-range shooting are improving rapidly. These are some of the first of Hornady's revolutionary ELD-X (Extremely Low Drag eXpanding), designed both for aerodynamics and to provide consistent expansion across a wide velocity spectrum.

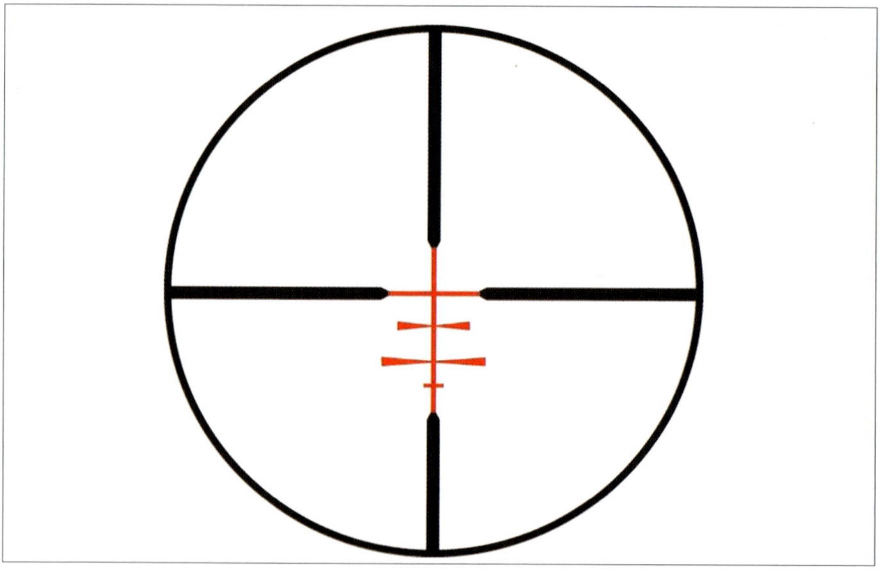

While dialing the range is the most precise method, for the average hunter using a reticle with additional aiming points is faster and more goof-proof. Almost every optics manufacturer has a range-compensating reticle, some simple and some complex. This is Leupold's B&C reticle, shown in illuminated version. It is one of the simplest to master.

shots became almost routine, and seemingly impossible shots were made with amazing frequency.

Among others, Chris Kyle came home a hero, wrote a bestseller, and was murdered for nothing worse than being a good guy. I believe he would have gone on to do marvelous things for the shooting sports, the sniper community, and for all veterans. His untimely death was a severe loss to us all, but, to be cold-bloodedly objective, as a martyr he was instantly catapulted into national hero status, with his book and movie, *American Sniper*, and the book written by his widow, Taya Kyle, *American Wife: A Memoir of Love, Service, Faith, and Renewal*, making Kyle a household name.

All of these factors have come together. Instead of the sniper being reviled, abhorred, or treated as the elephant in the room, the skills of the sniper and the long-range precision required is now fascinating to more shooters than ever. Please remember long-range shooting is nothing new. Thousand-yard competition goes back to the muzzleloading era. As a formal competitive game,

Nosler has jumped into the long-range game with their .26 and .28 Nosler cartridges, based on the shortened 7mm RUM case. Both are fast and efficient. Nosler also has a "long range" version of their excellent AccuBond bullet, intended to open reliably at velocities down to 1,300 feet per second.

Although I believe velocity gains have been very incremental during my lifetime, there have been gains. Lazzeroni's cartridges are the fastest in their calibers, and other small firms are making advances. The Tejas Magnums are very impressive! The .300 Tejas (bottom right) is an improved version of the .300 RUM; velocity averaged 3,679 fps with a 180-grain Berger . . . with a standard deviation of just 19!

The .338 Lapua Magnum (center) was developed as a long-range sniping cartridge. The intent was to bridge the gap between the 7.62 NATO (left), which is barely a 1,000-yard cartridge, and the .50 BMG (right). The .50 BMG can be used up to 3,000 yards, but its platforms are too heavy to readily carry.

it is probably more popular than ever, although increasingly limited by a shortage of thousand-yard ranges. On a more informal basis, long-range shooting is "in," with a tremendous number of riflemen and women desiring to extend their range envelopes and in some measure emulate the feats of our snipers.

This is actually a good thing. As mentioned much earlier, although relatively few rifle shooters actively pursue formal benchrest competition, the benchrest community has been responsible for much development that has benefited all of us: rigid actions, cartridge design, synthetic and laminated stocks, better barrels, and more. Similarly, long-range competitors and the military sniping community have given us enhanced bullet aerodynamics, better optics, and extremely useful cartridges such as the 6.5-.284, 6.5mm Creedmoor, and .338 Lapua Magnum.

In thousand-yard shooting it's a given that there will be yards and yards of bullet drop. How much doesn't really matter because, as I've said, past a certain point bullet drop is just a number. Remaining energy also doesn't matter. Instead it is desirable to be able to lie prone and not get kicked into next week.

However, it is extremely conducive to long-range accuracy to be able to reach 1,000 yards without the bullet dropping below the speed of sound (1,127 feet per second). This is because there is turbulence when crossing the sound barrier. In acceleration this happens long before the bullet leaves the barrel, so that turbulence is controlled; in deceleration it is unavoidable, but at exactly what range it takes place is manageable through both velocity and bullet aerodynamics.

It has long been known that the efficiency and high ballistic coefficient (BC) of a 6.5mm allows it to leave the barrel at fairly modest velocity (which means moderate recoil) yet remain supersonic beyond the 1,000-yard target line. The 6.5-.284, based on the oddball .284 Winchester rebated-rim cartridge, was a popular wildcat in thousand-yard circles long before Norma adopted it as a factory cartridge. The 6.5mm Creedmoor, developed by Hornady, is not quite as fast, but it remains supersonic beyond the thousand-yard mark. I've taken this little cartridge out to a thousand yards, and it's amazing what it will do at a minimal price in recoil.

The .338 Lapua Magnum is a whole different story. It is a big cartridge generating brutal recoil, developed as a sniper's cartridge that would bridge the range gap between the 7.62x51mm NATO cartridge, which becomes difficult to hit with beyond 800 meters; and the .50 BMG. In accurate rifles with good optics the .50 BMG can be effective out to 3,000 meters, but a .50 BMG platform has the major disadvantage of being almost too heavy to lug around. The .338 Lapua is rated effective to 1,910 meters, but our snipers have used it considerably farther. The current distance record for a confirmed sniper kill in combat is held not by an American, but by one of our allies. Craig Harrison, British Corporal of Horse, used a .338 Lapua to make an amazing shot at 2,475 meters, or 2,707 yards.

I think it's a wonderful thing that our snipers are now considered heroes rather than heels. Certainly they deserve it. And shooting at long range is a whole lot of fun. Although I've never competed, in recent years I've done more long-range shooting than I ever have. Ringing steel targets at a thousand yards and beyond is an awesome confidence-building exercise. However, I have

Based on the .416 Rigby case necked down, a .338 Lapua rifle must be fairly heavy, but the performance is amazing. This .338 Lapua built by Marc LeQuieu (top) was extremely manageable on the bench, and it produced superb groups.

major concerns about translating that capability on targets into actual extreme-range shooting at game animals.

I understand that not everyone will agree, but in my mind there are fundamental differences between sniping and hunting. Both the sniper and the serious hunter use the same credo: "One shot, one kill." But it's a bit different for the sniper. A fatal hit is not necessary for the sniper to accomplish his mission. It can be argued that a wounding hit is even better, because now it takes another enemy soldier or two to carry their comrade to safety. Snipers can be employed to take out specific high-value targets, but more common roles are to demoralize the enemy and break up troop formations. For the latter mission, near misses count.

For serious and ethical hunters, misses, whether near or far, count for nothing, and a wounding hit is far worse than a miss. The rangefinder has given us near-perfect knowledge of range (at least most of the time). The ability to get steady and to hold 'em and squeeze 'em is a matter of training and practice. In hunting, where only kill shots count, there are other factors at play.

As I wrote in the previous chapter, before compact rangefinders, we figured four hundred yards or perhaps a quarter-mile to be a very long shot. It was, and it is, but with more accurate rifles, better hunting bullets, much better optics, effective ranging, and *lots of practice*, such shooting is within the reach of most of us under good conditions. Some of us can take it a bit further, always depending on the conditions. Just recently I got on a nice New Zealand red stag at 485 yards. I knew the drop and I had plenty of gun, scope, and bullet, but the wind was gusting at least 30 miles an hour. Under those conditions that was "no shot." So I passed, and after four hours of hard work I got the shot—and the stag—at a bit less than three hundred yards.

It is not my place to say exactly how far is too far. It depends a bit on equipment, a lot more on skill, and even more on the conditions. Under reasonable conditions I'm very comfortable at 400 yards, and under ideal conditions with the right equipment I'm OK out to maybe 500 yards and change. My personal longest shot at an unwounded animal was 635 yards, and I've prevented the escape of wounded animals at slightly longer distances. Some riflemen I know are very comfortable at those ranges, and do it enough that I'm not suggesting they shouldn't. Much beyond that, *on game*, I'm not so sure.

On extremely open floodplains in Australia's Northern Territories, CZ's Jason Morton and I had a chance to use a CZ in .338 Lapua on water buffalo. We didn't push the cartridge's range envelope: No shots exceeded 450 yards. Even so, that's very far to be shooting at buffalo, and the several we shot went down very cleanly.

How far is too far is a very personal decision, but it's important that we all understand that the farther the shot, the more things stack up against us. And, no, we shouldn't take as gospel everything we read or see on the silver screen. For the written word, well, we have only the writer's word. Before rangefinders I think it was very common to exaggerate distances. Today there is no excuse, but I'm not convinced the practice has stopped. As for what we see on TV, well, we know what the screen shows and what the narrator tells us. Do we know we're being told the truth? And even if the distance given is real, do we know if we're seeing the first shot, the last shot, or the *best* shot? My advice: Take it all with a grain of salt.

If you are interested in expanding your range envelope, then you certainly can. But you cannot simply purchase the best equipment and instantly become competent at 400 yards, let alone twice that distance. Modern equipment helps, but you need an awful lot of range time at actual distances before you can start to translate range shooting to field shooting.

Wind is the greatest variable at longer ranges. You can measure wind speed where you are, but the wind can vary between you and the target, and the farther the target the more it can vary. Terrain features channel wind. Tim Fallon's SAAM ranges are in canyon country, and by using smoke canisters I've actually seen wind coming from three directions across just a few hundred yards. If you can't read the wind you can't make the shot, and reading wind is an art, not a science. At several hundred yards it doesn't take much wind to blow you off the target or, worse, turn a well-placed chest shot into a hit too far back.

At really extreme range there are other factors to consider. Again, in competition shooting and military sniping, residual bullet energy isn't a concern. In hunting, it's a big concern. Col. Townsend Whelen theorized that we should have 1,000 foot-pounds of energy at the target to cleanly take deer-size game. There is no way to know if that's genuinely valid, because shot placement and bullet performance (how that energy is transferred) are terribly important. But it's not a bad rule of thumb, and if it has validity, then perhaps we should have 2,000 foot-pounds of energy for elk-size game. There are plenty of cartridges that will carry 1,000 foot-pounds beyond 600 yards, and a few hard-kicking beasts that will carry a ton of energy that far. With really good

At the SAAM ranges, Caroline was able to "ring steel" at greater distances than she has ever shot. Shooting at long range is a lot of fun as well as a wonderful confidence-builder, but I think it's important to recognize differences between target shooting, sniping, and hunting.

bullet aerodynamics it is possible to get 1,000 foot-pounds at 1,000 yards, but it is very difficult to produce 2,000 foot-pounds of energy at 1,000 yards.

Honestly, these "energy requirements" are more theoretical than actual. The old .44-40 has accounted for unknown numbers of deer—considering the time it has been used (from 1873 forward), perhaps more than even the .30-30—but it develops less than 700 foot-pounds of energy *at the muzzle*. So energy requirements aren't locked in stone, but bullet energy is a factor, and as range increases, energy yields must inexorably diminish.

Bullet performance is another problem. At longer ranges, as velocities drop, terminal performance becomes erratic. All bullets designed to expand will expand less at lower velocity, and at some point will not expand at all. They will still penetrate (most of the time), but little of what energy remains will be transferred. This means that there will be much less reaction to the shot. In other words, at extreme range it becomes less obvious that a hit was made. Unless the strike of the bullet was observed, hunting ethics dictate that you have to go look. At, say, 800 or 900 yards, exactly how long will it take you to get there? When you get there, can you find the exact spot where the animal was standing? For the latter, in some terrain you can, and a companion on a spotting scope can usually walk you in. For the former, you'd better have plenty of daylight left before considering a very long shot.

None of this is to say that long-range shooting cannot be done. Of course it can, and with the equipment we have today it's more possible than ever. But it isn't just a matter of equipment. It's also a matter of the conditions. It takes time to properly set up for a long-range shot. You need time to get absolutely steady, read the range, determine the trajectory correction, and read the wind. In the field you'll start with the wind where you are, then you'll be studying leaves and grass to see if the wind remains constant. Even if everything else is perfect, on game uncertainty about the wind must lead you to a "no shot" decision.

Conditions aside, long-range shooting is also a matter of skill in using your equipment. That means lots of shooting at actual ranges. There is no substitute. I understand that relatively few of us have easy access to ranges that go way out there. In fact, many of us are fortunate just to have a hundred-yard range within easy access. This is a limiting factor. With a flat-shooting cartridge you

John Lazzeroni and I smile over our, sort of, double on coyotes . . . except that his was taken from over 500 yards, a brilliant and perfect shot. Lazzeroni walks the walk as well as talking the talk; he spends a lot of time shooting at actual ranges and knows exactly what he's doing.

can probably zero properly at a hundred yards and shoot with confidence to three hundred yards, possibly four hundred. Way out there, where the trajectory curve is steep, you probably shouldn't shoot at game unless you have spent a lot of range time shooting at the actual distances.

With long-range shooting so popular today, riflescopes have advanced wonderfully. Almost every optics manufacturer has some type of range-adjusting reticle, and most have turrets that allow you to "dial the range." Chronographs have also come a long way. When I was a kid, nobody had one. Today most serious rifle shooters have one, or at least know somebody who does. The chronograph will give you the true velocity of your load in your rifle. Armed with that knowledge it's pretty easy to go to a computer program and obtain the trajectory of your load.

So far, so good. In the old days we took an approximation of that data, usually based on published figures, and we guesstimated holdover. Today I am convinced that dialing the range on your scope's turret is the most precise method. I am also convinced that using additional stadia lines or aiming points in your scope's reticle is faster and, in the heat of the moment, more goof-proof. But it doesn't matter which method you use. It matters that you learn how to use it, and that you verify values at actual ranges. Not all scopes are exactly precise from one click to another, and little things like exact height of scope over the barrel become big things at extreme range.

There is simply no substitute for range time, and for shooting at actual distances. If you work at it, you can accomplish amazing things. Certainly there are far better riflemen than I who can shoot with both confidence and accuracy at far greater ranges than I am comfortable with. But my point remains: Hunting is not sniping. What constitutes "long range" differs for all of us, as does the question "How far is too far?" I won't try to define those distances. Ringing steel or punching paper at long ranges is a lot of fun, and you can bet the snipers we now admire did an awful lot of that before employing their skills in combat.

That's my friend and cohost of Guns & Ammo TV, *Kyle Lamb, next to me . . . on the rifle is our producer, Darin Narlock. With the filming done, we're having some fun seeing who can ring the 500-yard gong the quickest with a Ruger American .30-06 and Trijicon scope.*

Over the years I've done a lot of prairie dog and ground squirrel shooting. Shooting small varmints is probably the best "school" for learning to dope wind . . . it doesn't take much more than a breath to blow you off of a three-inch rodent at a couple hundred yards.

Hunting is a different game. Through practice we can expand our range envelopes, but in hunting, "almost" doesn't count. None of us are perfect. We all miss, and we can miss at close, medium, or long range. Unfortunately, over time, some of those "misses" will be nonfatal hits. In hunting these need to be kept to an absolute minimum, so regardless of range the question we all should ask ourselves is simple: "Are you *sure* you can make that shot?" Before pressing the trigger the answer must be affirmative. "Maybe" isn't good enough.

Climatic Changes and Other Variables

CHAPTER 22

Altitude, angle, barometric pressure, Coriolis effect, drift, humidity, temperature, wind deflection: These are the things that drive rifle nuts insane! Honestly, many of us don't need to worry about such things. If you are among the millions of American deer hunters who harvest your venison within, say, a hundred and fifty yards, don't lose any sleep over this stuff. Zero your rifle, aim for the shoulder or just behind the shoulder, and

Some days you're better off to stay inside! We were trying to hunt mule deer in southern Alberta, but with gale-force winds and zero visibility, not much was likely to happen.

make sure your knife is sharp. If you're an infantryman toting the standard-issue service rifle, make sure you have a proper battlefield zero (BZO) and concentrate on holding 'em and squeezing 'em—and keep your head down.

Even the most serious long-range rifle shooters, including our most elite snipers, don't need to worry about all this stuff. Coriolis effect and drift, for instance, are not significant enough to specifically factor into small-arms trajectory calculations. We'll put both on the table anyway.

Coriolis effect is, in simple terms, the movement of the target due to the Earth's rotation while a projectile is in flight. There is movement because nothing on Earth is actually stationary; everything in contact with the ground is moving as our planet spins. The Coriolis effect must be taken into account with long-range artillery, naval gunfire, and ballistic missile guidance. It is not a factor at small-arms ranges simply because the distance or, more properly, the time of flight, is too short for adjustment to be required. But those who thirst for arcane knowledge should understand that the Earth spins on its north-south axis, so for projectiles fired north or south the Coriolis effect is horizontal. For projectiles fired east or west it is vertical, and at all other angles it is both horizontal and vertical. For artillerymen, God bless the computer!

Although you may have heard the term *wind drift*, the proper term is *wind deflection. Drift* is something different: It is the natural movement of a spinning projectile in the direction of the spin. As we know, rifling imparts a spin to the bullet that stabilizes it in flight. After the turbulence of acceleration and departure from the muzzle, most bullets yaw a bit, essentially wobbling in flight. Yawing is constant, but if the spin is (reasonably) correct for the length of the projectile, it will settle down to a very slight and consistent wobble. Scientifically this is called the "yaw of repose," but accuracy freaks refer to the bullet as "going to sleep."

Now, in theory, if a rifle fired a one-inch group at 100 yards, then natural dispersion should allow it to fire a two-inch group at 200 yards. Often, however, we find that our groups increase in size more than that. It could be yawing from imperfect stabilization, or (more likely) it is simply human error because it's harder to hold tight groups as distance increases. Not infrequently, however, we find that groups at 200 and even 300 yards are relatively smaller in minute of angle (MOA) terms than 100-yard groups. For instance, that same "one-

It takes a lot of distance and flight time for the Coriolis effect of the earth's rotation to come into play. With small arms we don't need to worry about it, but the artillerymen manning these coastal guns on Corregidor Island had to factor it in to target a passing ship properly.

Temperature has a major impact on both ammunition and the flight of a projectile. Colder ammo develops less pressure and thus less velocity; and cold air is denser than warm air, thus creating more resistance.

inch" rifle produces 1.5-inch groups at 200 yards. If this happens consistently we could probably conclude that this projectile needed a hundred yards or so to "go to sleep."

However, while the gyroscopic spin is stabilizing the bullet, it is also very slightly forcing it in the direction of the spin. Traditionally most rifling has a right-hand twist, so drift is generally to the right, but left-hand-twist rifling is occasionally seen, and a bullet fired from left-hand twist rifling will drift to the left. Thousand-yard competitors probably unconsciously take this into account when zeroing, but even at extreme range the actual drift is small enough that this is usually not something to worry about.

If you're a long-range target shooter, an open-country hunter, or a sniper, the rest of this stuff is important to understand, and, when conditions apply, pay attention to. We finished the previous chapter with a discussion on the difficulty of judging wind, so we'll start with *wind deflection* because it is probably the most vexing and potentially most devastating variable.

Clinically and scientifically, wind deflection looks easy. Ballistics charts will give it to you, as will various computerized programs. You can even put an app on your smartphone. You can carry a pocket wind gauge, and it will tell you the wind speed where you're standing. But let's not underestimate the effect.

As I've said, over the years one of my "go to" cartridges—in several different rifles—has been the .300 Weatherby Magnum. A 180-grain .30-caliber spitzer bullet is fairly aerodynamic, and the .300 Weatherby is fast. This is important because *time of flight* reduces the wind's ability to work on the bullet. My load clocks 3,100 feet per second, and the bullet is a hunting bullet, not a match bullet, so it has a good (but not awesome) ballistic coefficient of .500. So let's say we have a nice, steady 10-mile-per-hour crosswind, which means we can feel the breeze, and see leaves and grass stirring gently. At 100 yards I've got less than an inch of deflection; at 200 yards I've got 2 inches. No worries; the

The wind was really howling when I shot this Wyoming pronghorn. The distance wasn't much more than 200 yards, and I was shooting the fast .270 WSM . . . even so, I gave it about 10 inches of wind deflection in order to place the bullet behind the shoulder.

Humidity and barometric pressure affect projectiles, but that isn't something to be concerned about until ranges get very long. On a day like this, the most immediate effect is that no laser rangefinder is likely to be able to give you a reading!

vital zone of even smallish big-game animals are plenty big enough to mask such minimal errors.

But the bullet is going to keep getting blown sideways. At 300 yards I have five inches of wind deflection, so I need to start taking it into account and consciously holding "a bit into the wind." At 500 yards I have 13 inches of deflection. Depending on how the animal is standing, if I don't take the wind into account I will either miss or hit too far back. At 700 yards I have 28 inches wind deflection. This is from a very mild breeze. If the wind is blowing 20 miles per hour we can double all those numbers. This is all provided that the wind is constant all the way to the target, and that it's really a straight crosswind, 90 degrees from the gun-to-target line.

On formal ranges there are almost always wind flags that make it fairly easy to estimate both wind speed and angle. In the field there are no flags. All we can be 100 percent sure of is how the wind is blowing where we are shooting from. Headwinds and tail winds are "zero value" wind, no adjustment needed.

The effect temperature has on propellants varies quite a bit. The Australian Outback ammo, though limited in calibers, is designed to remain consistent across a wide velocity spectrum. I put some cartridges in the freezer and heated others with a blow dryer, and I found that neither point of impact nor velocity shifted noticeably.

Except—guess what—downdrafts will push the bullet down, and updrafts will push the bullet up. In mountainous country these can be issues. Winds from, say, one, five, seven, and eleven o'clock are "quarter value" winds, more or less one-fourth the deflection of a straight crosswind. Winds from two, four, eight, and ten o'clock are "half value" winds, more or less one-half the deflection of a 90-degree crosswind. Provided, of course, that the wind is constant all the way to the target.

This is where the art comes in. What are the leaves and grass downrange telling you? Are there terrain features that might be channeling or limiting the wind downrange? Wind effect is greater during the initial part of a projectile's flight, but if we could know the wind speed and angle then it's all mathematics. Reality: We cannot measure downrange winds, so we must make the very best guess we can. The risks are huge. The hunter risks wounding a marvelous animal; the sniper risks giving away his position. I'm pretty good at guesstimating wind, perhaps from doing a lot of prairie dog shooting on windy plains. I don't recall ever missing—or losing—a big-game animal due to an incorrect wind call. On the other hand, there have been a lot of shots I haven't taken because I couldn't get a handle on the wind.

Even more perplexing is the business of *angles*—uphill and downhill shooting. It isn't necessary to *understand* the effect, but it is essential to keep it in mind. I have tried to explain it and have seen it explained a dozen different ways. Hey, I have an English degree, in part because I wasn't very good at mathematics! Once again, all good ballistics programs will give you the precise solution, and a Google search will give you so many different explanations that your hair will start to hurt. Let's take a simplistic approach: When shooting uphill or downhill the effect is the same: The strike of your bullet will be higher than you think it will be, so you must adjust your hold *lower* to compensate.

Failing to take the angle into account *has* caused me to miss game, including the biggest elk I've ever seen. Usually, of course, the error is to shoot too high, as in when I whistled a 220-grain 8mm bullet just over the back of a monstrous Arizona bull at 500 yards. The good news: You need a lot of distance or a lot of angle—or both—for this to make a significant difference. The bad news: Much shooting in the mountains requires distance *and* angle, so this is something long-range rifle shooters need to keep in mind.

As I said, all ballistics programs will yield hold variances for specific angles. You can try to cram the numbers into your overcrowded memory banks, but there are simpler solutions. One is to have a rangefinder that gives you the angle correction, such as Leupold's True Ballistic Range (TBR) system. I have another solution right here on my range card from the SAAM shooting school, again for my .300 Weatherby Magnum, expressed as a percentage of distance based on angle:

5–10 degrees	=	98 percent
15–20 degrees	=	95 percent
25–30 degrees	=	90 percent
35–40 degrees	=	80 percent
45 degrees	=	70 percent
50 degrees	=	65 percent
60 degrees	=	50 percent

This is a big no-no! Even on a cool day, cartridges left in the sun can heat up, and while genuine hazard is unlikely, a hot cartridge can cause a shift in the point of impact and, in extreme cases, sticky extraction.

Joe Bishop (left) and I hunted tur in southern Russia. Joe came from Steamboat Springs, Colorado, that has an elevation about the same as that of our hunting area. I came from sea level, but I zeroed "dead on" expecting a rise in point of impact. I guessed pretty close; these are our two bullet holes from checking zero, side by side. (Don't count on that happening all the time.)

Obviously this requires you to have at least an approximation of the uphill or downhill angle, but you'd better have that anyway. You can carry a device to read the angle precisely, or you can estimate it. Let's start right now. Put your arm out straight. That's 90 degrees. Now cut that in half; that's 45 degrees. Imagine a hillside, and it's pretty easy to see that genuine 45-degree angles are fairly rare in nature. Usually we overestimate the steepness of an angle, which means that we might be compensating when we really shouldn't, or overcompensating. Mind you, steep angles do occur; you could be on top of a cliff and shooting down, or vice versa. But this is not common. On that Arizona elk I knew it was 500 yards, but I was on a lower ridge and the bull was standing well up on the next, ascending ridge. The terrain fooled me, and only after I shot over him did I realize he was well above me. I held a bit of daylight over his back—a bit too much.

Years later I was a lot more careful when I shot my Suleiman markhor, clearly a very important shot. We were on a terrifying cliff looking down, and a group of markhor were bedded far below us on the next ridge. This time I had my SAAM range card, but I didn't yet have a rangefinder that would do it for me. The range wasn't extreme, 390 yards. The angle looked steep but, as usual, it wasn't as severe as it looked. I figured it had to be in the 25- to 30-degree range, so 10 percent of 390 is 39 yards. I should hold for 350 yards instead of nearly 400. I did, and took the mountain hunter's Holy Grail. Again, there are lots of ways to do it, but if you are combining angle and distance it's important to *think* and *evaluate*.

This was the place where I missed the biggest elk I've ever seen. I had the range, just over 500 yards, and I knew the trajectory . . . but I didn't take into account the uphill angle, and I shot right over him. Uphill/downhill doesn't come into play until the angle is steep and/or the range is long, but when either occurs, you'd better factor it into your equation.

When I left California to hunt in Greenland, it was still very warm. It was summer in Greenland, but there was still a 90-degree temperature swing. If you figure a shift of between one-half and one MOA per 20 degrees Fahrenheit of temperature, the change can be significant.

The rest of the factors that affect accuracy involve climatic conditions. Although their effects can be profound, how they impact you depends on your situation. For instance, my old friend Joe Bishop lives in Steamboat Springs, Colorado, cool country with elevation of nine thousand feet. If he zeros his rifle there on a normal autumn day he can take it to any mountain range in the world and expect little difference. Yes, of course he should check it when he gets there, but unless he drops down for a tropical hunt there's no reason why his point of impact should change. On the other hand, if I leave central California or southern Kansas, near sea level, on a hot September day and go to any mountain range in the world, I can expect a significant change in point of impact.

Pure climatic factors are: altitude, barometric pressure, humidity, and temperature. Of these, *temperature* probably causes the most radical changes, for two reasons. First, cold air is denser than warm air. Denser air means more resistance. Second, temperature of the ammunition affects velocity.

Warmer cartridges are, literally, hotter and faster. In the general sense this can cause problems. Even on a cool day cartridges left baking in the sun on your dashboard can warm up enough to cause sticky extraction. A handloader in Alaska preparing for a February safari in Cameroon can expect a temperature difference of more than 100 degrees, so it wouldn't be a good idea to approach maximum powder charges under Alaskan conditions.

In the more finite sense of accuracy, some propellants are more tolerant of temperature changes than others. Australia's Outback ammunition, unfortunately currently limited in cartridge offerings, uses very tolerant propellants. I put some of their cartridges in the freezer overnight and heated others with a hair dryer, and the difference was negligible. This is rare. As a rule of thumb you can expect one-half to one minute of angle difference for each 20 degrees Fahrenheit temperature change. The rule is obvious: Temperature up, bullet strike up; temperature down, bullet strike down. On any given day almost

Though widely discussed around the campfire, it's a fact that one wrap of tape over the muzzle will not change zero or alter accuracy. It's also a fact that taping the muzzle will protect the crown and keep gunk and precipitation out of the barrel.

anywhere a temperature change of 30 to 40 degrees isn't unusual, so this is a major variable at extreme range.

Altitude is another big one. We all know that air is thinner at high altitude. Less dense, less resistance, *higher* bullet strike. There are no absolutes, but you can expect a change in bullet strike between one-half and one MOA (higher) for every five thousand feet you climb in elevation, and the same difference (lower) as you descend. The good news is that it's pretty rare (and very difficult) to climb more than five thousand vertical feet in a day. So if you check your zero the first day in camp you should be in pretty good shape on elevation, and unless the weather changes dramatically you won't be too bad on temperature.

In 2011 Joe Bishop and I went to the Caucasus Mountains of southern Russia to hunt Kuban tur. Joe came from Steamboat Springs, similar in both elevation and weather. I came from central California, sea level and still very hot. I anticipated the difference and sighted in dead-on at a hundred yards. In the mountains Joe and I fired one sighter shot each, me with my Blaser in .300 Weatherby Magnum and Joe with his Sako in 7mm Remington Magnum. The two shots were side by side, almost touching, and just right for our respective 200-yard zeros. You won't often get that lucky.

Barometric pressure is related to altitude. Higher air is less dense, so barometric pressure, measured in inches of mercury, pretty much follows the altitude curve. Using a barometer rather than an altimeter is probably more accurate, since even at high altitude we still have the vagaries of "high pressure" and "low pressure" systems. However, here's the rub: For consistency and for weather forecasting, most barometric readings (and most barometers) are adjusted to sea level. So a "normal" barometric reading of twenty-nine to thirty-one inches of mercury is not a true reading at higher altitudes; actual unadjusted pressure will be several inches lower. Most computerized ballistics programs ask for either altitude or barometric pressure to be entered. The latter is more accurate, but only if it's the true reading and not the standard "adjusted to sea level" reading.

That leaves us with *humidity*. Humidity is actually counterintuitive in that humid air is *less dense* than dry air. Water vapor is lighter, which is why clouds float, so your strike will be a bit higher at high humidity than at low humidity. There are no rules of thumb for this and the difference is slight, but at the extreme ranges folks are shooting today, little things suddenly matter. A good ballistics program will allow you to input relative humidity. Minor changes matter little, but if you are taking ballistics data from a dry climate to one of high humidity and add in extreme range you may have a miss on your hands.

That's plenty to think about and plan for, so let's finish with a couple more things you *don't* have to worry about. As far as is known, precipitation has no effect on a bullet's flight. Snow and rain may well make it nearly impossible to see the target and will certainly make it almost impossible to use a laser rangefinder, but neither rain nor snow nor sleet nor hail shall stop either your U.S. mail carrier or your bullet from completing its intended mission. However, during a storm, humidity is probably going to spike, so guess what? In moist air, the bullet strike will be higher, though probably not by enough to matter.

Let's finish with the time-honored tradition of taping the muzzle of your rifle. Yes, you should. I don't recommend wrapping a whole roll of duct tape around your muzzle, but one strip of waterproof tape, whether electrician's tape, duct tape, or the adhesive portion of a Band-Aid *will not* alter your point of impact. (Honest, it won't!) It *will* prevent rain, snow, and dirt from polluting your barrel. In a worst-case scenario a plugged barrel can cause a dangerous explosion. Even in the best case, moisture or debris in the barrel can change point of impact. Equally important, a strip of tape protects that all-important muzzle crown. Every time I forget to do this I regret it, so just do it and don't worry about it. There are plenty of other things worth worrying about.

Technology Gap

CHAPTER 23

If you had the good fortune to be involved in Scouting, do you remember trying to start a fire without matches? I managed to get it done with flint, steel, and tinder, but I never got it done with the older friction method. I am not against technology. Matches are great, butane lighters are better, and sprinkling a little "Scout water" (diesel or Coleman fuel) on damp tinder doesn't bother me in the least.

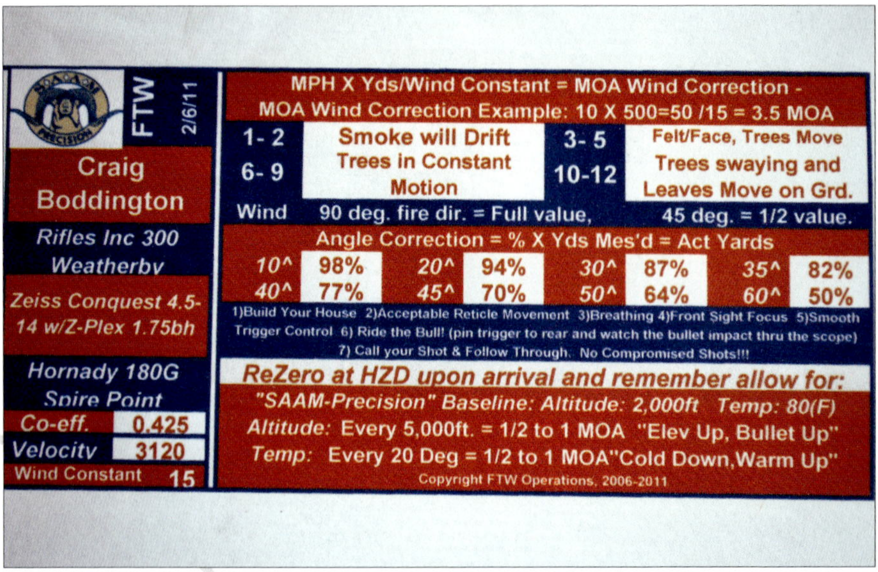

While I draw some personal lines, I do believe in using tools and technology. If you know the ballistic coefficient of your bullet and the velocity of your load, several different computer programs will give you a trajectory chart you can print out. This is one of my "range cards" from the SAAM course for a .300 Weatherby Magnum load, and it's full of all kinds of good info. I usually carry both!

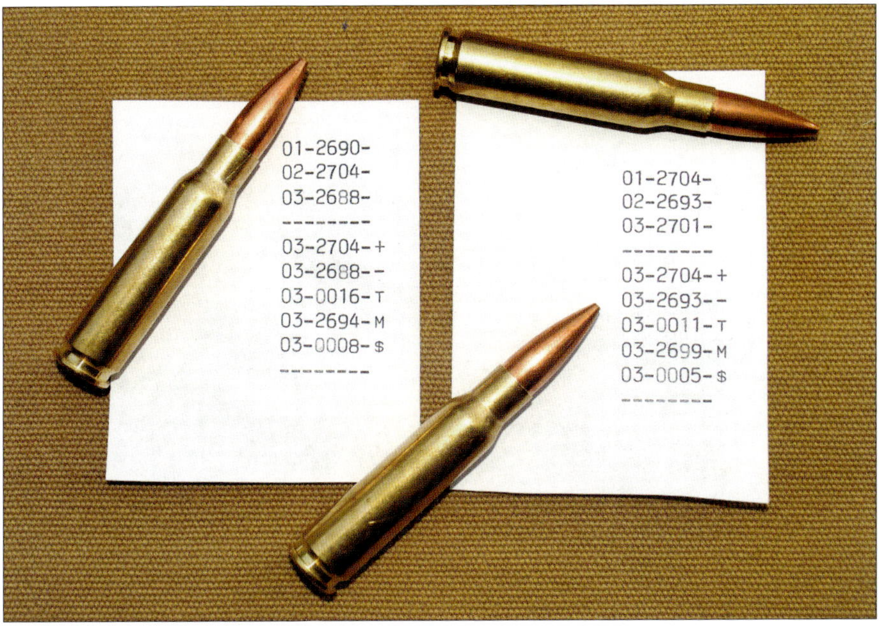

While velocities haven't increased much in my lifetime, ammunition really is better! My Oehler chronograph printout for this factory *match load, .308 with 168-grain bullet, shows a velocity spread of just 11 feet per second, with a standard deviation of 5. Ammunition doesn't get much more consistent than that!*

I embrace laser rangefinders, and I'm all for the best optics you can afford. I'm all for really good rifles, too. I have no issues with carrying range cards or computerized trajectory readouts. In fact, on open country or mountain hunts where longer shots might be possible I usually have both. Although I have no issues with them, I have never carried a wind gauge, although I did carry a device for reading angles for a while. It worked, but I never actually used it, so it's no longer in my pack. Actually, I have no problems at all with whatever you want to carry that will give you confidence to make the shot when your chance comes.

For me personally, I draw some lines. On the range I'll try anything, but in the field I'm not going to carry a computer or use a smartphone application, and as I said earlier, I'm not going to hunt with a laser within a scope, or a self-adjusting scope. All these things are emerging technologies, and I'm sure we'll be seeing more of them in the field in the future. They're not for me in the time I have left. Part of the reason is there are only so many new tricks an old dog can learn. Part, too, is that, aside from playing on the range, which is a lot of fun, I have no desire to shoot at anything quite as far away as the new technology may enable (at least with enough training and practice, and the ability to recognize the right conditions).

My reasons were stated earlier, but I'll restate them: Although I was a Marine infantry officer for thirty-one years, I was never and am not a sniper. At heart I am primarily a hunter. I haven't lost my desire to take game, not in the least, but I feel it essential to take game cleanly and efficiently. We have better rifles and better optics, and we have computers. Bullets are better, too, but cartridge technology hasn't changed much in nearly a century, and it's not going to change significantly so long as we use nitrocellulose propellants. Velocities haven't increased and trajectories haven't flattened materially since the 1940s. Wind deflection remains the same, time of flight hasn't changed,

Doug Pritchard on the spotting scope at the SAAM shooting school, is getting ready to make a wind call. Snipers almost always work in two-man teams, one spotting and one shooting. The importance of the spotter is often underestimated, but in many ways spotting—calling the wind and helping orchestrate the shot—is the more difficult of the two jobs.

Leupold's Custom Dial System (CDS) uses a turret calibrated for your load. With a 200-yard zero, all you need to do is dial the range. Given a good scope with consistent adjustments, I am convinced "dialing" is the most precise method for longer-range shooting, but it takes a lot of practice.

and beyond about six hundred yards we can still measure bullet drop in yards or meters. For me there are too many variables at long range.

There was a sequence aired on television showing a lovely ram pole-axed at an amazing distance, as I recall something over 800 yards. Great shot? Not really. The shot would have landed well to the right, but while the bullet was in the air, the ram turned and walked into it. I really don't care what you or anyone else does so long as it is legal, but for me I want some certainty that, if I do my job, my bullet will bring the animal down. Understand, that applies to hunting, which is my personal passion. In military applications, bring on the drones and laser designators, and give our snipers the tools to take these guys out as far as possible.

I suppose, being a bit old-fashioned, I am also concerned by the seductive and pervasive belief that skill can be replaced with technology. Without question technology helps. Contemporary heroes like the late Chris Kyle use far more advanced equipment than was available to Carlos Hathcock. But

Kyle and his contemporaries weren't just issued the latest in rifles and optics and sent into combat. They train and train, and shoot and shoot, and only then, when skill matches equipment, are they sent into harm's way. Hathcock didn't have that advantage. In his day there was no formal sniper training and no designated specialty as such, but the Marine Corps had a very good rifle team, of which Hathcock was a part. Filling a need, competitive rifle shooters became snipers, with "on the job" training. Only later, with the help of people like Gunnery Sergeant Hathcock, was formal training instituted, including, eventually, a genuine sniper school. Today's sniper training is very, very good.

I can't speak for the other services, but in the Marines a young trooper must first be a good shooter to qualify for the Scout/Sniper school. Then

Most optics companies have some type of reticle with additional aiming points to make holdover consistent. It doesn't really matter whose system you use since they all work, but all require shooting at actual ranges to verify values.

Here Chris Bilkey and I pose with a very nice New Zealand red stag. Earlier in the day I had taken a shot at 485 yards. I had the scope all dialed in, but it was just too windy to attempt the shot. Several hours later we managed to close the distance to 300 yards.

training makes him better—and still better—before he is awarded the Military Occupational Specialty (MOS) of Scout/Sniper. Those of us who seek to emulate these folks are trying to fill very big shoes. It's not an unsound goal because today's snipers are extremely good at what they do, and are worthy of our admiration.

But let's understand: Shooting is their *job*. It might also be a passion, but it's not a hobby or an avocation. It is what they do, and what they are paid to do. Timing in military service is somewhat random, so many trained snipers never test their skills in combat, but they train for that test day in and day out, week in and week out, month in and month out, in many cases for years. It is very difficult for hobbyists to compete with this level of concentration.

Typically they work in two-man teams, one as spotter and the other as shooter. Again, speaking only for the Marines, the training of the two is generally identical. In some cases seniority or experience might determine which is which; in other teams, they might rotate. In some ways the job of spotter is actually more difficult because the spotter will do much of the calculation and calling of the wind. So in some teams the division of work—shooter or spotter—will fall to who is better at which task.

Snipers don't work for medals or "score." History has shown they are unlikely to win medals for doing their jobs, and they can only count coup if verified by a third party. Thus, many hits will be unrecorded. This doesn't matter. The sniper's job is to kill the enemy, or at least take him out of the fight. Today they have the very best tools and latest technology to help them accomplish this job, and they have spent countless hours learning how to use those tools and technology, so that employing them properly has become second nature.

These guys are the professionals. There are two problems with we amateurs employing this technology in the field. First, we often lack the training to make it goof-proof. As I've said, I have no interest in and little patience with using computerized systems to shoot game animals. For me it seems to defy the meaning of the word "hunt." But if I were placed on a hillside with a world-record elk at nine hundred yards and given the tools I'd surely be tempted. However, I reckon that elk would be fairly safe, because I wouldn't have much of a clue how to go about hitting him. That isn't a mission I've trained for.

A better example of our typical lack of training is the dial-up turret. Depending on quality of optics, they work very well, and with really good scopes they work almost perfectly. Thanks to the laser rangefinder we know the range, so simply dialing the range with the turret is almost certainly the most precise way to hit at long range. Sure, but talk to the guides. With "dialing the range" commonplace today, they all have stories about hunters misdialing and missing, when a simple hold with a little daylight over the backline would have gotten the job done.

Right now, for the first time in my career, I'm working very hard at learning to "dial the range." The impetus has been Leupold's Custom Dial System (CDS), with a turret calibrated to my load. The concept isn't new, but in the past I've relied on reticles with multiple aiming points as distance increases. This system has worked well for me, and although it's always possible to choose the wrong stadia line, that seems to hold a bit less risk than dialing up for a long shot and losing your place, or forgetting to dial

Dave Leonard and I pose with a gorgeous grizzly from Arctic Alaska. This was a tough situation: The bear was something over 200 yards away, a long shot on a bear. There was no way to get closer, and snow was falling too fast to allow a rangefinder to work. I figured 250 yards was the worst-case scenario, so that was my hold.

back down if you *don't* shoot. I've been playing with these turrets for nearly three years now, using them first on my Blaser in .300 Weatherby and, more recently, on a Legendary Arms Works Model 704 and a Jarrett Ridge Walker, both in .300 Winchester Magnum.

Oddly, although I've put in a lot of range time with these turrets and am developing a lot of confidence in them, I still haven't used a turret to "dial the range" in the field. The closest I came was just now in New Zealand. I had the range dialed, but I felt it was too windy to take the shot. So I returned the turret to my 200-yard zero, and when we eventually got the shot I simply held about five inches high to adjust for the 300-yard drop.

Or maybe it's not so odd. I shoot at long distances at shooting ranges every chance I get, but in the field I don't seek long shots, and it isn't all that often that I'm called upon to make them. The range I use most is limited to 200 yards. In that, I suppose I'm fortunate; many of us are limited to hundred-yard ranges. Either way, the only way to prepare for long shots is to shoot at long distances. So I make the opportunity as often as I can. Once again, though, each of us is entitled to our own definition of "long range." I still think of 400 yards as a long poke, but whether I'm using a reticle or a turret, I try to verify my data out to 600 yards. I have taken game at longer distances, but I consider that my theoretical limit.

As I said, I don't seek long shots, and I think to do so is a bit crazy, but I'm not afraid of them, at least to my personal limit. That said, I'll definitely get closer if I possibly can. Usually I can. Even on mountain game there are a lot of shots between 250 and 400 yards, and in my experience fewer beyond 400 yards. In fact, although I prepare for such shots, it's been a while since I've needed to take one.

But sometimes it's a long shot or nothing, and a few years ago I had a bit of a run on them. In 2011 I took my Kuban tur at 450 yards in Russia's Caucasus Mountains. I was shooting with a Zeiss 4–12X scope and a Rapid-Z 800 reticle on my Blaser in .300 Weatherby Magnum. I knew the reticle and I knew the rifle and cartridge. The light was good and it was very calm, so it wasn't really a difficult shot.

Since 2010 the Blaser with a .300 barrel has been a favorite for open-country hunting where long shots might be possible, but the first time I used it was in Nepal's Himalayas. I had the same Zeiss scope on it with the Rapid-Z 800 reticle, and I had verified the stadia lines out to 600 yards.

Himalayan tahr are found right at timberline in Nepal (about 12,500 feet elevation); blue sheep live much higher, on the open slopes. Earlier I wrote about my shot at a fine tahr, about 460 yards with some right-to-left wind.

I was pretty pleased with myself, but I was hoping I'd draw a much easier shot on the blue sheep. Instead it was worse. We were on the crest of a knife-edge ridge. There was a really good ram in a small group across a valley, pretty much the same level, distance initially 495 yards. So far so good, except on our ridge the wind was howling.

I studied the valley and the far ridge, and I was pretty sure the wind was strongest where we were, dying in the valley and just barely stirring the grass over where the sheep were. It was probably a foolish shot to try, but we were above 15,000 feet and we'd gone as far as we could go that day. There was no cover between us and the sheep, so I could take the shot or we could come back

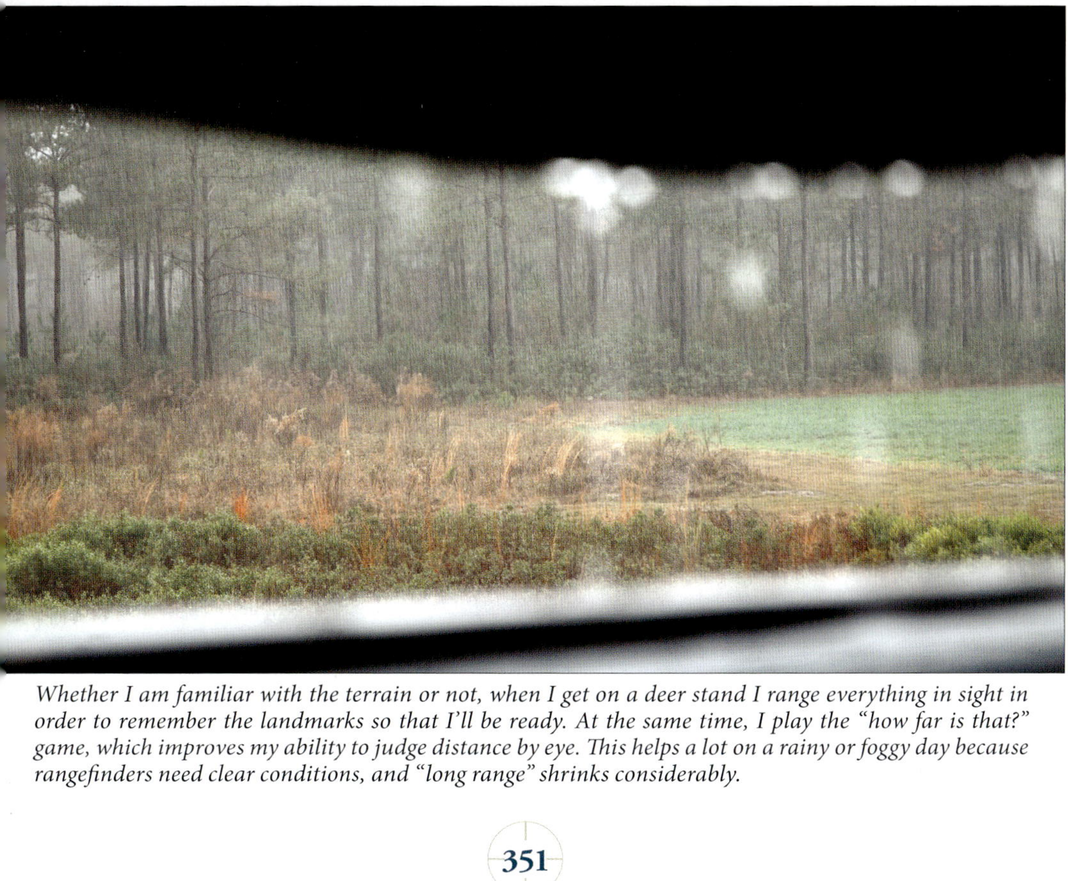

Whether I am familiar with the terrain or not, when I get on a deer stand I range everything in sight in order to remember the landmarks so that I'll be ready. At the same time, I play the "how far is that?" game, which improves my ability to judge distance by eye. This helps a lot on a rainy or foggy day because rangefinders need clear conditions, and "long range" shrinks considerably.

another day. The sheep were feeding slowly up the far ridge, and the distance was 510 yards before I had the big ram broadside, facing left. This time I held a bit of daylight between the ram's rump and the vertical wire. The hit was slightly low and just a bit back, but I didn't know that. Using pretty much the same wind call, I hit the ram again as it quartered away, and was just about to shoot again when he went down.

I had good technology and knew how to use it, but there was just a bit of magic in calling the wind correctly. Or maybe—probably—I just got lucky. I am not totally convinced that's a shot I should have tried, but I was certain there was a lot less wind across the valley. In most situations, as range increases, technology alone won't cut it. You need to know how to use everything you've got going for you, and you need all the experience you can draw upon, whether range, field, or both. And what about those times when technology fails?

The laser rangefinder is a wonderful tool that, without question, has extended our sensible range envelope. However, there are many situations where you can't get readings. Sometimes it's a distance issue or inability to find a properly reflective target, but the biggest limitation is probably weather. It is impossible to get a laser rangefinder to read in fog, rain, or snow. Usually this is self-limiting; our own visibility, and thus range, is also restricted. But at a certain distance you shouldn't shoot unless you're very sure of the range, and there are times when you have to do things the old-fashioned way, so don't get too spoiled.

One of the worst situations I ever faced was on a grizzly in Arctic Alaska, near the Noatak River. The bear was on a moose kill in the center of a wide-open bowl of a valley. Bears can be stalked if the wind is right, and we were in snow camouflage. But this bear had sentries: There were ravens perched nearby. The ravens would see us coming and alert the bear, so we had to shoot from the top of the ridge. It was snowing hard, nearly horizontal, and there was no way to get a rangefinder reading. I was shooting a Kimber in .325 WSM. Now, nobody takes long shots at grizzlies, but "long" is a relative term. Fifty yards is a very long shot on an elephant; a hundred yards is a long shot on a buffalo; and anything beyond 200 yards is a far poke on a grizzly. I'm certain this bear was well beyond 200 yards, but I'm reasonably sure he wasn't farther than 250.

The Noatak area is great grizzly country, but in the spring you have to hit it just right, when the bears are first out of hibernation and you can catch

We were somewhere above 15,000 feet in elevation in Nepal's Himalayas when I took my blue sheep. The distance was about 500 yards and the wind was strong from right to left on our ridge. I studied the situation carefully, and I felt certain the wind diminished across the valley. It was either a good call or a very lucky shot . . . maybe it was both!

them on moose kills. This was my third attempt, and this was a good bear. I was going to shoot, but I sure wish I could have known exactly how far the shot was. I couldn't, so I held for 250 yards. One part was pretty easy: The horizontal snow made a pretty good wind gauge! Although my first shot wasn't very impressive, I kept shooting and got the bear.

That shot wasn't far enough that I really needed to know the range, although it would have been comforting. Truth is, although most open-country hunters carry rangefinders these days, on most shots at game with modern cartridges, you really don't need to know the range. Often knowing the precise range is a confidence-builder, but with a proper zero it shouldn't matter whether an animal is standing at 175 or 225 yards. Also, there are situations where you should be shooting rather than messing with the rangefinder. Use technology, but don't become a slave to it.

The Essential (and Accurate) Rifleman

Chapter 24

The skill you need with a rifle depends on what you intend to do with the rifle. Aside from casual target shooters, America's largest group of rifle shooters is almost certainly our ten million whitetail hunters. The great majority of these folks hunt from tree stands, many of which incorporate a safety rail that can double as a rest. Of course, many whitetail hunters don't use centerfire rifles, at least not all the time. Some are part-time or full-time bow

To millions of American hunters, "field shooting" means shooting from a tree stand. This Ameristep stand is one of our Kansas setups, complete with safety bar that offers a very nice rifle rest for about 180 degrees of the circle. When getting into any stand, I try to visualize all potential shots, then I figure out how to make those shots.

In America's East and upper Midwest, a great many deer hunters are required by law to use shotguns with slugs. I admit to little familiarity with the slug gun, but there have been times when I've used one, as when I hunted this Barbary wild boar in Tunisia. I used a Benelli slug gun with rifled barrel and scope, and the rules are the same: I worked with the loads, established the optimum zero, and practiced.

hunters, others use muzzleloaders, some choose handguns, and millions are obligated by law to use shotguns. Effective range thus varies, but the situations are similar.

In familiar stands, such as my own on my Kansas place, I already know the ranges and the most likely angles. Although I'm left-handed, I don't consciously set my stands for left-handed shooting. I do try to keep the angles neutral or somewhat ambidextrous, but we have a few stands where the most likely shots are right-handed. I use them, but I know that if a buck shows up from certain directions I'll either have to be a contortionist or shoot right-handed. But even on unfamiliar stands, such as on a buddy's place or an outfitted hunt, the distances and shot angles become quickly apparent as soon as it gets light. Other than that, most stand hunting—no matter where you are or what you are hunting—is fairly similar.

Retired Sergeant Major Kyle Lamb with a coyote he took with a Smith & Wesson M&P 15 "Viking Tactics," a rifle he helped design. Kyle is one of the best all-round shooters I know, but what impresses me the most is how effortlessly he switches from his strong right side to shooting left-handed . . . almost as accurately.

Two great friends, unfortunately gone now—Gary Sitton and John Wootters (right)—flank me with a nice Texas whitetail taken with the great old Winchester 1894 in .30-30. Late in life Wootters lost his right eye to a detached retina and had to switch to left-handed shooting, a difficult task that might have been easier if he'd spent more time practicing from his weak side.

Clearly, if that's the way you do most of your hunting, that's where you should concentrate your training (or *practice*, if you prefer that word). Many of the concepts in this book may be quite foreign to the stand hunter, and very possibly of limited utility if that is your primary use for the rifle. But there is still training to be done. Many of my friends who are serious bow hunters take the smart step of putting a tree stand in their backyard archery range. This is for the obvious reason that, whether standing or seated, drawing a bow is a whole lot different from a tree stand than from a proper target stance on the ground. Not so obvious is that, with short-range equipment with very arcing trajectories, that uphill/downhill business is greatly exaggerated. This does not apply to flatter-shooting firearms at typical tree stand shooting distances, but complete training should include *practicing* from the kind of stand you expect to use. You need to know how to get your bullet- or arrow-launching device into position slowly, silently, and sometimes quickly.

At the SAAM school, Bruce Keller looks on while Doug Pritchard uses a wind gauge to check wind speed and direction. The problem with all wind calls is that you only know the speed and direction of the wind where you're standing. Especially in broken ground, wind can be quite different between you and the target.

In the tactical world, most shooters spend at least some time learning how to shoot effectively from the weak or support side. This is done for two reasons: First, in a real-world gunfight there is always the possibility that your strong or shooting-side hand, arm, shoulder, or even face may be injured or disabled, but you still need to be able to defend yourself. Second, among the endless variations of cover and barriers that you might wish to shoot from behind, many will specifically dictate either a right or left-handed shot, either for greater protection or surprise. During the many "shoots" we've done together for *Guns & Ammo TV* I have learned an awful lot from retired special ops Sergeant Major Kyle Lamb. I can hold my own against him with a rifle (never with a pistol!), but one of the most impressive aspects of his shooting is how effortlessly and effectively he is able to shift from right to left-handed shooting.

My guess is that relatively few *hunters* consciously practice shooting from the support or weak side. In my day this was never taught in the Marines, either. As a lefty, I almost never attempted any right-handed shooting until I was nearly thirty. After I went to work for Petersen Publishing there were numerous occasions for "photo ops" where it just looked too weird to pose left-handed with a right-handed rifle. So I figured I'd better learn to shoot right-handed. Mind you, whether an action is right-handed or left-handed, I am a left-handed shooter and I do most of my shooting (and all of my best shooting) from the left side. But in those days I was primarily a Western hunter, totally unfamiliar with tree stand hunting. Armed with the knowledge that I can shoot right-handed if I have to, there have been several times over the years where I've taken white-tailed deer and turkeys right-handed. It has always been a split-second decision, made because the shifting necessary to bring a left-handed shot to bear was too likely to spook the game. However, while I'm sitting on a stand evaluating potential shots I'm always thinking and making mental notes. As in, "Craig, if a deer comes from *that* side, you'd better take him right-handed."

So I think complete preparation, regardless of your intended purpose, should include at least some capability for shooting from the weak side. One great benefit to this: We never know what unkind tricks life may play on us. In a long shooting life I've known a fair number of people who suffered accidents or ailments to one side of the body, and in order to keep shooting had to switch sides. It's a whole lot easier if you already have at least passing skill.

We're in western Tanzania, and there's a great sitatunga out in the marsh. PH Jaco Oosthuizen is acting as "spotter." I'm on the rifle, ready as I can be: My sticks are set low for a tripod, and I have my shooting elbow supported by a pack. Jaco's sticks are also set up high, so I can stand if I need to see over low brush.

One comment: Take it easy! Especially if you're already an experienced shooter you will probably find your weak side both unaccustomed to and highly susceptible to recoil. One of the worst things I ever did to myself was for one of those G&A shoots back in the early 1980s. My old friend Payton Miller was on the camera, and we wanted a photo of a .460 Weatherby Magnum in full recoil. (It must have been sort of like Tom Sawyer and the picket fence; I can't remember why I had to do the shooting while he held the camera, but I guess he's smarter than I am!) Of course the rifle was right-handed, so I shot it four or five times right-handed. I was black and blue for days! Start with a .22 and work up slowly. Today I shoot pretty well right-handed, but even the mild .308 Winchester still has unpleasant recoil on my right shoulder.

If you're serious about extreme-range shooting, your practice regimen is a whole different deal. I've mentioned Carlos Hathcock several times, not only because he was one of our great snipers from Vietnam, but also because I met him on several occasions, and he was a really good guy. He was also an extremely accomplished rifleman in all ways, and exceptionally gifted in his ability to read the wind. However, the way he was employed was a bit different than the way it is normally done today. Hathcock was often sent out on solo missions to take out specific targets. Since his day most serious long-range shooting has evolved into a team sport, both in sniping and hunting. The role of the spotter is extremely important. Whether it's a sniper team or a couple of hunting buddies, it's the *spotter* who is most likely to employ the tools—wind gauges, rangefinders, computerized ballistics—while the *shooter* goes about the work of getting steady, "building his house," and preparing for the shot.

Again, today's snipers are highly trained. I have expressed my misgivings about transferring military sniper skills to hunting, simply because of the increased risk of wounded animals, which is not a concern in military applications. However, it is being done, it will be done, and under ideal conditions with the right equipment *and* the right skill sets, it certainly can be done. I submit, however, that it remains a team sport. It is not something that should be done alone. This is partly because, as in military sniping, it's helpful to have a buddy work with the tools and assist in figuring the shot, but it's also a matter of ethics. Because of recoil, the spotter on a spotting scope has a much better opportunity than the shooter to call the shot. With a clear miss the strike can often be observed and a correction made. Unless the animal drops or is observed to go down, hits are harder to call, so ethics dictate that you have to go look. At long range this becomes very difficult for a lone shooter, but a spotter can stay on the spotting scope and direct the shooter to the exact spot to look for sign.

Some guides are very good at this. I'll be totally honest: The only shots I've ever attempted at *unwounded* game beyond six hundred yards were with my friend Kirk Kelso as spotter. He is a master at long-range shooting, and without his coaching I wouldn't have tried. John Lazzeroni is also very good at this. I've seen both of them coach hunters into amazing shots on open-country game such as Coues deer and pronghorn, and I've seen them do it themselves. But unless you have a hunting and shooting buddy that you train with, this stuff isn't for everybody in all places.

Whether you're sniping, having fun at long range, or hunting with a guide or buddy, this is a typical situation—one shooter on the rifle (me), and in this case outfitter Hunter Ross is acting as the spotter. Ross will confirm the target, call the range, and recommend a wind call if needed. In many ways this is more difficult than simply making the shot.

Because of the hunting conditions, ranges are often quite long in the mountains of Asia. I've mentioned several fairly long shots that I've taken over there, and there are reasons for it. Unlike most North American sheep and goat country, a lot of Asian mountain ranges are extremely open at high elevation; the terrain makes it hard to get close. It's made harder by the fact that, instead of just you, or you and your guide, in Asia you often have an entourage on the mountain with you: interpreter, multiple guides, packers, hangers-on. Eight or more people isn't unusual. Stalking close with a mob like that? Forget it. But when it comes time for the shot, you can also forget about good coaching. There will be an extreme language barrier, and in many cases very limited knowledge of ballistics, wind deflection, the whole works. When it comes time to shoot you are on your own.

I've done very little "extreme range" shooting outside of targets on ranges, but if you're serious about really expanding both your own capabilities and your hunting horizons, then you need to work hard at expanding your personal range envelope. As I've said, for mountain hunting I try to set up myself and my equipment so that I can shoot to 600 yards if I really have to. I've almost never had to push that envelope, but if I feel OK at that distance then I'm a whole lot more comfortable in the 400- to 500-yard window, which is much more likely.

In order to get there you need to spend a lot of time shooting at actual distances with your rifle and your load. You also need to spend a lot of time working with wind, which remains the greatest variable. Absent ready access to a long-distance range (which few of us have) there are at least two good ways to do this. One is to spend as much time as you can shooting varmints. A prairie dog town is the best classroom I know of. Prairie dog country almost always has at least some wind, and you can get in a lot of shooting in a relatively short time. It doesn't take much breeze to blow a bullet clear off a prairie dog. But here's the deal: An entire prairie dog is considerably smaller than the vital zone

There are many options for long-range shooting, and I've tried a lot of them, but I've pretty much settled on a fast .30-caliber, largely because I understand the trajectory and capabilities. I took this big Dagestan tur from Azerbaijan with my Rifles Inc. in .300 Weatherby Magnum.

One of the secrets to all shooting is practice, but for long-range shooting, it's important to practice at actual distances. Access to longer ranges is a problem for many—but there is no real solution. At his range in Georgia, Zack Aultman has targets to 500 yards, and he spends a lot of time getting dialed in.

on even a pronghorn. If you can reach a point where you are reasonably deadly on prairie dogs at, say, three hundred yards, then a deer, sheep, or pronghorn a couple hundred yards farther shouldn't be daunting.

The other option is to *get training*. With good long-distance ranges ever more scarce, a lot of great shooting schools have sprung up. Gunsite, founded by Jeff Cooper, remains the most famous, perhaps still best-known for pistol training but with equally good rifle courses. The school I know the best is Tim Fallon's Sportsmen's All Weather, All Terrain Marksmanship (SAAM) courses. Tim's FTW Ranch in the Texas Hill Country is a network of wonderful ranges, and the instructors are great. There are many others scattered around, but here's the point: It doesn't matter how experienced you think you are. Even the most experienced among us either have or will occasionally develop bad shooting habits. I've been to the SAAM courses a half-dozen times and will go again soon. Good rifle marksmanship cannot be developed overnight, but a "cram course" with good instructors can work wonders. I've learned a lot at the SAAM courses, and I'm still learning.

As I've said, each of us must define our limits. In the field I have no interest in extreme-range shooting, but a lot of fine riflemen and successful hunters consider my own range parameters as being too far. Part of being a complete and effective rifleman is knowing what you can accomplish with reasonable certainty, and what you have no business attempting. I can talk endlessly about my theoretical range window, but it always comes down to the conditions. If the atmospherics won't allow a range reading and you can't be reasonably certain of the wind all the way along the bullet's path, then your theoretical maximum range just shrank to a much shorter practical limit. Tools help, of course. I have Leupold's new Wind Plex reticle on the VX-6 I'm using right now. I'm still training myself with it, but it has a series of hash marks on the horizontal wire that allows a full ten minutes of angle with precise aiming points. Great tool for long-range shooting, but you still have to be able to read the wind all the way to the target.

There's one more thing: You have to be able to get steady. This applies universally, whether you're a hundred-yard whitetail hunter, a 300-yard mule deer hunter, a 400-yard elk hunter, or a 500-yard sheep hunter. All skills are important, but because it applies everywhere, and for everything, I am

Part of the secret to shooting accurately is being as creative as possible in one's practice, and this means getting away from the bench and shooting from a variety of positions. At our range Donna practices a variety of potential field situations.

Practice from weird positions on the range pays huge dividends in the field. Donna had a rock to use for a rest, but the slope made it weird and uncomfortable. Her practice paid off when she took this very fine Himalayan tahr on New Zealand's South Island.

Shooting small varmints like prairie dogs, ground squirrels, and gophers is some of the best practice one can get. These small targets teach you a lot about wind, and the learning curve is even better if you get away from portable benches and shoot from actual field positions.

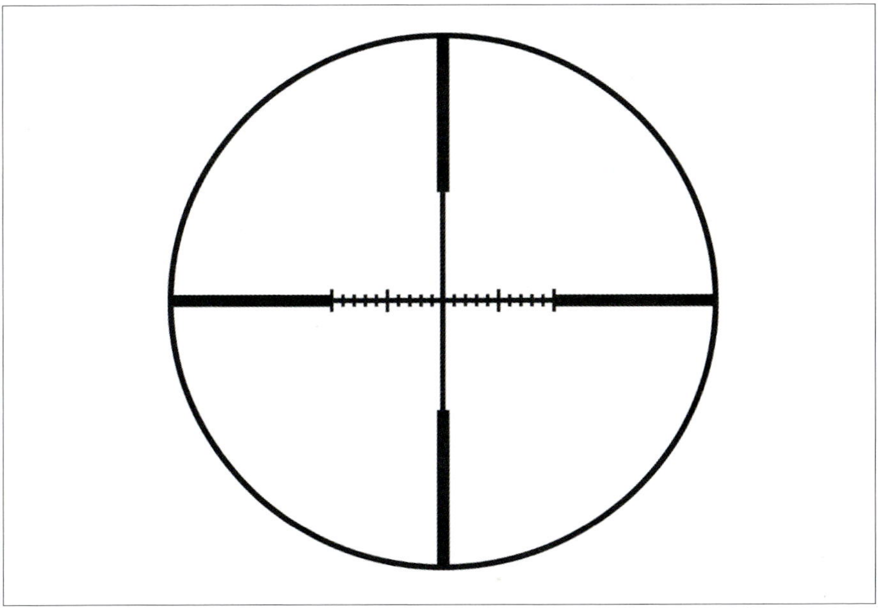

This is the Leupold Wind-Plex reticle, with ten minutes of wind adjustment in one-minute hash marks on the horizontal wire. Intended to be used with Leupold's CDS dial-up turret, it allows a precise hold, but you must still know the wind deflection of your bullet, and you must still be able to "call the wind."

convinced that the most critical skill in rifle shooting is to know how to get steady, quickly, in almost any situation.

Obviously the degree of steadiness required changes dramatically with both size of target and distance. Unless you're David Tubb, the standing position is useless at 200 yards, but you should be able to stand on your hind legs and place a 60-yard shot on a whitetail or a buffalo. At a hundred yards most of us need some extra stability, and much beyond that we all do.

The larger your repertoire of ways to get steady, the more successful you will be. The options are nearly endless, but nothing works under all circumstances. Terrain, vegetation, shooting angles, and more dictate that no one shooting position or preferred method for getting steady will work under all conditions. The more options you have practiced on the range, the more options you will have in the field, and the less likely you are to get into a funk when an opportunity arises. It should be a matter of quickly studying the situation and then building the best house you can in the time you have and under the conditions you must deal with.

Note: Not all sightings of intended targets can yield a shot. There is a time element in that the target must be visible and in range long enough for you to set up for a steady, educated shot. However, the more quickly you can get steady, the better your chances.

This was really brought home to me recently in New Zealand. A friend of ours, an emergency-room doctor, went with us, and she wanted a tahr. She's a studious and dedicated shooter. I've watched her on the range, and I've seen her make brilliant shots off of sticks. But she had never done a mountain hunt, and she had never shot prone off a pack. Since she does all things with a doctor's precision, she had also never missed an animal before. We had a bit of a train wreck on the mountain. Getting steady for an uphill shot off a pack was totally unfamiliar to her. No surprise, she missed. Also not surprising, it messed up her confidence, so she missed a couple more times.

Luckily, we then spent a day hunting fallow deer at Ritt Richards's place. A longtime follower of Jeff Cooper's Gunsite training protocol, Ritt teaches shooting courses for the New Zealand forces. He gave my friend a brilliant hour of instruction on shooting prone, with and without a pack, and she got to practice by shooting uphill at gongs on his range. The last day she went back up

Just prior to a hunt for Punjab urial sheep, I had a chance to verify my data at Kyler Hamman's range (bottom). He has eight-inch gongs out to 500 yards, an appropriately small and difficult target. My actual shot in Pakistan was 250 yards. That isn't a "chip shot" on smaller animals like this, but I had confidence and made the shot (top).

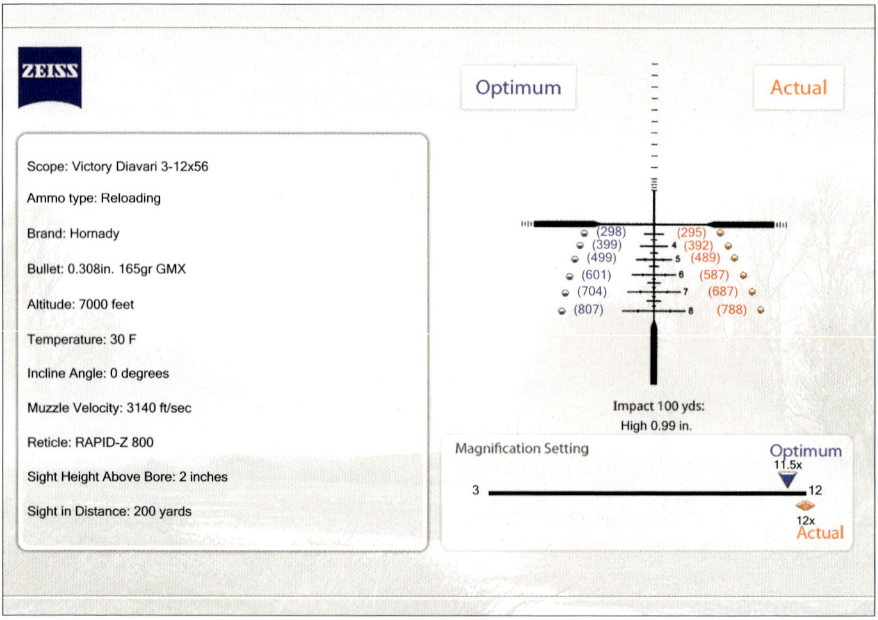

These days it's easy to chronograph your load and get a printout. This will get you close . . . but all data still need to be verified at actual ranges. This is the Zeiss Rapid-Z 800 reticle (bottom), a reticle I've used a great deal, along with a computer printout (top) for Hornady's 165-grain GMX load for the .300 Weatherby Magnum.

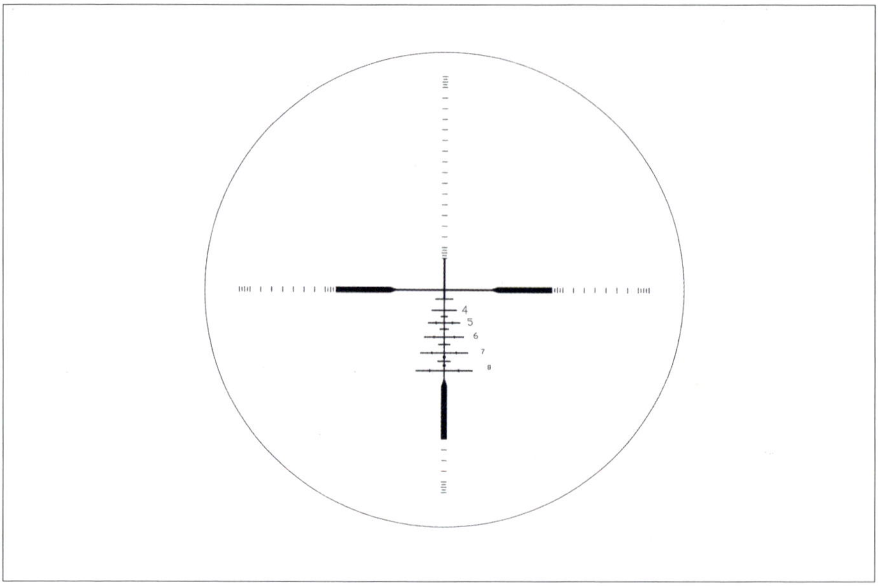

In unfamiliar territory it's essential to verify data, especially if altitude and climatic factors change. Usually this is an impromptu range session, but my outfitter in Kyrgyzstan was that rarity in Asia, a serious rifleman with a good benchrest and long-range targets. This was a real blessing before we set out to hunt ibex and sheep.

the mountain and shot a great tahr, prone off the pack, at 235 yards. Now, with renewed confidence, she has a much better idea of the kind of practice shooting she needs to do.

People in my business, me included, throw out all kinds of examples of awesome shooting at outlandish ranges. These are the exceptions. Most police sniping is done at less than a hundred yards. Unless you have the misfortune to be in urban combat, most military sniping is done at much longer range—we really don't want our snipers engaged in close combat.

In field shooting, as I've said, most shots are on the near side of 200 yards, and relatively few are at 300 or 350. These are not "bragging" distances, but under field conditions all of them can make for very difficult shooting. You have to get steady, and you have to overcome the jitters. Hunters who have been doing this stuff for decades have enough experience to overcome buck fever (at least most of the time). The average hunter who gets chances at maybe two or three animals in a year has an awful lot going on in his or her head when that rare chance comes along. It isn't easy.

My friend Kyler Hamman in Paso Robles is an extremely fine rifle shot, and although he's more into selling real estate now, for years he was one of our very best local outfitters for hogs, deer, and tule elk. Like me, Kyler doesn't buy into extreme-range shooting on game, but he's not afraid to reach out a bit. On some family property in the area he found two adjacent ridges, one to shoot from and one where he could put up steel gongs. It's a very simple range: Eight-inch steel gongs at 250, 300, 350, 400, and 500 yards. On the "shooting ridge," there is bare ground. No benches. What a great and sensible test of field-shooting capabilities! You can lie prone, you can use a pack, you can drag up a couple of logs, and there are a couple of handy stumps, but no benchrests. Shooting from this range brings home two important points: First, if you can actually hit an eight-inch gong at 500 yards from a field rest, you're doing something. If you can't (and few of us can, consistently), then you have some idea of your genuine *field shooting* capabilities.

I had a chance to use his range just before I went to Pakistan for a Punjab urial sheep in February 2015. I wasn't real keen on making a fool of myself in front of Kyler and some of his friends and family, but I wanted to verify the values on my scope one last time. My stadia lines were perfect out to 350 yards, but beyond that the wind was a bit tricky, as it always is in canyon country. I misread it on my first shot at 500 yards, then corrected and got a solid hit with the second shot. I knew to quit while I was ahead!

Urial sheep are not big targets, but they aren't animals of the high mountains. They're really sheep of the Asian foothills, where vegetation and terrain usually allow stalking. I was armed with the knowledge that the values on my scope were good, but I was hoping a long shot wouldn't be necessary. We found a great ram feeding up out of a valley, range about 250 yards, which is really a classic distance for a lot of open-country hunting around the world. I lay down over my pack, scrunched the butt into my shoulder with my right hand, and held for 250. Although the ram went straight down, the shot hit maybe two inches higher on the shoulder than I'd intended. Not perfect, but in field shooting I'll take that result any day of the week. And, no, I didn't consider backing up a couple hundred yards.